Building Walls, Constructing Identities

The Cultural Lives of Law

Edited by Austin Sarat

Building Walls, Constructing Identities

Legal Discourse and the Creation of National Borders

Marie-Eve Loiselle

Stanford University Press
Stanford, California

Stanford University Press
Stanford, California

Printed in the United States of America on acid-free, archival-quality paper

Library of Congress Cataloging-in-Publication Data

Names: Loiselle, Marie-Eve, author.
Title: Building walls, constructing identities : legal discourse and the creation of national borders / Marie-Eve Loiselle.
Other titles: Cultural lives of law.
Description: Stanford, California : Stanford University Press, 2024. | Series: The cultural lives of law | Includes bibliographical references and index.
Identifiers: LCCN 2024013673 (print) | LCCN 2024013674 (ebook) | ISBN 9781503640610 (cloth) | ISBN 9781503641112 (ebook)
Subjects: LCSH: Emigration and immigration law—United States. | Border security—Law and legislation—United States. | Nationalism—United States. | Walls—Political aspects—Mexican-American Border Region. | United States—Boundaries—Mexico. | Mexico—Boundaries—United States.
Classification: LCC KF4819 .L65 2024 (print) | LCC KF4819 (ebook) | DDC 342.7308/2—dc23/eng/20240402
LC record available at https://lccn.loc.gov/2024013673
LC ebook record available at https://lccn.loc.gov/2024013674

Cover design: Michele Wetherbee
Cover painting: Karen Black, *Bed Mess*, 2017, acrylic and oil on linen, 152.5 x 122 cm. Courtesy of the artist and Ames Yavuz.
Typeset by Newgen in 11/14.5 Adobe Garamond Pro

Contents

List of Illustrations vii
Acknowledgments ix

Introduction 1
A Wall Building (a) Nation

1 Looking at the Wall through the Law 14

2 Drawing the Contours of the Nation 30

3 The Wall We Need 75

4 The Wall as Law 113

Conclusion 148
Looking Back to the Future

Appendix: A Tour of the US-Mexico Borderland 159
Notes 167
Bibliography 217
Index 245

List of Illustrations

FIGURE 2.1: Observation tower erected in 1937 45

FIGURE 2.2: Design for a fence at the border between California and Mexico, 1954 50

FIGURE 2.3: Location of two proposed fences in Texas in 1953 50

FIGURE 2.4: Location of sections 1 and 2 of planned fence near Brownsville, Texas 51

FIGURE 2.5: Location of section 3 of planned fence near Brownsville, Texas 52

FIGURE 4.1: Littering at Border Field State Park, California 130

FIGURE 4.2: Debris swept by the sea at Border Field State Park, California 131

FIGURE 4.3: Gate of Friendship Park, located within Border Field State Park, California 132

FIGURE 4.4: Line of petunias marking the border between Stanstead, Canada, and Derby Line 140

FIGURE A.1: Gap by design in the fence at Sabal Palm Sanctuary along the Rio Grande, Brownsville, Texas 160

FIGURE A.2: Border fence in El Paso, Texas 161

FIGURE A.3: Border fence cutting through Ambos Nogales 162

FIGURE A.4: Border fence near Yuma, Arizona 163

FIGURE A.5: Border fence stopping abruptly near Yuma, Arizona 163

FIGURE A.6: The US-Mexico border fence (the "Sand Dragon") snakes through sand dunes 164

FIGURE A.7: The border fence built southeast of San Diego in the 1990s 165

FIGURE A.8: Border fence at Border Field State Park, California 165

Acknowledgments

Completing this book has been an enthralling experience, and I am in debt to so many scholars and friends who have provided me with support and advice throughout the project. *Building Walls, Constructing Identities* is the last of many iterations of what started as a doctoral research project. I could not have hoped for a finer scholar to guide me through this journey than Hilary Charlesworth. Hilary has been an inspirational supervisor who offered me rigorous advice and guidance while always giving me the freedom to explore my own ideas. I am grateful for this freedom and her enthusiasm toward my project, which was my greatest source of encouragement in times of doubt.

Several institutions and people have made the book possible. At the Australian National University, I would like to give a special thanks to John Braithwaite, Michelle Burgis-Kasthala, Kathryn Henne, and Desmond Manderson for their careful reviews and comments on earlier drafts of the chapters that make up this book. I am truly grateful to Mareike Riedel for her constant encouragement, as well as to Jeremy Farrall, Benjamin Authers, Emma Larking, Christoph Sperfeldt, and Suzanne Akila for their insights and engaging discussions, at both academic and personal levels. At the Max Planck Institute for the Study of Religious and Ethnic Diversity, I would like to extend my gratitude to Ran Hirschl, Benjamin Boudou, Ali Emre Benli, and Alexander Hudson for their advice on earlier versions of some chapters. Their comments contributed to the publication of the article "The American Border Wall: A History of Legal Division," which appeared in the journal *Law, Culture and the*

Humanities. My time at the Harney Program in Ethnic, Immigration, and Pluralism Studies at the University of Toronto was critical to completing this book. I am thankful to Phil Triadafilopoulos for steering me toward stimulating readings that made me see my subject in a whole new light. Finally, a very special thanks to Ayelet Shachar for her thoughtful comments and support during the completion of the book.

I also want to acknowledge the generous financial assistance of the following institutions: the School of Regulation and Global Governance (RegNet) at the Australian National University, Macquarie University, the Max Planck Institute for the Study of Religious and Ethnic Diversity, and the Transformations of Citizenship Leibniz Research Group at Goethe University, Frankfurt.

Finally, there are many people I want to thank closer to home. My mother, Louise. Melissa, for always being there *au bout du fil* despite the geographical distance that separates us. Bosco, for his quiet and soothing presence during extended periods of writing. Most importantly, I want to thank my wonderful husband, Benjamin, for his unwavering support during these several years of research and writing.

INTRODUCTION

A Wall Building (a) Nation

Over the last two decades, we have become accustomed to the sight of the wall at the border between the United States and Mexico. Following the passage of the Secure Fence Act in 2006, hundreds of miles of border walls were added to the few border fences built in the 1990s, south of San Diego and in El Paso. Then, in 2016, Donald Trump made the expansion of the border wall the central theme of his presidency. During his term as president, media reports abounded about the enhancement or construction of a new section of the wall, tensions between the Trump administration and Congress concerning the funding of the wall, as well as its effects on citizens and migrants. It was with great fanfare that the then president unveiled eight steel and concrete border wall prototypes in 2017, each measuring an imposing thirty feet in height. Images of these striking concrete blocks along with pictures of the actual border wall have travelled the world.

The wall's length is impressive too. As of 2023, it ran along approximately seven hundred miles of the border's length, covering roughly one-third of the 1,954-mile divide between the United States and Mexico.[1] Although the publicity surrounding this contemporary wall has been deafening, we know little about early American walling projects.

The construction of fences and barriers between the two countries is not new—far from it. As I was exploring the US National Archives, I was surprised to discover that Congress had already adopted legislation authorizing the erection of barriers along a substantial length of the southern border during the first half of the twentieth century. As I dug deeper into the records of the Immigration and Naturalization Service, I was struck by how similar the arguments in support of such fences in the early 1900s were to those deployed today. Immigration, disease, and crime have appeared as recurring justifications for the wall, both then and now. Yet, over the span of a century, the sociopolitical and legal contexts surrounding the demands for border walls have changed. Proposals to fence the border during the first half of the twentieth century were made against a backdrop of territorial consolidation following the not-so-distant Mexican-American War. Contemporary walls are erected along a settled territorial border—at least from a formal legal perspective. This made me rethink the function of the wall between these two countries. Could the wall perform a more fundamental function than its often-stated role as an instrument for the governance of movement in an era of globalization?

To be sure, walls have been used for centuries as a form of protection against a variety of threats, both real and perceived. As historian Claude Quétel notes in his *Histoire des murs*, walls have been present throughout human history.[2] They are built to defend against theft, invasions, and threats to cultural identity. An early example is the Great Wall of China, built by a succession of dynasties between the seventh century BCE and the seventeenth century CE. Walls may appear as a rational strategy for structuring space and movement in these historical contexts. Today, however, in an era of sophisticated border control technologies, the erection of walls to prevent movement between spaces appears anachronistic. Nevertheless, despite states increasingly relying on biometric systems, e-passports, and virtual detection assemblages at the border and beyond to monitor and control the flows of people and goods, walls remain a popular instrument of spatial division. This is so even for a country like the United States, with access to some of the most advanced surveillance technologies.

The United States is not alone in erecting physical walls at its borders. As of 2020, at least seventy-two fences and walls edged national borders worldwide.[3] Nearly all continents have them. Walls divide Israel and Palestine, Serbia and Hungary, and Iran and Pakistan, to name only a few.[4] Surely, something unites these various structures. In fact, a rich body of literature on border walls has emerged over the last two decades that seeks to understand what motivates countries to build these physical partitions.

This is an interesting question, and this book contributes to that debate. However, this is not the book's main objective. Instead, *Building Walls, Constructing Identities* focuses on the US-Mexico border wall, tracing its genealogy and the legal discourses surrounding its erection to identify its function as a marker not only of territory but also of identity.

Relying on an interdisciplinary approach that brings sociolegal studies into dialogue with critical race theory, history, geography, and philosophy, this book contends that past and present walls and fences between the United States and Mexico have participated in cementing an American national identity.[5] In doing so, it provides an alternative understanding of the relationship between the law and wall building by demonstrating how the law provides a unique site for communicating meanings about space and national identities. Informed by two episodes of wall building in American history—the Act of August 19, 1935, and the adoption of the Secure Fence Act of 2006, both authorizing the erection of walls at the US-Mexico border—the book identifies two discursive processes by which the law and the wall come together to communicate legal knowledge about the territorial limits of the state and questions of national identity and belonging: legal words and legal matter.

First, I argue that oral and textual legal discourses about the construction of a US-Mexico border wall—including legislation, US Congress deliberations, and administrative reports—have provided sites for the deployment of narratives that have contributed to constructing the Mexican neighbor in opposition to a selectively white American identity. Building on the work of critical legal scholars and race theorists attentive to the role of rhetoric and discourse in law's formation and its communication,[6] I argue that legislation authorizing the construction of walls at the US-Mexico border is the outcome of a legislative process that feeds on colonial discourses to justify wall building. Once adopted, the text of these laws become discourses that authoritatively suggest meanings about how the world ought to be interpreted and how we should conduct ourselves within it. I focus on the legal discourses that were deployed during legislative debates concerning the authorization to build a wall at the southern US border. I analyze the justifications that were developed in favor of or against the border wall in oral debates and the policy documents that informed them. I also question the discourses found within the text of the law itself and reflect on the messages they communicate. This review demonstrates how Mexican identity was transformed into a threat to be curtailed through the language of racial and cultural difference, which relied on generalizations, stereotypes, and metaphors around themes such as criminality, licentiousness, dirt, and disease. This repertoire for understanding Mexican identity was regularly contrasted with an idealized expression of American character portrayed as industrious, law abiding, and virtuous. What is more, the review of these two episodes of wall building highlights the persistence of these discourses today.

As such, this book questions the epistemological distinction found in the literature between walls built before the end of the Cold War and those built after. Most authors acknowledge that old and new walls have a similar defensive function, but new walls, they argue, are erected to stop nonstate threats—crime, terrorism, unregulated migration—while older walls were erected against threats from other states.[7] New dynamics of globalization that favor the mobility of people, goods, and ideas are perceived as facilitating these new and potentially dangerous cross-border flows, which can undermine a state's sovereign control over its territory. Consequently, the scholarship on border walls often conceives of its object as an answer to the tensions arising in an increasingly interconnected world. In this respect, the US-Mexico border wall is no exception. Yet, this approach risks missing parallels between older and contemporary walls at this border. To be clear, I am not suggesting that globalization has played no part in boosting the popularity of border walls. It has certainly raised the level of anxiety about the permeability of state borders to the mass arrival of foreigners, ideologies, and other perceived threats to the nation. These anxieties—exacerbated by the media's sustained attention on the US southern border since the 1970s—help explain why, as this book demonstrates, border wall proponents in the twenty-first century succeeded in obtaining substantial funding for the construction of a wall, whereas their predecessors mostly failed. But, at least in the context of the southern US border, we are forced to recognize that the appeal of both old and modern walls is founded on similar grounds.

Scholarly accounts of the US-Mexico border usually identify the 1990s as the period when the first border walls were erected; however, as previously mentioned, Congress was already considering plans to fence large parts of the border during the first half of the twentieth century. The literature rarely considers these plans that, in the 1940s, sought to erect walls along close to 900 miles of the US-Mexico border. Only a few authors have studied fence-building projects that occurred during the first half of the twentieth century, and their accounts remain partial. For instance, Deborah Kang's interest lies not so much with fencing but with the broader history of the US Immigration and Nationalization Services, while Oscar Martínez's focus is on the erection of two fences: one between El Paso and Ciudad Juárez and one between San Ysidro and Tijuana, between 1978 and 1979.[8]

In this book, I pay attention to these early projects to provide a historical account of the US-Mexico border wall. In doing so, I argue that we need to redefine the timeline for its study. By considering the Act of August 19, 1935—an early federal legislative authorization to erect a wall between the United States and Mexico—I seek to demonstrate the longtime yearning for the physical severance of the two national territories. Based on thorough archival research conducted at the US National Archives on congressional debates, federal agency reports, bills, and individual submissions to members of Congress considering plans to erect fences at the US-Mexico border, this book illuminates the implications of the border wall in the formation and sustenance of a (white) American national identity.[9]

What appears from this book is how deeply entwined today's border wall is with America's settler-colonial history. To recognize the relevance of settler colonialism in the context of the US-Mexico border wall, it is important to understand that the object of settler colonialism is territorial gain.[10] This is what distinguishes it from colonialism. Whereas colonialism consists of the domination of a people from the outside, the aim of settler colonialism is different: it seeks to remove the indigenous population to make space for the settler. Historian Lorenzo Veracini acknowledges that similarities exist between the two phenomena but insists on their distinctive structures and outcomes.[11] The colonizer moves to establish a relationship of economic domination governed exogenously from the capital. The colonizer comes and goes; nonetheless, the exploitative relationship requires permanency, that is, the continuity of the colonizer-colonized configuration. By contrast, the settler colonizer moves to a foreign territory to stay.[12] However, because the objective of settler colonialism is the displacement of indigenous people, unlike colonialism, its success depends on its very extinction. As Veracini remarks, "Colonialism *reproduces* itself. . . . Settler colonialism, by contrast, *extinguishes* itself."[13] Settler colonialism can thus be understood as a process of erasure. Indeed, most scholars of race accept Patrick Wolfe's claim that settler colonialism is not an event but an ongoing structure that seeks to end indigenous presence through various practices, including physical elimination, forced territorial displacement, confinement, and assimilation.[14] This is from that perspective that we can see the wall and the legal discourses that surround its erection as part of an ongoing process of colonial settlement.

Since people of Mexican descent are not all indigenous to the land, it may appear improper to consider the relationship between them and Anglo-Americans through the lens of settler colonialism. I argue otherwise. When referring to settler colonialism, I follow Rita Dhamoon's understanding of the term as an ongoing process that supports and consolidates "hierarchies of otherness."[15] In the US context, this hierarchy undoubtedly implicates the relationship between white Anglo settlers and indigenous people. But as I show in chapter 2, it also concerned Europeans' interactions with other groups, including Spaniards, Mexicans, and Mexican Americans, as the territorial limits of the United States and Mexico were being drawn. This is a view shared by sociologist Evelyn Nakano Glenn. Glenn explains that in regard to the US, the mobilization of race in settler colonialism extends to other groups considered undesirable—notably, Mexicans. Without assuming the commensurability of the experiences of native people and Mexicans, she recognizes that the political, economic, and social factors that underpin settler colonialism are present in the confrontation between the latter and Anglo-Americans at the US southwest border.[16] What is more, we must recognize the connections between the Mexican and Native American histories and experiences of white settlement in North America.[17] Gloria Anzaldúa's reflections on Mexican and Chicano identities, which I return to throughout the book, call attention to this. Mexican nationals and Mexican Americans, she observes, are the offspring of unions between Mexicans, Native Americans, and Spaniards.[18] As she explains,

> As a culture, we [Americans of Mexican descent] call ourselves Spanish when referring to ourselves as a linguistic group and when copping out. It is then that we forget our predominant Indian genes. We are 70–80% Indian. We call ourselves Hispanic or Spanish-American or Latin American or Latin when linking ourselves to other Spanish-speaking peoples of the Western hemisphere and when copping out. We call ourselves Mexican-American to signify we are neither Mexican nor American, but more the noun "American" than the adjective "Mexican" (and when copping out).[19]

This passage not only underlines the indigenous heritage of many people of Mexican descent but it also articulates the complexity that makes out what I loosely call the "Mexican people" or "people of Mexican descent" for practical reasons while acknowledging the inadequacy of these terms to represent such a heterogeneous group of peoples. Cognizant of the intricate ties that connect Mexican and indigenous identities, this book uncovers the settler-colonial rationality that pervaded legal discourses surrounding the emergence of the wall at the US-Mexico border in the early and mid-1900s. In turn, these discourses contributed to shaping a racial hierarchy that privileged Anglo-Americans' whiteness. Yet, more importantly, what the book suggests is that these settler-colonial undertones never truly disappear—the process remains ongoing. These undertones found their way into contemporary discourses about the border wall, albeit in a more subdued form largely expunged of direct references to race and ethnicity. As the language of racial difference merged with the walling discourse, I argue that a precedent is established about how we think about the southern US border and the Mexican neighbor. In this respect, my point rejoins E. Tendayi Achiume's argument that international borders are racial borders. Achiume sees walls as part of a border infrastructure that creates a mobility divide between the Global North and the Global South.[20] She shows us how race underpins the legal discourses about international borders deployed by liberal democracies such as the United States. Especially, Achiume highlights how colonial, including settler-colonial projects, are echoed in contemporary regimes of border control such as the wall. These racial borders, she notes, are enabled by seemingly race-neutral laws and policies that perpetuate the racial injustices of the past by conferring unequal mobility rights that favor whiteness.[21]

Legal matter, especially the "walled landscape," is the second site of legal normativity the book identifies—a space where discourse and process combine to convey legal meanings about categories of thought and social relationships in relation to space. Here, the book moves away from the strict division between discourse and materiality often present in Western thought. Instead, it advocates for an understanding of discursivity that takes the role of matter and social practices seriously. Work in and around the field of legal materiality is crucial to my argument as it fleshes out not only how law inscribes itself in the physical world but also how matter itself possesses normative qualities.[22]

The walled landscape, the book argues, materializes the notions of national and social order that its aesthetic qualities impart through symbolic meanings, on the one hand, and sensory experiences, on the other. One way in which the wall communicates the law is by translating sovereign order into space.[23] The walled landscape symbolizes the state's power and right to control its territory and decide who it admits. The wall also implies division, distrust, and protection against a perceived enemy; it signals danger. In this sense, it translates the language of legal texts authorizing the construction of a wall at the US southern border into a material form. The wall is a visible sign that remediates the law's "invisible presence."[24] Yet the normative power of the border wall is not limited to its embodied symbolism. By merging sociolegal research, human geography, and work in the field of law and the humanities, this book evaluates how normative meanings also flow from a combination of sensory experiences and feelings.[25] This last aspect of the wall's normativity adds a layer of complexity to the legal analysis of the border wall that requires considering the law through its various modes of creation, enunciation, and action. It is not only state law, communicated through legal texts, that matters, but also the experience of the law and the practices that emerge around it.

Before going further, I wish to make a note about terminology. Although I mainly use the terms *wall* and *walled landscape* when referring to contemporary structures found at the US-Mexico border, I more readily employ the words *barrier* and *fence* for older constructions. These terms better capture the material qualities of early divisive architecture. Whereas a semantic analysis shows commonalities between these three terms, they distinguish themselves in their material composition and level of permanence.[26] The term *wall* usually refers to a masonry structure, whereas *fence* suggests a see-through structure made of wood, wire, or mesh. Among the three terms, *barrier* is the most generic since it comprises all of the common elements.[27]

Still, this semantic analysis fails to account for why one term is preferred over another by a speaker. First, it obscures the fact that in the case of border walls, speakers are often not so much interested in using the most precise term as they are in using language rhetorically and metaphorically in order to mold reality. As legal scholar Albane Geslin explains, the preference for one term over another is inscribed in a politic of performativity that cannot be ignored.[28] *Wall*, *fence*, and *barrier* have different connotations. The concept of a wall may impart a sense of definitive division mirroring the Berlin Wall, evoking authoritarianism.[29] It also appears to be more efficient at blocking threats. The repeated use of *wall* by former president Donald Trump, including in his Executive Order 13767, is certainly an instance of the use of the term for its performative effect.[30] Conversely, the term *fence* has a less definitive and negative overtone. A fence evokes images of farmlands or peaceful neighborly divisions. It may appear more temporary than a wall since it is less expensive and more easily erected or dismantled.[31] *Barrier* is also used to avoid the negative connotations that come with the word *wall*.[32]

Second, authors acknowledge that technological advances increasingly blur the distinction between these three terms.[33] Contemporary see-through fences and barriers may be more efficient than any given concrete wall at stopping bodies from crossing. With these considerations in mind, there will be times in the following chapters when I will use the term *wall* to refer to a structure that shares the material attributes of a fence if its material consequences align more closely with that of a solid wall, or if I want to emphasize its performative quality. Likewise, when discussing earlier fences, I might use the term *wall* if what I wish to impart is the more general idea of a division between two nations or races.

• • •

The next chapter outlines the theoretical basis for a novel approach to the legal analysis of border walls that questions the role of the law in the erection of a wall at the southern US border. Building on critical legal theory, the contributions of sociolegal legal scholars working at the intersection of law and language, legal materiality, and geography, the chapter argues that the law does not flow from a single and abstract authoritative source; instead, its origins are plural and derive from our physical experience of the world. Hence, it offers a richer account of normativity that combines a range of theoretical frames, methodologies, and material to develop the premise for an account of how the walled landscape operates in constructing national identities.

Chapter 2 provides the relevant historical and cultural context for understanding today's wall running along the southern US border. This chapter aims to demonstrate the long-standing appeal of the wall as an institutional technique of spatial and cultural division in the making of the US-Mexico border, rooted in US settler-colonial history. The first part of the chapter underlines the importance of race and culture in drawing the new border between the United States and Mexico following the Mexican-American War of 1846–1848. It presents the range of legal innovations deployed since the Treaty of Guadalupe Hidalgo to define the spatial, cultural, and racial limits of the American and Mexican nations. This includes the creation of the border patrol, the criminalization of undocumented entry into US territory, and the adoption of legal provisions granting enhanced powers to arrest aliens entering outside the law. The chapter situates the adoption of the Act of August 19, 1935, which authorized the US secretary of state to erect fences and other structures at the border with Mexico, within that process.

The second part of the chapter turns to a close reading of the legal debates leading to the adoption of the 1935 act and subsequent funding requests under its authority to analyze arguments in favor of walls. The archival material studied in this chapter includes legal texts, debates and proceedings of the US Congress, reports from US federal agencies, and communications between public servants, members of Congress, and members of the public. Noting that there was no unified voice for or against border fortification, the episodes examined show that legislative debates became a site where beliefs about race and culture infiltrated the legislative process to influence the meaning of Mexican identity and its rapport with an imagined American community. During these debates, the repetition of stereotypical tropes on issues such as morality and crime accentuated a racial hierarchy that favored Anglo settlers and contributed to the reaffirmation of America's territorial expansion following the Mexican-American War. The chapter closes by emphasizing the importance of the walling discourse in the production of US nationalism within the specific settler-colonial circumstances and the distinct structural paradigm that animated US-Mexico borderland politics in the early twentieth century.

Chapter 3 illustrates how the legal framework governing the authorization to build border walls evolved at the turn of the twenty-first century to become increasingly ambitious and prescriptive about the scale of the walling project. At the outset, the chapter gives an account of how narratives targeting Mexico and its inhabitants, present from the 1920s to 1950s, persisted in the second half of the century and beyond, eventually tainting debates surrounding the adoption of the Secure Fence Act of 2006. I argue that while the vocabulary of the narratives may have changed—race is mostly absent in contemporary debates—the discourses in support of today's walls remain grounded in ideologies about race. This introductory part serves to bridge past and contemporary episodes of wall building taking place at the US-Mexico border.

The chapter then turns to a close reading of the legal debates that preceded the adoption of the Secure Fence Act. It explores how legal discourses were colored by two specific visions of immigration: one that promoted a border-enforcement-first approach and another, more sympathetic to migrants, that defended a comprehensive approach to immigration. I argue that the enforcement approach prevailed and was reflected in the form and language of the act, which was developed around three justificatory themes: the border as a dangerous space, alien criminality, and spatialized terror. Jointly, these three themes gave further credibility to a narrative that represents southern migrants as a threat to the nation. This chapter stresses how the text of the Secure Fence Act was built in such a way as to trigger emotions that reify distinctions based on race. In turn, the act established a precedent for how we think about and regulate movements at the southern border, as the recent "build the wall" campaigns and congressional bills attest to.

Chapter 4 is the last substantive chapter of the book. While the previous two chapters focus on oral and textual legal discourses, the central argument of chapter 4 is that materiality too is discursive, meaning making, and therefore normative. The chapter begins by developing this argument through the reading of sociolegal scholars whose works consider the aesthetic and spatial dimensions of the law. The analysis contrasts this literature with a positivist account that conceives the law as a set of immaterial and ideational norms transmitted through language rather than as something material, out there in the physical world. It argues that the material world is an extension of the legal discourses that shape the legal text. The material rendering of the law is what gives it its sensory force and makes the law more readily knowable to those unfamiliar with the legal text. The walled landscape embodies and materializes notions of national and social order and authority, which it communicates through an aesthetic discourse resting on symbolism and the physical experience of the space.

To illustrate this point, the chapter compares the aesthetic experience of the US-Mexico border with the US-Canada border. This comparison illustrates how the materiality of the walled landscape, its texture and shapes, informs meanings about territoriality and identity. This parallel between the two borders not only highlights the different treatment accorded to each but it also illustrates how the materiality of the wall conditions the prospects for cross-border interactions or, on the contrary, inhibits them by shutting off pathways for exchange. The striking contrast between the closed southern border and the openness of the northern borderland substantiates the argument presented in chapters 2 and 3 regarding the racial and cultural underpinnings of walling discourses that privilege whiteness. However, the chapter also notes that the wall's inherent exclusionary nature can sometimes be mitigated by the contesting performances of communities along the border that challenge norms set in state law, further showing the plurality of normative sources.

The fifth and concluding part of this book summarizes the findings of the preceding chapters and discusses how these contribute to a better understanding of the role of the law in the construction of a border wall. It further contextualizes the book's findings by considering past and present legislative episodes of wall building together. The chapter outlines structural similarities in legal discourses justifying the wall, which were spurred on by anxieties about the southern neighbor and expressed through racialized discourses. Drawing on the notion of legal precedents of injustice to characterize these legislative episodes, the chapter highlights the importance of the past in understanding today's legal appreciation of the wall. It argues that through legal precedents, persistent racial hierarchies informed by a legacy of imperialism and settler colonialism have crystalized and infiltrated contemporary legal debates about a southern "other" imagined as standing in opposition to a distinct American identity. Building on the values, language, symbols, and practices enshrined in or imposed by these precedents, each new legal text authorizing the construction of a border wall heightens the perception of its necessity and risk of it becoming a self-fulfilling prophecy.

ONE

Looking at the Wall through the Law

The legal scholarship on border walls is relatively sparse when compared to other disciplines such as political science, sociology, geography, and border studies. Indeed, since the mid-2000s, a growing body of work in these fields has critically engaged with the phenomenon of border walls as an autonomous subject of study. Many scholars have underlined the cognitive and symbolic dimensions of walls. Border study theorists address how borders and walls are socially constructed through practices and discourses, as well as how "people perform notions of territoriality, cultural identities and power relations" in relation to them.[1] Political scientists and geographers are also interested in the wall and its role in the construction of national identity.[2] They highlight the performative function of walls, notably as a theatrical stage for the expression of state power and national unity. Some of these contributions specifically consider the US-Mexico wall. By contrast, legal scholars engage less readily with the symbolic nature of border walls, their emotional forces, and their roles in forging and maintaining national identities.[3] Their contributions often adopt a positivist approach that is primarily concerned with the status of walls in international law and their legal consequences for territories and rights.[4] This literature recognizes such walls' potential to interfere with fundamental human rights and other rights recognized by the state.[5] For instance, scholars note that the US-Mexico border wall affects indigenous rights[6] since it undermines native people's freedom of movement across tribal lands spanning the two states' territories and thus restricts their access to sacred sites and resources.[7] It also encroaches on environmental law. Since 2008, eighty-six federal laws and regulations for the protection of the environment, culture, and health and safety were waived to permit the construction of sections of the wall.[8] Property rights are also challenged by the construction of the border wall on private properties acquired through the federal government's exercise of its eminent domain power.[9] Nonetheless, most legal scholars are reluctant to attribute any normative force to the wall. Hélène Ruiz Fabri argues that walls are neutral: "What is not neutral is the legal rule that expresses the choice to prevent or allow circulation."[10] Indeed, legal experts have largely resisted treating walls as legal objects. This silence is consistent with Margaret Davies's point that although we interpret the construction of a wall as a statement that "the law is here," we do not understand the wall itself as law.[11]

This book provides an alternative reading of the relationship between the US-Mexico border wall and the law. To show how entwined the border wall is with the settler-colonial history of the United States, I pay close attention to the legal discourses that justified its construction over the last one hundred years to reveal how they have worked to draw the contours of the nation in both material and immaterial ways. Importantly, instead of conceiving of the wall as a simple representation of the text of the law—which it also is—I approach the wall as law. In the remainder of this chapter, I explain my theoretical approach to understanding the normative power of legal discourses and the wall itself in order to establish the foundation for an exploration of their role in shaping American national identity in the following chapters.

Moving Beyond Legal Positivism

There is an enduring myth that law is rational and objective, produced out of scientific inquiries into observable facts.[12] This, in turn, sustains the belief that law is untainted by the subjectivity of ideological and political designs.[13] Legal positivism follows this rationale when it claims the law's neutrality, which then contributes to its authority since its legitimacy resides in its perceived universality and rationality. According to that reasoning, the law is seen as an abstract system of rules never understood as existing in the physical world.[14] The law is created and managed by state institutions and imposed upon the subjects of the law. Within this "legal-bureaucratic structure," lawmakers' choices are objectified; that is, their choices are severed from life experience, considered instead as the outcome of an ends-means analysis.[15] This view also leaves legal subjects with no agency to shape the content of the imposed set of rules.[16] However, these accounts fail to pay attention to whose legal knowledge is informing the emergence of state law, what the cultural biases are that influence the legislative process and content of state law, and how legal knowledge is communicated, interpreted, abided with, and contested.[17]

By contrast, the work of sociolegal scholars, critical legal scholars, and—most recently—researchers interested in legal materiality challenges the positivist model by demonstrating not only the subjectivity of law but also how legal rules come into being through the interactions of people, materials, and spaces.[18] As Margaret Davies points out, legal meanings appear

> from concrete human relationships as well as from the dynamics of human-world engagements. This is as true of state law as it is of general social normativity, though perhaps the causal links are less obvious for state law. Because social normativity is the material basis for state law, it is impossible to conceive of state law without this material support.[19]

This approach recognizes that the law does not flow from a single and abstract authoritative source; instead, it derives from a diversity of foundations rooted in our physical experiences of the world. Hence, it provides a richer account of normativity. Critical law theory and work in the field of law and the humanities open new avenues for identifying these multiple sources of law by combining a range of theoretical frames, methodologies, and materials, including narratives, symbolism, metaphors, spaces, history, and experiences.[20] The perspectives provided by these frameworks are particularly useful here because they give coherence to a study of law that bridges the ideational with the material. Indeed, this helps make sense of the normative roles of social relations, discourses, matter, technologies, etc., and how these feed into each other.

Because I am interested in the various modes by which law is produced and deployed, I approach the law, including the wall, as a form of discourse that influences social relations. On the one hand, I argue that state laws authorizing the construction of walls at the border between the United States and Mexico are the outcome of a legislative process that feeds on rhetorical discourses and narratives influenced by the settler-colonial history that shaped the relationship between the United States and Mexico. In turn, these legal texts constitute authoritative discourses that convey meanings about identities and relations of power, thereby informing conduct accordingly. On the other hand, I posit that the material wall constitutes a form of discourse in itself. Using insights from legal materiality in particular, I uncover the normative power of the wall; that is, its capacity to communicate legal meanings that include—but also go beyond—state law.

Legal Words

Some critical legal scholars conceive of law as language. Law is informed by language and is often transmitted by it.[21] James Boyd White argues that the law is usefully seen as a branch of rhetoric that establishes, maintains, and transforms communities and cultures.[22] Law's creation is an empirical process.[23] Through this process, legal actors use the resources available to them, including "maxims, general understandings, conventional wisdom" to justify their positions about the kind of community we should establish.[24] Hence, the law is a creative and communicative process, a discourse whereby real-life events and experiences are narrated in a way that gives them meaning—a meaning that is contingent and never final because it can always be altered by new discourses and practices.[25] In other words, law "emerge[s] from social meanings built up over time and drawn into law through its processes of interpretation and application."[26]

Language is crucial to this understanding of law as a creative discourse process. For linguist Joshua Fishman, language is an important carrier—and thus a producer—of meanings about how social relations ought to be imagined:

> Language is not merely a means of interpersonal communication and influence. It is not merely a carrier of content, whether latent or manifest. Language itself is content, a referent for loyalties and animosities, an indicator of social statuses and personal relationships, a marker of situations and topics as well as of the societal goals and the large-scale value-laden arenas of interaction that typify every speech community.[27]

This understanding of language applies to any form of discourse, including legal ones. To a large extent, law is created by categories and definitions expressed in language. Therefore, as Michelle Burgis-Kasthala writes in *Boundaries of Discourse in the International Court of Justice*, "Once we apply this sensibility about language to international law, the result is indeterminacy: there can be no external reference point and no rule that is beyond choice; all rules are rooted in politics."[28] What is more, the choices expressed in legal language are usually those of groups that dominate political discourses and who tend to repress alternative voices.[29]

Although these remarks are made in relation to politics as a source of law within the specific context of international law, this applies equally to national law, which is also closely entwined with politics. Indeed, while the national legislative process is often relegated to the realm of politics, it is nonetheless an intrinsic dimension of the law; legislation is produced through a political process.[30] State law comes into being through debated decisions made by legislative assemblies. As Teemu Ruskola aptly notes, "More than just a set of rules for regulating behavior, law in this larger sense is a structure of the political imagination."[31]

Debates that precede the adoption of a legal text are rhetorical exercises that use language to construct discourses or narratives that describe facts in a particular way to justify and create meaning. Indeed, "no set of legal institutions or prescriptions exists apart from the narratives that locate it and give it meaning," Robert Cover says.[32] State law, Cover argues, consists of a *corpus juris* but also language and myths (narratives) drawn from material experiences to justify the former.[33] We can think of the legislative process as a practice through which stories and narratives are created. These narratives, drawn from the world of experience, justify the law and serve to counter claims about its subjectivity. At the same time, the law's mythical character, its assumed neutrality and objectivity, gives authority to what it prescribes. This circularity underlies the law's subjectivity; during legal debates, facts are presented in a certain way to persuade of the objectivity and inevitability of the rules, while the force of the legal text as a narrative aims to give these rules the appearance of normality.

Critical legal scholarship recognizes the discursive nature of the law and the legal text, as well as their power to communicate values and ideologies to communities.[34] Indeed, it has demonstrated how the law regulates social relations through the creation of categories—especially social ones.[35] Immigration law creates the immigrant and the illegal alien; national security law, the terrorist; criminal law, the felon. The law "invents" and defines the contours of these conceptual categories and "becomes [a] routine part of our vocabulary."[36] In doing so, the text of the law enjoins us to see the world in a specific way and adopt a specific conduct; it structures our experiences of the world by mapping the limits of the possible, the lawful, and the unlawful. It tells us where we belong in the world, and in space, and shapes our relations to others. Yet, legal narratives are rarely innocent or neutral; they are presentational.[37] They present events in such a way as to influence our understanding of them and their meanings. Therefore, the narratives found in legal texts are exclusionary because any action or value on which they rest is the outcome of a selective process that favors certain facts or experiences while rejecting others. This ties in with Davies's claim that "the whole point of law is to enable distinctions to be drawn at the level of facts, which facts are relevant to a legal issue and which are not."[38]

In this respect, legal and settler-colonial discourses operate in a similar way, and indeed, they often merge. They both strive to promote specific representations (e.g., of a territory, of a people, etc.) through discursive coherence and the elimination of alternative visions to fix the discursive limits of their object.[39] White notes that legal discourses can act as a form of constitutive rhetoric that informs conceptions about who we are.[40] Constitutive rhetoric gains credence by drawing on maxims and common perceptions that circulate in the community. It processes in a way that resembles the othering discourse described by Edward Said in his book *Orientalism*, whereby the European subject produces itself in opposition to the Orient in totalizing terms, often based on stereotypes.[41] Ruskola provides a powerful illustration of the infiltration of Orientalist discourses in the law by showing how legal discourses contribute to producing China as a nonlegal subject.[42] In making his argument, he contends that material conditions support and give rise to such legal representations and ideologies.[43]

Although these representations are certainly not immutable, they can be stubbornly enduring. The prescriptions that come to figure in state law and the stories they tell are potent discourses that become part of the normative universe, the *nomos*.[44] They may not always correspond to the views of a majority; instead, they are the result of a competitive political process that depends on the many variables inherent in politics. Nonetheless, because of the authority and assumed legitimacy of the law, the views reflected in acts, statutes, and other forms of state law benefit from a particularly effective communicative medium.[45] Their significance goes beyond the rights and obligations they prescribe. These narratives, or "myths" to use Cover's words, "establish a repertoire of moves" by associating actions to norms and norms to actions; doing so creates the conditions under which we submit, contest, disgrace, and dignify.[46]

The idea of precedents of injustice developed by Eve Darian-Smith is helpful in understanding the enduring influence of past legal discourses in the context of racial discrimination. I will develop this concept further in the last chapters. For now, I simply wish to underline the point Darian-Smith makes: as the law develops, it produces specific forms of knowledge that set precedents—comparable to a legal judgment—about race that constrain the possibilities for alternative meanings to emerge.[47] To reveal the foundational "myths" at the origin of our contemporary laws, she warns, we must pay attention to the historical context in which they arose and the stories that were told to justify one legal outcome over another. Achiume's *Racial Borders* offers a valuable demonstration of how precedents of injustice, rooted in settler-colonialism, have contributed to the development of our contemporary mobility regime through a variety of legal techniques—such as literacy tests and passports—and legal texts.[48] She notes that "a related injustice of the contemporary system of racial borders is that it perpetuates a historic injustice rooted in the constitutive debt [caused by colonial extraction] that First World nation-states owe Third World persons—a debt that is racial in nature and that is sustained in part by migration and mobility controls."[49] Close attention to the text, how it reads, and how it feels is required to uncover these inequalities, often couched in seemingly race-neutral language.

Desmond Manderson explains that legal texts have their own structure and rhetorical devices through which we can grasp a text's meaning and motivation.[50] The presence of certain words in a text, as well as the absence of others, the way in which language is used, and the style of the writing, all have implications on the meaning of a legal document and the message it seeks to convey.[51] Through an analysis of the meaning of written words, the connotation of the text, even its form, we can perceive the purpose of the law. For Manderson, legal texts have a "mood" that can be analyzed similarly to a work of art. Like a painting, the mood of a written law tells us about how it "'looks at' observers, the way in which it tries to entice them into its world, or alternatively, exclude them."[52] The legal subject may feel the mood of the law toward him or herself. In that sense, legal texts perform a normative function as they attempt to persuade the reader, through words and narratives (and omissions), to adopt specific beliefs about the world, including social relationships.

To assert that a written law possesses a mood is to recognize its power to trigger feelings and emotions. This resonates with Sara Ahmed's observation that emotions in narratives about others serve an important role in defining the contour of collectivities.[53] There is, she explains, an "emotionality" to texts that works to reinforce associations between specific emotions and others. Ahmed uses an anti-Semitic text on the website of Aryan Nations (a US white supremacist organization) to illustrate her point that narratives that imagine the other as the source of fear and hate are particularly useful in delimiting the body of the nation.[54] She argues that a reading of others as the source of threats and fear contributes to the making of an inside and an outside between individuals and between communities. Nations are formed in part by these readings and the emotions they trigger. The fear of losing wealth or security, for instance, or being replaced can bind an "imagined white subject and nation together."[55] In *Political Emotions*, Martha Nussbaum makes a similar argument when she acknowledges the potency of fear in discourses aimed at bringing together or dividing societies.[56]

Although no legal text is likely to express fear, anger, and hate as explicitly as the text that Ahmed refers to in her paper, the law can trigger negative feelings against certain groups of people. In turn, these feelings influence how we think about those the law points its finger at. As I argue in chapter 3, part of the text of the Secure Fence Act of 2006, which authorized the erection of fences at the southern US border, has this effect to a certain degree. By associating negative emotions about the southern "other" and the border (notably fear and anger), the text of the law implicitly works to mark a divide between the American nation and its southern neighbor. The Secure Fence Act reinforces the sense of an American community by making reference to the negative characterization of those south of the border that the United States shares with Mexico. The concrete, mortar, and barbed wire of the walls constructed under the authority of that law only intensify the fear and hostility the text conveys.

Legal Matter

Western thinking often distinguishes between discourse and matter. During the "cultural" and "discursive" turns of the late 1900s, Western thinkers overwhelmingly reverted to language for explaining the transmission of social knowledge.[57] For feminist theorist Karen Barad, this insistence on language has undermined the importance of the material in shaping our understanding of the world: "The linguistic turn, the semiotic turn, the interpretative turn, the cultural turn: it seems that at every turn lately every 'thing'—even materiality—is turned into a matter of language or some other form of cultural representation."[58] She notes that discourse is not only about language and calls for an approach that recognizes the role of matter in the production of meaning:

> The relationship between the material and the discursive is one of mutual entailment. Neither is articulated/articulable in the absence of the other; matter and meaning are mutually articulated. Neither discursive practices nor material phenomena are ontologically or epistemologically prior. Neither can be explained in terms of the other. Neither has privileged status in determining the other.[59]

Other scholars have reacted to the focus on language to the detriment of matter. Ernesto Laclau and Chantal Mouffe reject the distinction between linguistic and behavioral aspects of social practices in the production of meaning and, therefore, the differentiation between discursive and nondiscursive practices. Rather, they advocate for an understanding of discourse that takes seriously the role of matter and dissolves the distinction between discourse and materiality.[60] The sociologist Benno Herzog considers the distinction between language and other forms of discourses useful for social research but notes that even nondiscursive reality, such as social practices and objects, can be understood as discourses.[61] With regard to discourses about race more specifically, cultural theorist Stuart Hall makes a similar argument when he criticizes the "awkward" opposition between ideology and practice: "Far from signaling just talk, as if to say we are dealing with nothing but language, the term 'discourse' suggests exactly the breaking of the distinction between these two levels of 'pure ideas' and 'brute practice.' . . . All human, social and cultural practices are always both, that is, they are always *discursive practices.*"[62]

What does this mean for legal discourses? If there is little contention about the discursive, ideational nature of the law, stating that law is material is a more controversial assertion. Still, legal discursivity, far from being opposed to an understanding of law as material, is deeply intertwined with it. Goodrich underlines the power of material objects to physically represent the law. Indeed, we need to appreciate the "plastic presence" of the law to fully grasp how it is inscribed in everyday life.[63] For Goodrich, the visual forms of the law allow us to feel what is otherwise invisible.[64] In certain circumstances, the aesthetic qualities of the image (and the object, I would add) gain more power than the content of the law itself, since very few read the text.[65] This is a point made by the author:

> A reading of the legal text which ignores the power of its imagery or the aesthetic of its reception is a reading which is in many senses beside the point in that it ignores precisely that dimension of the text and its context which performs the labour of signification and so gives the text its effect.[66]

Materiality is, therefore, essential to the law since no law can be normative if not communicated.[67] The communication of legal knowledge is an aesthetic endeavor that appeals to the sensations and perceptions, and thus to people's physical experiences.[68] I understand aesthetics in a specific sense, not as the "realm of beauty" as Hegel describes it, but rather in line with its Greek etymology *aisthetikos*, referring to perception and sensation.[69] An understanding of matter as normative calls for a consideration of its aesthetic qualities and affect: "how people read and experience signs, symbols, smells, images, and stories and how these comprehensions influence human behaviors and social relations."[70] On this analysis, this book argues that the material wall holds normative content, state law or otherwise, that it communicates through experience.

Experience operates in two distinct yet complementary modalities: a normative experience may flow from the symbolism of an object, a monument, a landscape, etc., or it can result from a combination of sensorial experiences and feelings.[71] Often, the experience of a place is mediated through a combination of these two aspects. In Manderson's words, "the process of aesthetic experience is this union of senses and symbols—of the utterly present and the necessarily absent."[72] This goes to the heart of the questions critical geographer Yi-Fu Tuan addresses in his work on space and place about how people experience and understand the world and how they attach meaning to place.[73] For Tuan, meaning emerges through experiences. Spatial meaning can be imparted through our indirect experience of conceptual messages (e.g., symbolic) or a direct experience of space.[74] That is, objects and space can be representational, embodying long-established meanings, but they can also create meaning without holding symbolic power. In the absence of a symbol, a person knows and constructs reality through sensorial experiences that he or she then processes; that is, through impressions made on the body mediated by the senses of vision, touch, smell, and hearing. Experience, as Tuan notes, implies the ability to learn from what we have undergone.[75] This involves a coming together of sensations and feelings. Feeling is both the qualities we perceive from things or persons and a manifestation of how these affect us. So, the softness or roughness of a surface, the heat, the cold, the pain, or the pleasurable touch we feel trigger emotions that are processed by thought. Heat, for instance, becomes suffocating, pain can be light or brutal, an unobstructed vision can be felt as freedom, or to the contrary, may impart a sense of exposition and vulnerability.[76]

Tuan argues that architectural forms, like language, influence people's feelings and consciousness.[77] The body, he notes, is responsive to basic architectural features such as mass, volume, horizontality and verticality, and the sharpness of angles. Without the built environment, space remains diffuse and fleeting:

> Consider the sense of an "inside" and an "outside," of intimacy and exposure, of private life and public space. People everywhere recognize these distinctions, but the awareness may be quite vague. Constructed form has the power to heighten the awareness and accentuate, as it were, the difference in emotional temperature between "inside" and "outside."[78]

Like language, the built environment contributes to define and refine sensibilities.[79] Tuan contends that architectural space can inspire awe or otherwise instruct by a direct appeal to the senses.[80] Some objects, for instance, attract, while others repulse.[81] So the disposition of the built environment, like that of people in space, contributes to our spatial knowledge and how we perform within it. Design and architecture, as well as the décor, send signals about social categories and social relations.[82] In chapter 4, I explain how the material chosen for the construction of a wall influences our reading of the communities it separates. For instance, the degree of accessibility allowed by the built environment signals our attachment to others. We tend to limit obstacles that hinder contact with those we care about. By contrast, we put distance between us and those we fear or dislike. Distance, often apprehended through measures of time, is also affected by the materiality of space.[83] Indeed, "Space is not the [only] measure of distance."[84] Other considerations, such as travel costs and effort, are also part of the equation. Verticality, for instance, increases the efforts needed to progress from one place to the next. Hence, the built environment, for instance, in the form of a wall can act as a substitute for geographical distance, like the prison that separates the "bad" population from the "good."

To bridge Tuan's comments on space with the law, the field of legal materiality (also referred to as *materiality-inflicted approaches*) is useful. This area of legal inquiry explores the relationship that exists between the law and the material world; it seeks to resituate law and the human in relation to the physical environment. It builds on works from various fields, including critical and sociolegal theory, legal geography, spatial justice, legal aesthetics, object-oriented ontologies, and things theory.[85] Very few scholars have explicitly situated their work under the label of legal materiality. Nonetheless, their concerns for the material dimensions of law make their work relevant to legal materiality. What counts as the material of law may vary among authors, but most of the work done in this field has associated the material with legal practices, social interactions, corporeality, texts, and objects.

Critical legal geographers have been among the first to articulate the co-constitutive nature of the relationship between law, space, and the material. The early body of work that addressed the subject was either interested in how geographical conditions could affect law and legal systems (Bodin and Montesquieu) or, inversely, how law shaped space (Derwent Whittlesey).[86] By contrast, Blomley points to the mutual character of the relationship: law shapes space and vice versa.[87] On the one hand, the law affects spatial configurations, while on the other, the particularities of certain spaces give the law its "meaning and saliency."[88] The law identifies territories and defines jurisdictional spaces: property laws allow or exclude people from specific spaces, as do zoning laws. At the same time, space contributes to shaping the law:

> A prisoner without a prison, even a virtual one, is of course, not a prisoner. A legal category such as the "citizen" is meaningless without the spatial category of "territory." In turn, land without an owner is an impossibility (at least within the West). When we think about it, it becomes hard to isolate the "legal" from the "spatial."[89]

Philippopoulos-Mihalopoulos acknowledges the importance of the work of legal geographers but argues that the literature on spatial justice has focused too heavily on the geographical dimension of space, therefore neglecting its other aspects, such as architecture.[90] For him, the law regulates any object found in the physical world to some degree. The law "spreads on pavements, covers the walls of buildings. . . . Every surface, smell, colour, taste is regulated by some form of law, be this intellectual property, planning law, environmental law, health and safety regulations, and so on."[91] Law consists of things and symbols, bodies and ideas. There is legal "matter" and then immaterial legal knowledge; the two dimensions are distinguishable but operate in parallel.[92] In this respect, his work has some resemblance to that of Davies, who similarly builds on new materialism, posthuman theories, and object-oriented ontology to question the common distinction in law between the material and the immaterial. Davies expresses doubts about that conceptual binary since any ideas about law and its meaning are enmeshed in a network of physical objects. She does not entirely relinquish the distinction since she recognizes that there is a domain of "perceptible things" that includes text, human bodies, brains, landscapes, and so on. But her point is that because legal meaning, usually perceived as immaterial and conceptual, can only emerge through material interactions between perceptible things, it cannot be completely isolated from that dimension.[93] Hence, both Philippopoulos-Mihalopoulos and Davies argue that law is found in and created through social and material assemblages, practices, and interactions constituted of both human and nonhuman bodies that occur at a specified time and place.

I use these insights from legal materiality to conceive of the US-Mexico borderland as a space of interactions between people and objects, which I call the *walled landscape*. This expression derives from my reading of Darian-Smith's analysis of the relationship of law with the landscape in her ethnographic analysis of the construction of the channel tunnel between England and France.[94] In *Bridging Divides*, Darian-Smith demonstrates how the English space/landscape was woven together with the law to sustain the rationalization of a bounded English nation and identity. The work of Darian-Smith is informative for understanding how crucial the normativity of the physical space is for the construction of the nation-state. Her account of the landscape shares many features of Tuan's critical observations about the spatial experience while insisting on the law's presence in space. For Darian-Smith, the landscape is both a discourse and a process. It is discursive, she explains, because it is constituted of aesthetic components that convey legal meanings that "make[s] tangible categories of thought and spatially articulate social relations."[95] Law defines the use of space, its value, and its appearance and, therefore, regulates the quality of the experience one lives through it. In the landscape, monuments and architectural styles provide an emotional and sensory dimension to a place that conveys social, legal, and political knowledge. In particular, Darian-Smith highlights how the landscape is a "constructed social space" with the potential to reflect a certain ideology, such as national identity.[96]

At the same time, the landscape is also a process because identities are formed through the discursive practices that take place within it.[97] I build on the notion of the landscape proposed by Darian-Smith, as well as insights from aesthetic and legal materiality, to assess how we can conceive of the wall landscape as a legal discourse that contributes to shaping the identities of communities confronted by it. The work of Irus Braverman is also relevant in this respect. In *Planted Flags*, Braverman argues, as I do in this book, that not only do legal discourses influence the construction of physical landscapes but the law also possesses a physical dimension that is transposed to the landscape to support settler-colonial ambitions.[98]

Braverman demonstrates how the manipulation of the landscape through laws regulating the planting and uprooting of pines and olive trees in Israel and Palestine serves to visually reaffirm territorial claims. Each type of tree symbolizes people's rootedness in the land: the pine tree for the Israelis and the olive tree for the Palestinians. The planting and uprooting of these trees inscribe dominance over the space—a mark of ownership and control, like the wall.[99]

Beyond the symbolism of the walled landscape, I consider how its material qualities influence performance and movement within it. The concept of de jure pathways developed by Davina Cooper is particularly relevant here. It helps explain how the wall functions as a legal object that imposes constraints on movement by foreclosing earlier de facto paths that had emerged organically through the repeated "trampling of the same soil."[100] Building on the work of Gloria Anzaldúa and Sara Ahmed, I show how these new de jure pathways particularly affect nonwhites.

Conclusion

While the academic literature devotes considerable attention to the symbolic qualities of the border wall on the one hand and its legal consequences on the other, the question of how these two aspects relates to each other remains underexplored. The positivist understanding of the law's relation to the wall provides only a partial account of how the law is related to border walls. It does not, for instance, explore the normative influence of legal processes associated with the construction of the border wall, nor how the material wall may impart legal meanings and thus become normative. A legal engagement with the phenomenon of border walls would gain greater depth if an interdisciplinary and critical approach to the law was taken to address these questions. Hence, *Building Walls, Constructing Identities* moves away from a positivist approach that restricts the definition of law to a normative system of textual rules that emanates from the state and its institutions. It is attentive to the legal discourses that have contributed to the construction of walls along the US-Mexico border, including legislative debates and legal texts. It also considers the normative power of the wall as a material structure that holds discursive qualities. In doing so, it instantiates common assertions about the symbolic power of the wall that often neglect to question and explore how that power is deployed. Bringing insights from the field of legal materiality to the study of border walls, the book recognizes that the law is also material; that is, legal knowledge is conveyed not only by the text of the law but also by its material context. In this sense, I argue that the wall, as a material object, constitutes a legal discourse that flows from both its symbolic—or representative—nature and the physical experience of its presence. What is more, by paying attention to the legal discourses that surround the construction of the wall, I can uncover missing accounts that have obscured some of the complexities that characterize the ideological and material divides between the United States and Mexico today. The next chapter offers a historical reflection on the US-Mexico borderland that exposes the traces of a colonial past in today's wall.

TWO

Drawing the Contours of the Nation

This land was Mexican once,
Was Indian always and is.

—GLORIA ANZALDÚA, *BORDERLAND/LA FRONTERA*, 17

Territory is an essential feature of statehood. The modern concept of the nation-state connotes the very idea that a specific territory incorporates a specific people distinct from those that populate spaces beyond the pale of the state. In this chapter, I explore how the US-Mexico border and its early fencing projects have worked as a contested site for the negotiation of a bounded US national identity. As Benedict Anderson reminds us, national identity is "imagined."[1] There is nothing determinate or preordained about who has the privilege to be part of that exclusive community, or, indeed, what the spatial limits of the national expanse will be. Instead, nationalism "invents nations where they do not exist."[2] This notion of creating a national identity *where* it was previously absent is particularly relevant in the case of the US-Mexico border and its walling. If we accept that a nation must be bounded, then the process by which the line is traced is of utmost relevance in understanding the rationalization of national identity. In recent years, border theorists, including John Agnew, have warned us to be attentive to the historical contexts from which a territorial state emerges, including its border. Agnew is particularly critical of analyses that ignore the "historical consciousness about the appropriateness of particular spatialities."[3]

I agree with Agnew and further argue that it is useful to study the southern US border and its wall from the perspective of settler colonialism's utmost imperative: territorial appropriation. Territorial appropriation, as

Patrick Wolfe notes, is what distinguished settler colonialism from colonialism. Territoriality, Wolfe states, is "settler colonialism's specific, irreducible element."[4] A crucial aim of settler colonialism is to ensure that territory and national identity map onto each other. In the US context, this implied the dissolution of native societies to install Anglo settlers on expropriated lands.[5] America's settler-colonial society is indeed built on the displacement or elimination of indigenous peoples—euphemistically translated into the "frontier myth" as the site of unremitting struggle for expansion conceived as a battle of civilization.[6] US settler colonialism also entails a contest for territorial control with Mexico, a former Spanish colony that gained independence in 1821. In that space—and as reflected in the epigraph above—Native American, Mexican, and Anglo-American claims to the land collide.[7]

One aim of this chapter is to place the contemporary issue of the border wall between the United States and Mexico in its historical context. I analyze early projects by the US federal government to build physical barriers at the border between the United States and Mexico from the late 1920s until the end of the 1950s. During that period, federal agencies and Congress considered, almost yearly, building fences at the southern US border. Little is known about these projects, and by contrast with the contemporary fences erected under the Secure Fence Act of 2006, they have received little scholarly attention.[8] Nonetheless, these projects must be seen as part of America's continuous process of articulating and reaffirming its national identity.

Keeping in mind that US nationalism emerged from the particular context of settler colonialism, I pay attention to how legal discourses about the construction of border fences express particular hierarchical orders between Americans and Mexicans. Like Evelyn Nakano Glenn and Rita Dhamoon, I consider settler colonialism to be an ongoing and continuous process aimed at assigning meanings and organizing material structures that support and consolidate specific racial hierarchies.[9] What is particularly helpful in their accounts is that settler colonialism not only implicates the encounter between settlers and the native population but also creates hierarchic distinctions between settlers and other people of color, and between different people of color. With respect to the US-Mexico border, this inclusive conception allows us to extend the conceptual lens of settler colonialism to the encounter between two former colonies—the United States and Mexico—and native groups.

This chapter has three sections. Section one maps out the events surrounding the delimitation of the border following the Mexican-American War of 1846–1848. Then, it identifies the social and demographical consequences that arose from a redrawing of the boundary. It reveals that the delimitation of the border between the United States and Mexico participated in the definition of American territory and identity, which inevitably entailed the definition of its relationship with people of Mexican descent, including those present on territories annexed by the United States. The second section describes the developments leading to the adoption of the Act of August 19, 1935, authorizing the US secretary of state to erect fences and other structures at the border with Mexico.[10] It also surveys the principal attempts made to barricade the border under the authority of that act. The final section considers more attentively these legal debates about the construction of a border wall between the United States and Mexico. This review of congressional debates, official reports, and correspondence between lawmakers reveals how the grammar of race and culture was essential to the sustenance of legal discourses that participate in the dynamic and continuous process of territorial appropriation and the reaffirmation of a claim to acquired space that remains relevant today.

Unsettled Identities in a Disputed Space

Most of the existing boundary between the United States and Mexico was defined at the outset of the Mexican-American War. During the war, Mexico lost half of its territory—including most of what is today Arizona, California, and New Mexico, as well as parts of other states. The drastically redrawn territorial limits of the two countries did not follow the social, cultural, and ethnic heritage of the people living along that new border. Indeed, in this process, about one hundred thousand Mexican nationals found themselves in US territory overnight.[11] The Treaty of Guadalupe Hidalgo, the peace treaty signed on February 2, 1848, between the United States and Mexico, concluded a sustained period of US territorial expansion that was crucial to the rationalization and naturalization of the demographic alteration of the two states.[12] It became the source and authority that defined the territorial limits of the United States and Mexico and their populations, as envisioned by the former. It provided a detailed description of the course of the border, starting from the mouth of the Rio Grande to the Pacific Ocean. This spatial delimitation was integral to the definition of an American community: who is a member and who is not.[13]

Indigeneity, the ethnic makeup of an expanded US territory, and ideological convictions were crucial in influencing the delimitation of the border between the United States and Mexico. At the time the two countries were negotiating the peace treaty, various American Democrats and expansionists, emboldened by a belief in their "manifest destiny" as the chosen people called upon to spread democratic rule, favored the complete annexation of Mexico.[14] However, racial considerations eventually undercut these ambitions. Indeed, others convinced of Mexicans' racial inferiority—explained notably by the miscegenation of Spanish settlers with indigenous populations—advocated for only a partial annexation of Mexican territory so as to limit the number of people of Mexican descent to come under US jurisdiction.[15]

The analogy between Mexicans and indigenous tribes conveniently transposed the logic that had for decades sustained the extermination of indigenous Americans. It did so by rationalizing the war against Mexico in mythological terms as a war of civilization between a cultured society fit for self-rule and an outside barbarian.[16] Conceived in this way, the racial distinction between Mexicans and Americans secured the mystical "liberating" character of the war waged against Mexico. This was achieved by casting Mexicans in the language of a "unitary racial antagonist" made up of Spanish renegades and Mexicans of "Indian" blood.[17]

Yet, the same racialization process forced Americans to reassess their commitment to anti-imperialism and democratic equality when annexing new territories. The widely shared conviction of US Democrat president James K. Polk that America's strength as a nation rested on Anglo-Saxon Protestantism stood in tension with the prospect of granting citizenship to "Mexican-Indians" in newly conquered territories. For instance, the *Democratic Review*, an influential American political-literary monthly, claimed that "the virtues of the Anglo-Saxon race made their political union with the degraded Mexican-Spanish impossible."[18] One Southern senator fretted at the possibility that with the territorial annexation of Mexico, the United States would have to integrate not only white Mexicans but also "peon, negros, and Indians of all sorts . . . as equal citizens of the United States."[19] However, incorporating these populations in enslavement or peonage would undermine the US commitment to civic values.[20] The question about the delimitation of the border also underlined the tension within the Union about slavery. As Slotkin explains, the issue of incorporating Mexicans into the US Republic raised questions about the treatment of other excluded groups in the United States. On the one hand, the United States could espouse the principle of racial equality, grant Mexicans American citizenship, and extend the same rights to Black and Indigenous people. On the other, it could recognize slavery as a feature of the American state.[21] According to historian Peter Guardino, this dilemma could have disrupted the sectional balance between Southerners in favor of slavery and Northerners opposed to its expansion.[22] In the end, concerns about Mexicans' racial inferiority outweighed sectional tensions and US officials decided to limit territorial annexation.

The conviction that the incorporation of "millions of dark-skinned Catholic American citizens" would weaken the US project informed the decision to annex only the most sparsely populated Mexican territories.[23] As Guardino notes, it is ironic that "the most racist and anti-Catholic statements made in the US Congress during the war were made not to justify unlimited American expansion but instead to advocate limiting it."[24]

As prescribed in the Treaty of Guadalupe Hidalgo, the delimitation of the border sought to reconcile the tensions described above. By limiting America's annexation of Mexico to its northern regions, it also limited the number of Mexicans nationals it would be compelled to accept as citizens. As it established the dividing lines between America and Mexico, the treaty provided that populations residing in territories previously belonging to Mexico had one year to expressly state their intent to retain their Mexican citizenship; otherwise, they would become US citizens.[25] The extension of citizenship rights to nonwhites was significant at the dawn of the Jacksonian period, a time when the national naturalization law excluded non-"free white persons." Still, the incorporation of former Mexican citizens within the Union was not on an equal footing with US citizens who enjoyed the full rights that come with citizenship. Instead,

Article IX of the Treaty of Guadalupe Hidalgo provided that Congress would decide at a later date when citizens of Mexican descent would gain access to "the enjoyment of all the rights of citizens of the United States, according to the principles of the Constitution." In the meantime, they were merely "maintained and protected in the free enjoyment of their liberty and property and secured in the free exercise of their religion without restriction."[26]

The artificiality of this new border made control of the borderland a challenge as it fueled secessionist sentiments on both sides of the divide. As Michael Dear explains, individual definitions of identity and allegiance "were frequently opportunistic, responding to business opportunities, political convictions, or simply to survival needs."[27] At the dawn of its independence, and well into the first years of the twentieth century, Mexico struggled to assert its control in the northern parts of its territory, where the population called for greater autonomy.[28] The United States was not spared from political upheaval and secessionist unrest. Several factors frustrated the US government's attempt to stabilize the borderland: filibusters undermined the terms of the peace agreement by launching attacks in Mexico, while Mexican Americans resisted US control in newly acquired territories.[29] The American Civil War, fought from 1861 to 1865 between the Union in the North and the Confederacy in the South, also undermined control of the borderland.[30] In this context, the governments of Mexico and the United States asserted control over their territories along the border with the establishment of strategic military bases (in the case of the United States) and the promotion of urban and economic development.[31]

Trade and commerce growth in the second half of the nineteenth century led to the appearance of twin towns along the border and strengthened the integration of the two communities.[32] These twin towns facing each other on opposite sides of the border entrenched the mutual reliance of their communities while reinforcing their cultural integration.[33] Everyday life in the twin towns of Brownsville, Texas, and Matamoros, Tamaulipas, was one of frequent friendly incursions across the border. For instance, Matamoros residents developed the habit of receiving and sending their mail at the Brownsville post office, which was more reliable than its Mexican counterpart.[34] The same communal spirit was present in the twin towns of Nogales, Sonora, and Nogales, Arizona, where only a street marked the divide between the two countries. As for the twin towns of Calexico, California, and Mexicali, Baja California, the two cities' fire departments responded to calls from either side of the border.[35] The neighborly attitude that characterized the relations between the inhabitants of the twin towns led historian Linda Gordon to depict the population of the borderland as "border people" living in a "border culture . . . as if the border itself were their nationality."[36]

This romantic picture of the borderland should not obscure the tensions that existed between Anglo-Americans and Americans of Mexican descent in the United States. North of the border, xenophobia certainly tainted their rapport. Several Anglo-Americans considered Mexicans as "racially inferior, lazy, and criminal."[37] Despite the rights and protections granted to Americans of Mexican descent by the Treaty of Guadalupe Hidalgo, their property rights were often breached in practice, partly due to structural inequalities in land ownership laws as well as outright fraud.[38] Those who lost their land turned to unskilled work in mines, farms, and the railroad industry for survival.[39] Thus, the integration of the Mexican population into the US economy alienated them as second-class citizens and providers of cheap labor.[40] Segregation in housing and schools, and other forms of institutionalized discrimination, exacerbated the estrangement of the Mexican population and tensions between the two communities.[41] As late as 1915, Mexicans residing in the United States, along with Mexican citizens, rioted in public places and at ranches owned by Anglo-Americans to protest against the living conditions of Mexicans in the United States.[42]

The Mexican Revolution that erupted in 1910 further frustrated border relations. As the revolution intensified over the decade, violence spilled over the border into US territory, provoking diplomatic clashes between the two nations and undermining the transborder economy.[43] Historian Rachel St. John observes that the resulting instability fed hostility and suspicion between Mexican and American border residents and between the two nations more generally. Mexico was uneasy about US economic superiority and frequent territorial encroachments, while the United States dreaded the effects of a cascade of political violence from Mexico. In that context, "the national divisions that border people had successfully blurred remerged with stark clarity."[44]

The First World War exacerbated the strain on the relationship between Mexico and the United States. American authorities worried about the vulnerability of the border, especially the risk of enemy agents infiltrating the United States through the southern border.[45] The initial response of the US government was to tighten its border controls. In 1917, Congress adopted the Immigration Act of 1917, which restricted immigration from Asia and southern and eastern Europe while also imposing a head tax and literacy test for individuals seeking admission into the United States.[46] A year later, it adopted An Act to Prevent in Time of War Departure From or Entry Into the United States Contrary to the Public Safety (the Passport Act), requesting that travelers show a passport or a visa when crossing the border.[47] The Bureau of Immigration and the Public Health Service also introduced a system of health inspections at some southwestern border stations. Migrants crossing at those stations were subjected to invasive triage and cleaning procedures to identify diseases or "defects."[48] These new measures for screening and restricting entrants severely impacted the ability of Mexican migrants to enter the United States and were met with protests by border residents who previously crossed the border freely and by industries reliant on Mexican labor.[49] Soon restrictions were eased to accommodate the crossing of local populations and the social and economic needs of the southern borderland.[50]

It was only in the late 1920s that nonimmigrant cross-border movement at the southern land border became a primary concern for US authorities.[51] While many Americans in the 1910s–1920s recognized that Mexican workers benefited the country's economy, this changed when, owing to the Great Depression (1929–1939), unemployment in the United States reached six million in 1930.[52] In parallel, Mexican migration levels rose sharply before and around that period. In 1924 alone, the United States admitted nearly eighty-eight thousand Mexican nationals.[53] In California, Mexican immigration tripled between 1920 and 1930.[54] The soaring number of Mexican workers entering the United States, combined with the effects of the Great Depression, led to a period of American chauvinism.[55]

Against this backdrop, the United States intensified efforts to consolidate control over the border with Mexico. The US Border Patrol was created in 1924.[56] Then, a year later, Congress adopted the Act of February 27,

1925, which gave Border Patrol agents the power to arrest without warrant any "alien who in his presence or view is entering or attempting to enter the United States."[57] These measures along with the adoption of the Act of March 4, 1929, criminalizing entry into the US territory "at any time or place other than as designated by immigration officials" or by eluding examination or inspection by immigration officials, had severe consequences for Mexican immigrants.[58] Intense repatriation campaigns of Mexican nationals, sometimes through coercive force, occurred between 1930 and 1939.[59] It is estimated that in the early 1930s, nearly four hundred thousand Mexican nationals were repatriated.[60] Congress's specific authorization to build fences at the border with Mexico in 1935 was one additional measure taken during that period to enforce control at the southern border.

Race and Wires: Making the Imaginary Line Visible

Adoption of the Act of August 19, 1935

In 1935, Congress adopted a federal law explicitly authorizing the construction of fences at the southern border: the Act of August 19, 1935. The adoption of the act did not occur in a vacuum. The fence and the barbed wire had since the late nineteenth century played an essential role in the westward expansion of the Union. The fence proved essential in forcing native tribes to the west and separating them from Anglo settlers. It was not specifically defensive; rather, it worked as a settler-colonial tool in the subdivision of land—notably under the Dawes Act of 1887, which provided for the breakup of indigenous lands into individual plots—that participated in a strategy to negate the foundations of a nomadic society.[61] The fence was essential to the practice of forcing private ownership of land upon native tribes and consequently promoted the dispossession of these tribes from their lands.[62]

Still, in the early twentieth century, before the adoption of the Act of August 19, 1935, the border between the United States and Mexico remained mostly open.[63] Ranchers and railroad companies had erected private fences along small sections of the border. The US government also built a few fences in cities along the border to prevent smuggling and crossing at ports of entry outside opening hours.[64] Yet, there had been no serious attempt at physically closing the border between the two countries.

This changed in the 1920s. The First World War (1914–1918) spurred fears that radicals and alien enemies could enter the country through the southern border. In addition, due to the growing number of migrants from Mexico crossing the southern border, European arrivals at Ellis Island ceased to monopolize the attention of policymakers in Washington.[65] This revived interest in the southern border, coupled with the expansion of the state bureaucratic apparatus, led to frequent debates in Congress and among federal and local officials on the need to strengthen the control of movement from and to Mexico. One recurring issue was the erection of fences along the southern border.

In the late 1920s and early 1930s, the US Immigration Service considered fencing the border along the twin cities of Nogales, Arizona, and Nogales, Sonora, and between El Paso, Texas, and Ciudad Juárez, Chihuahua. What emerged from the debates, reports, letters, and testimonies about border fencing at the time was a discourse heavily reliant on stereotypes that centered on the purported perversion and lawlessness of the Mexican people. This generalizing viewpoint about Mexican identity appears most clearly in a 1928 letter by R. M. Cousar, the inspector in charge of the Nogales office of the Immigration Service, to his district director, where he explained the rationale for the construction of a fence at the border between the twin cities of Nogales more impermeable than the fence already in place. In the letter, stereotypes around the themes of crime, vice, and diseases figured prominently. The danger of an open border was that Nogales, "like all Mexican Border communities . . . draws persons of the criminal tendencies, who take up their residence there and steal and rob on the US side and then flee to Mexico."[66] Although no evidence was provided to support the claim, it was "safe to say" that many aliens deported from the United States, including "prostitutes, procurers, burglars, murderers, rapists, convicts, illiterates, aliens afflicted with syphilis, tuberculosis, gonorrhoea [*sic*], leprosy, trachoma, insanity, and other diseases," would reside in Nogales, Mexico.[67] The fence would discourage these undesirable aliens from entering the United States. The US Immigration Service insisted on similar considerations when it considered a blueprint for the installation of observation towers and a fence along most of the border between El Paso, Texas, and Ciudad Juárez, Chihuahua, two years later, in the spring of 1930. However, in that area,

Mexican involvement in smuggling activities, especially in response to Prohibition, served as the most potent justification for the construction of border fences.[68]

In 1933 and 1934, there was a growing momentum to build fences in populated areas along the border in the US cities of San Ysidro, Calexico, Naco, Nogales, Douglas, and El Paso, foreshadowing the adoption of the Act of August 19, 1935.[69] At the time, a few influential Texas residents demanded that their congressional representatives ensure the construction of wire fences along the border to combat smuggling.[70] In December 1933, R. G. Folk, a prominent El Paso businessman, suggested to Democrat Representative Robert Ewing Thomason of Texas the construction of "a strong wire border" to deter rum smugglers. The letter emphasized the violence engendered by smuggling activities, "which forcibly brings home to us the hazardous life that these men lead," hinting at the physical violence crossing the border.[71]

To respond to these demands, Daniel W. MacCormak, the new commissioner general of immigration, commissioned a report by Immigration Services on the feasibility of an 8.6-mile international border fence between El Paso and Ciudad Juárez.[72] The report, produced in February 1934, provides valuable insights into the rationale for the construction of a fence along the international border in El Paso.[73] The authors of the report stressed the necessity of the fence to stop the thousands of aliens that crossed into El Paso between ports of entry each year. In particular, they noted the high concentration of criminal aliens previously deported back into Mexico that remained in Ciudad Juárez waiting to cross back surreptitiously into the United States to "rob, murder and what not."[74] The fence, the authors of the report argued, would help deter these criminals from entering, as well as narcotic smugglers, juvenile delinquents, thieves, beggars, undocumented workers, and aliens seeking medical care in the United States.[75]

Racial considerations shaped the report and indirectly served as a justification for the proposed fence. The intersectionality of race and gender contributed to form a narrative that posited the fertility of Mexican women as a social problem, conflating issues of citizenship, welfare dependency, opportunism, and crimes. The report noted the case of women "of the immoral classes" seeking admission at the El Paso City-County hospital to give birth, which, "[aside] from the cost to taxpayers, the element of their offspring being American citizens of probable criminal propensities is cause for serious thought."[76] At times, race alone appeared to explain criminal predisposition. The assumption that behavioral characteristics are either innate or culturally specific was merely concealed, particularly when the report notes that these children most likely contributed to the high numbers of "criminals of the Mexican race" in US prisons.[77] Hereof, if US authorities had taken measures to prevent these births in the past, "our penitentiaries would not be housing so many thousands of criminals of the Mexican race who were born in this country and who in the main enjoy a dual citizenship status."[78]

Perhaps the most revealing aspect of this passage is the discordance between legal citizenship, gained through jus solis, and national belonging. Tellingly, the authors of the reports alluded to the border region between El Paso and Ciudad Juárez as "a city of one hundred and ten thousand Mexicans, one-half of which is in Mexico and one-half of which is in the United States."[79] It is not citizenship, in the minds of the authors, that informs one's membership and allegiance to the American community, but a racial identity that rests on biological and cultural referents. What the report reveals is the assumption that "persons of the Mexican race" living in El Paso would almost naturally side with Mexican nationals who cross into the United States because of their shared biological attributes. Indeed, those seeking to cross illegally, the report noted, '"are well aware of the fact that when once [*sic*] they reach an abode shack in south El Paso, they will be among persons of their own race who, although total strangers, will usually conceal them and assist them in evading apprehension."[80]

This statement speaks to the question asked by Elizabeth Theiss-Morse in her book *Who Counts as an American?*. According to Theiss-Morse, not all Americans are treated as equal. There are "true" Americans, who benefit from all the opportunities and benefits of membership.[81] Then there are marginalized Americans, whose inclusion in the national group is contentious despite their legal citizenship.[82] Building on David Miller and Benedict Anderson's conception of national identity as a shared or imagined belief in a common bond, Theiss-Morse questions the value of legal citizenship as a decisive factor in the ascription of national identity.

Indeed, certain groups may well have full citizenship rights, yet they remain beyond the pale of the national community. According to the author, the positionality of one group within the national imagination is highly dependent on how this group corresponds with or deviates from the prototypical American. In the US context, ethnocultural factors that conceive of Americans as white, Northern European, and Christian (and at the time of the report, Protestant) compete with legal citizenship in the construction of American identity.[83] Returning to the report, we see how it underscores the tension described by Theiss-Morse between legal citizenship based on place of birth and national identity based on the racialized body, with the latter seemingly trumping the former. Here, it is Mexican race—not US citizenship—that is the constitutive element of belonging. In this respect, the report echoes Theiss-Morse's point that the intensity of the commitment felt toward fellow citizens may vary depending on whether a group fits the norms and stereotypes representative of the nation (i.e., those of the Anglo-Saxon male).[84]

Alongside questions of race, the Great Depression also influenced the report, especially with regard to the cost of illegal crossings and the threat it posed to the state and local economies. In that regard, two main criticisms were leveled against Mexicans: First, the discourse concerning Mexican women's abuse of the US welfare system was extended to their male counterparts. The authors of the report indicated that it was "a well known fact that many residents of Ciudad Juárez enter surreptitiously for the sole purpose of securing free medical and/or surgical treatment at public expense in El Paso."[85] The fence, the authors argued, would help deter their entry.[86] It would also reduce public expenditures associated with the trials of aliens in local federal district courts, the cost of sending Mexican juvenile delinquents to US state reform schools, and other charges that flowed from feeding "indigents" and caring for incapacitated aliens, all borne by American taxpayers.[87]

Second, the flow of illegal labor from Mexico would certainly have a negative impact on wages in the vicinity of El Paso. Undocumented workers, the report noted, tended to accept "starvation wages," sometimes by force out of fear that they would be reported by their employers if they complained about their working conditions.[88] This situation, the report argued, did not only take away employment opportunities from American workers but also lowered wages in the area of El Paso in comparison to those paid for similar work farther north.[89]

Finally, the report noted that in recent years, several Border Patrol agents had been killed trying to enforce customs and immigration regulations. In the opinion of the authors, it would be impossible to post enough agents at the border near El Paso to prevent unauthorized crossings and the smuggling of goods and narcotics. Sending agents to patrol the border without proper equipment, they noted, was pointless—akin to "put[ting] a body of troops in the field in an enemy's theatre of operation without artillery, observation planes, trucks, ammunition and other weapons."[90] The fence, in their opinion, was "the correct solution to the problem."[91] Following these considerations, the report concluded that fencing the border between El Paso and Ciudad Juárez was of "primary importance" and recommended the construction of the barrier and observation towers. A few weeks after the report was received by the district director of the Immigration and Naturalization Service (INS) in El Paso, the US Department of Labor recommended the allotment of $50,000 for the construction of the fence.[92]

A year later, on March 6, 1935, Democrat Representative Milton West of Texas introduced H.R. 6453, which would become the Act of August 19, 1935. The bill notably provided the United States–Mexico International Boundary Commission (IBC) with the legal authority to construct fences along the border.[93] Until then, the IBC had been building fences without the proper legal authorization. The bill primarily constituted an amendment to a previous act on the equitable use of the water of the Rio Grande between the United States and Mexico.[94] Since the IBC was responsible for the delimitation and demarcation of the border, a provision was inserted into the law to authorize the secretary of state, acting through the US commissioner of the IBC, to construct and maintain fences between the United States and Mexico.[95] Representative West explained to the House Committee on Foreign Affairs that the purpose of the bill, aside from its primary purpose for the division of water with Mexico, was to stabilize the boundary line between Mexico and the United States along the Rio Grande and properly mark the international border in California, Arizona, and New Mexico, "where there is just an imaginary line."[96] While little appears in the records of the proceedings about the section of the act that concerned the construction of fences, the IBC commissioner reveals the defensive purpose of the measure when he specified that the construction of fences will be undertaken "on our own side for our own protection."[97] After a negotiation between the two houses, Congress adopted the bill in August 1935.[98]

In parallel to these congressional debates, the INS, under the umbrella of the Department of Labor, worked actively toward the elaboration of the plan to fence sections of the Mexico-United States border. The INS extended the recommendation contained in the report of January 23, 1934, to erect a border fence between El Paso and Ciudad Juárez to several segments of the border, including at Naco and Nogales, Arizona, and various points in California.[99] Then, on August 26, 1935, a week after the adoption of the Act of August 19, 1935—and following consultation with the Department of State—Frances Perkins, the secretary of labor and a Progressive-era reformer in the Roosevelt administration, submitted to the Works Progress Administration (WPA), a New Deal agency that employed job seekers on public projects to alleviate the effects of the Great Depression, a request for the allotment of $3,422,725 for eighty-five miles of concrete and steel fencing at six locations along the border with Mexico.[100] The WPA did not fund the international fence project but provided funding to the INS to install observation towers in El Paso.[101] This setback forced the INS to turn to Congress in the following years to fund fencing projects along the border with Mexico.

Proposed Fences under the Act of August 19, 1935

Despite the Department of Labor's failure to obtain funding from the WPA to build border fences, the adoption of the Act of August 19, 1935, provided the legal basis for federal agencies to seek funding for the project through the normal process of congressional appropriations. For three decades, fencing projects were regularly brought forward to Congress. In the 1930s and early 1940s, the Subcommittee of the Committee on Appropriations debated two parallel projects.[102] The first was limited in scale and once again aimed at fencing the border between El Paso and Ciudad Juárez, at Cordova Island, where the INS estimated that more than 37 percent of all undocumented migrants apprehended

FIGURE 2.1: Observation tower erected in 1937 under the Work Progress Administration in El Paso, Texas. US National Archives File 55606/519 RG 85.

in the United States entered.[103] In 1941, Congress allocated to the State Department $6,500 for this project.[104]

The other fencing project, often referred to in congressional documents as the international boundary fence project, was much more substantial and provided for the construction of barriers along close to 75 percent of the border, a longer portion of the border than what the Secure Fence Act of 2006 provides for. From 1937 until the end of the 1940s, the State Department requested funding almost every year on behalf of other US agencies for the construction of fences along the border with Mexico. US officials from the INS, IBC, and Department of Agriculture appeared before Congress to justify a border fence that would be erected progressively, with priority given to strategic points. They believed, as does the Department of Homeland Security today, that a fence along the entire length of the international border was impractical. Instead, they proposed fencing areas of the border where crossings were more likely, whereas in mountainous terrain and where there were no roads, they deemed fencing unnecessary.[105]

For two consecutive years, in 1938 and 1939, Congress granted $25,000 for the construction of sections of the international fence, enabling the State Department to erect about seventy miles of fencing on the international border between Arizona and Mexico.[106] Then, in 1941 and 1942, Congress granted $40,000 to build just over fifty miles of fencing in New Mexico, close to El Paso and at Antelope Wells, a remote area along the border.[107] Controlling the entry of aliens and stopping smuggling were the main reasons for erecting fences in El Paso, while in Antelope Wells, stopping the smuggling of animals into the United States and the stealing of cattle were the primary concerns of the US livestock industry, which demanded the fences.[108] With regard to the movement of cattle, the livestock industry's interest in the fence coincided with that of the Department of Agriculture, which saw the fence as a tool to assist in its work on plant quarantine, the inspection of cattle, and the control of diseases that could spread from Mexico into the United States.[109]

The Second World War halted these projects, but plans to wall the border were resurrected in late 1945. At that time, US officials started to refer to the plan as two separate projects: the Western Land Boundary Fence Project, which provided for the construction of approximately 576 miles of fencing along the border from El Paso to the west, (91 miles was already built); and the Rio Grande Border Fence Project, which sought the erection of approximately 415 miles of fencing along the Mexico-Texas border.[110] In November 1945, the commissioner of the IBC requested congressional funding for the two projects as a matter of urgency under a deficiency appropriation bill.[111] Justifications for the fences were similar to those provided in the past, including concerns about smuggling.[112] Yet, this time, the threat of smuggling was intertwined with the fear of cattle disease spreading north of the border from Mexico. A statement by Representative West—who had introduced the bill that became the Act of August 19, 1935, ten years earlier—during a House Committee hearing illustrates how these two issues were merged:

> The Government is spending a tremendous amount of money every year for tick eradication. Recently there was a smuggling gang that came across the river. They had a load of liquor to be delivered 150 or 200 miles from the border. That is unsettled cattle country. They have lost their way. They were coming in on horseback. Some of the horses were tick-infested, and they infested about 800,000 acres of cattle country with ticks. . . . It is utterly impossible to stop smuggling unless we put in fences.[113]

If Representative West failed to convince Congress of the urgency of the matter at the time, an outbreak of foot-and-mouth disease in Mexico in November 1946 reinvigorated the debate on the border fence and served to strengthen the argument in favor of fencing to combat the spread of animal diseases. In early 1947, Democrat Senator Carl Hayden from Arizona introduced S. J. Res. 46 on behalf of a few border states' Democrat senators (i.e., Texas, New Mexico, and Arizona). This resolution requested funds, permissions, and waivers to facilitate and expedite the construction of the border fence.[114] S. J. Res. 46 provided $2,600,000 in funding for the Western Land Boundary Fence Project and the Rio Grande Border Fence Project.[115]

Notably, S. J. Res. 46 was not limited to the funding of the construction work. As in the debates of the 1990s and 2000s surrounding the border wall, the walling of the southern border was constructed as an emergency measure that called for an extraordinary process that would permit the expedient construction of the fences. The draft text provided the International Boundary and Water Commission (IBWC) with the authority (through its commissioner) to acquire real and personal properties—including rights of way—through the power of eminent domain when necessary for the construction of the boundary fence and patrol and maintenance roads.[116] It also waived the legal requirement for the US attorney general to first give an opinion on the validity of a title before the commencement of the work, if the commissioner believed that it would unduly delay the construction program.[117] A second waiver was incorporated that authorized the commissioner to hire personnel for the conduct of the project "without regard to personnel ceilings otherwise imposed, and without regard to the civil-service laws or regulations or laws or regulations requiring the employment of American citizens."[118]

Despite the stated purpose of the fence as an emergency measure to prevent the spread of foot-and-mouth disease, issues of illegal immigration, crime, and smuggling were just as prominent during the hearings. Members of the Subcommittee of the Senate Committee on Foreign Relations expressly requested that both the assistant commissioner of immigration and naturalization (at the Department of Justice)[119] and the deputy commissioner of customs testify on the desirability of the project for immigration and customs purposes.[120] The committee gave ample consideration to the number of apprehensions at the border and whether the fences would support the work of the Border Patrol and Customs. Members questioned whether the design and location of the fences would help prevent human crossing and cattle smuggling. Testimonies also provided accounts of criminal activities at the border to justify the erection of the projected fences.

In parallel to congressional hearings, the controversial House of Representatives Un-American Activities Committee (HUAC), established in 1938 to investigate alleged communist activities, fueled support for stricter border enforcement, contending that communist figures had likely crossed the border into the United States at locations along land border with Mexico. Following a tour of the southern border, and in the midst of the second Red Scare in June 1947, HUAC member Republican Representative John McDowell of Pennsylvania recommended in a letter to Attorney General Tom C. Clark that a fence between Calexico, United States, and Mexicali, Mexico, be repaired to prevent surreptitious entries.[121]

The narrative of national emergency deployed by a few border-state senators and federal agencies, however, failed to move the House of Representatives. While S. J. Res. 46 passed the Senate and was referred to the House Committee on Foreign Affairs for consideration, it appears that the latter decided not to introduce it to the entire House for a vote.[122] Most likely, members of the House assessed that the binational eradication campaign of foot-and-mouth disease underway in Mexico, which Congress authorized in February 1947, would be a more effective response to the crisis.[123] Still, demands for funding for the construction of border fences had not yet ended.

A report produced in March 1953 by David Snow, the Brownsville area patrol inspector in charge, contended that the "construction of a boundary fence . . . was almost imperative" in his area to control the entry of agrarian workers in addition to preventing smuggling activities, burglaries, and the crossing of "subversive elements," notably sex workers.[124] Snow attributed the crime situation in and around the city of Brownsville to the "undesirable and criminal elements of Mexico."[125] The Mexican city of Matamoros, he explained, "is loaded with professional burglars, thieves, pickpockets, prostitutes, narcotics peddlers, beggars, bums, shoe shine boys and child thieves from all over Mexico."[126] Alien prostitutes coming from the legalized red light district of Matamoros were seen in the dance halls, beer parlors, and cheap hotels of Brownsville.[127] The report predicted that a well-designed and appropriately manned ten-mile fence would eliminate these classes of "undesirable" foreigners, illegal crossers, "and other juvenile urchins, women, family groups with women and small children, the citizen housewives and other citizens" crossing between ports of entry to avoid entry fees and taxes on alcohol.[128]

In September 1953, US Army engineers, the INS, and IBWC assessed the feasibility of fencing this segment and another section of the border with a double fence complete with concertina wires.[129] They also considered whether the US secretary of defense could declare the project a defense measure or if the president might issue an executive order to avoid requesting funding from Congress.[130] Concurrently, twenty-six miles of new fencing and six miles of reconstructed fencing, equipped with twenty-five observation towers, were planned in California (in San Ysidro, Tecate, Calexico, Andrade, and San Luis) to prevent smuggling and the

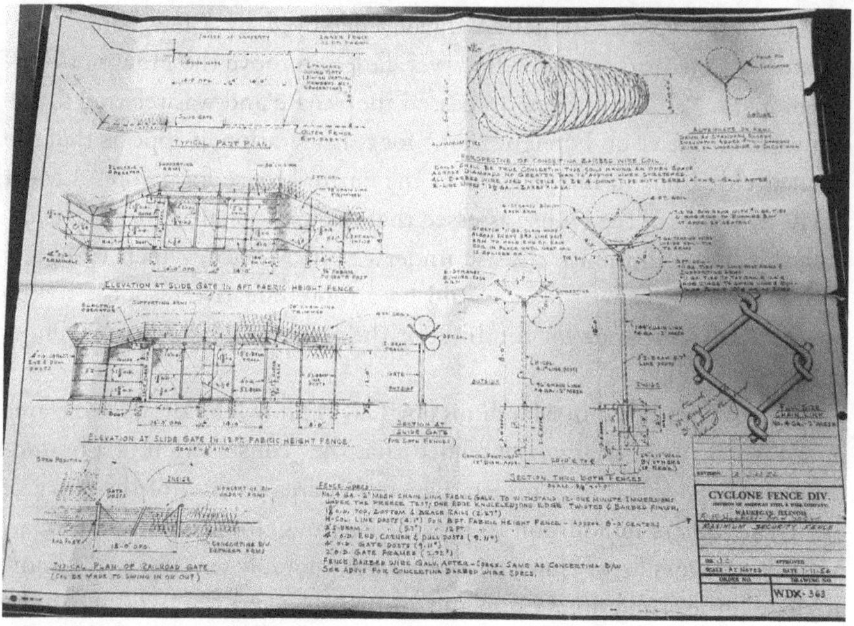

FIGURE 2.2: Design for a fence at the border between California and Mexico, as envisaged in 1954. US National Archives File: 56364/44.14, RG 85.

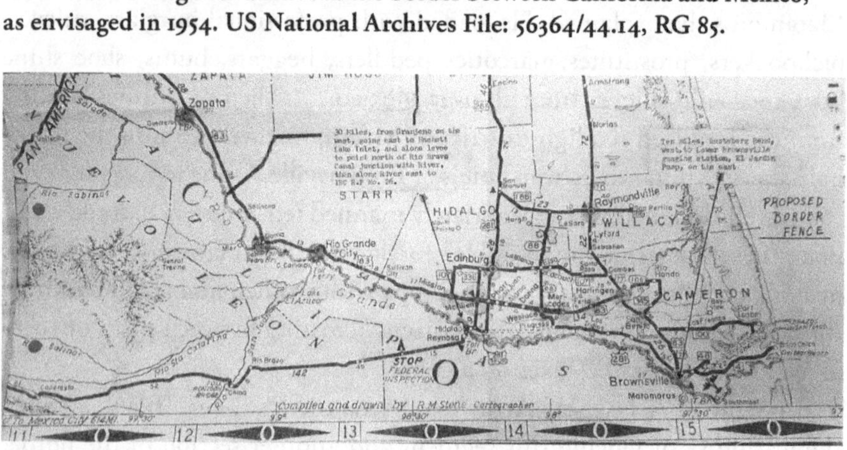

FIGURE 2.3: Location of two proposed fences in Texas in 1953. US National Archives File: 56364/44.14, RG 85.

crossing of undocumented workers.[131] No construction occurred in 1953, but the federal authorities resubmitted projects to erect fences along the border in Brownsville and in twin cities in California in 1954 and 1955 to address the "wetback problem."[132]

FIGURE 2.4: Location of sections 1 and 2 of planned fence near Brownsville, Texas, 1953. US National Archives File: 56364/44.14, RG 85.

The INS, Border Patrol, State Department, Attorney General's Office, and members of Congress continued to debate these plans in the following years. In a 1956 letter to the secretary of state, the US attorney general explained that 60 percent of illegal crossers in El Paso, where a fence was planned, were "women and children who pose a constant threat to the health and welfare of the community," recalling anxieties expressed in

FIGURE 2.5: Location of section 3 of planned fence near Brownsville, Texas, 1953. US National Archives File: 56364/44.14, RG 85.

the 1930s and the association of the Mexican neighbor with diseases.[133] Short stretches of fencing were erected between Calexico and Mexicali and between El Paso and Ciudad Juárez.[134] Eventually, the INS erected more fences in the US cities of Nogales, Naco, Douglas, Columbus, San Ysidro, and San Luis.[135] Nonetheless, these projects were very modest in comparison to the original plan proposed by the INS to fence 75 percent of the border.

Despite the insistence of several US federal agencies to erect fences along the US-Mexico border for over three decades, very few miles of barrier were built during that period. Several factors explain why these projects never gathered enough support to be completed. Historian S. Deborah Kang notes that contrary to the widespread view, the INS and its predecessors were rather weak entities. Moreover, these enforcement agencies were often at odds with each other. Early in the creation of the Border Patrol, tensions arose between the Border Patrol, set on enforcing strict border controls, and the immigration inspection unit inclined to overlook laws that would undermine the transnational quality of the borderland.[136] The INS also had to contend with the lack of support for its policies from federal policymakers, local residents, and southwestern businesses, as discussed below.

Pragmatic considerations also undercut plans to build substantial border fencing. Steel was in short supply, especially following the Great Depression (1929–1939), and members of Congress believed this material could serve better uses in factories to prevent imminent shutdowns.[137] Interestingly, arguments offered against the fence at the time echo contemporary critics of today's border wall. Some were doubtful that the fence would achieve any of its stated objectives, whether regarding disease control or crime and immigration control.[138] Officials noted that existing fences were cut through by people determined to cross into the United States, a situation that persists in the twenty-first century. Willard F. Kelly, the assistant commissioner of immigration and naturalization, noted before the Senate subcommittee considering S. J. Res. 46:

> East of Calexico there is a fine chain-link fence that was built before I went down there. It extended several miles. That fence is now just chock full of holes. It has been repaired and repaired, and when they have a very nice hole here that you think would satisfy them, you still find them cutting another hole 15 or 20 or 25 paces away. That fence is just ripped.[139]

Hence, the prevailing view was that the cost of fences outweighed their benefits.[140] Nonetheless, these projects testify to a desire for containment that existed long before the erection of a thirteen-mile-long fence between San Diego and Tijuana in 1990, often considered the point of departure of the American fencing project. In the end, officials came to see the fence as a possible solution to a wide range of anxieties that conflated issues of crime, immigration, and disease and translated into a racialized narrative targeted at the Mexican neighbor.

Settler-Colonial Myths and (Legal) Walling Discourses

The discussion presented in the previous section illustrates how legal debates about border fences were sites that allowed lawmakers, public officials, and members of the American public to integrate their beliefs about the border and those crossing it into law. A variety of actors influenced the adoption of these laws, including department officials from the INS,

Department of Agriculture, and IBWC, with certain individuals making recurring appearances at debates.[141] Interest groups, notably from the cattle and crop industries, engaged actively and provided rhetorical ammunition in favor of or against the fencing of the border—as did local residents.[142] Some testified before Congress or sent written requests to congressional representatives to press their demands. This process reveals the instrumentality of racially grounded stereotypes in support of legislation that would crystallize the imaginary line into a physical border. It illustrates how, far from being severed from the lived experience of the borderland, state law developed out of it. This may seem like an obvious statement, yet, as critical and sociolegal scholars have pointed out, too often, state law is objectified, and the process by which it comes into being is viewed as a bureaucratic activity isolated from emotion and experience.[143] The legislative episodes examined previously contradict this view. They show that legislative debates became a site where experience, emotions, and beliefs about race and culture infiltrated the legislative process to influence the meaning of Mexican identity and its rapport with an imagined American community. During these debates, narratives emerged that formed part of the mythical aspect of the law that Robert Cover insists upon, the language and myths that draw material experiences into the law-making process in an attempt to justify the *corpus juris.*[144]

Constructing Mexican Difference

The process of defining one's identity in relation to that of another has been extensively analyzed in postcolonial, feminist, and cultural studies, and law.[145] A common thread throughout the literature is that we define who we are largely in contrast to others. For structuralists, an opposition between concepts creates meaning. According to Ferdinand de Saussure, concepts are "purely differential. That is to say, they are concepts defined not positively in terms of their content, but negatively by contrast with other items in the same system. What characterizes each most exactly is being whatever the others are not."[146] In a similar process, the formation of identity is largely the result of exclusion based on differences. Davies writes, "Recognition of the self as a totality is predicated on recognition of otherness: by appreciating difference and learning to exclude, we come to recognise ourselves as separate bodies of meaning."[147] The same othering process contributes to the tracing of boundaries between communities.[148] The desire to identify with fellow community members relies on an illusion of sameness about values and a shared way of life. This wholeness is only imagined since the ideal of the community generally overlooks the differences that exist between subjects of the same group.[149] By contrast, we tend to exaggerate the differences we assume between us and outside groups. This is notably the case when establishing the boundaries of national identity.[150]

Whether at the individual or community level, language is essential to the formation of identities through exclusion.[151] Legal discourses are not immune to this process of othering and, in fact, endow it with authority by institutionalizing the differences expressed. Proponents of fencing the southern US border used belittling and deprecating language to frame the Mexican people in opposition to what was perceived to be American nature and the American way of life. This mode of differentiation is perhaps most famously expressed by Edward Said's concept of "Orientalism" to describe a discursive process that makes "essentially reductive negative generalizations" about the Orient.[152] Influenced by the Foucauldian notion of discourse, Orientalism can be understood as a system of statements that circumscribes the boundaries within which knowledge about the non-European subject is produced.[153] More precisely, Orientalism is a technique whereby the Occident distinguishes itself from an Oriental subject through representations shaped by political and cultural forces.[154] Through this process, the other group's identity is molded either in opposition to the West or as a reflection of undesirable elements of Western society—the delinquent, the insane, the poor—as "problems to be solved."[155] Essential ideas that are central to Orientalism revolve around the Other's "sensuality, its tendency to despotism, its aberrant mentality, its habits of inaccuracy, its backwardness—into a separate and unchallenged coherence."[156]

Although Said was interested in the relationship between the Occident and Orient, the discursive process he describes has a much broader application. The insistence on the ideological nature of the orientalist representation, and the operation by which such a representation is held to be true despite its stereotypical and at times caricatured nature, provides a useful framework for identifying the imperialistic undertones of discourses beyond the epistemological distinction identified by Said between the Orient and the Occident.[157] Homi Bhabha extends Said's construction of otherness outside the East-West binary. In doing so, he also complexifies Said's conceptual contribution by introducing the notion of ambivalence to account for the tension between two elements of the colonial discourse: "What is always 'in place,' already known, and something that must be anxiously repeated . . . as if the essential duplicity of the Asiatic or the bestial sexual licence of the African that needs no proof, can never really, in discourse, be proved."[158] This ambivalence, Bhabha explains, is contained in the stereotypes deployed to represent the Other, which, through repetition, contribute to fixing its ideological representation.

One aspect of the Orientalist discourse that I wish to emphasize is its normative character as a form of bounded knowledge or frame of reference for a given community that creates a "discursive coherence" about a given subject.[159] As Moustafa Bayoumi and Andrew Rubin describe,

> [There] are certain unwritten (and sometimes unconscious) rules that define what can and cannot be said within a discourse, and the discourse of Orientalism had many such rules that operated within the area of convention, habit, expectation, and assumption. In any attempt to gain knowledge about the world, what is known is overwhelmingly determined by the way it is known; the rules of a discipline determine the kind of knowledge that can be gained from it.[160]

To conceive of the othering discourse in such a way—that is, as a bounded system of knowledge—rejoins the argument made by James Boyd White regarding legal rhetoric introduced in chapter 1. In *Rhetoric and Law*, White defines rhetoric in an unusual way, as "the central art by which community and culture are established, maintained and transformed."[161] At the same time, he proposes a reframing of the law and governmental processes as constitutive and rhetorical.[162] The legal process (or the role of the legal actor) consists of three elements: First, a set of culturally relevant persuasive resources, including idioms, maxims, general understandings, and conventional wisdom. Second, law as creative: it draws from seemingly objective external experiences that in fact are "always uncertain" and thus in need of a defense through argumentation—or as

Bhabha would argue, repetition.[163] Finally, law as an argumentative activity is constitutive of communities: "The law is an art of persuasion that creates the objects of its persuasion."[164] Consequently, legal processes are not only creative; they are also *educative* since they instruct about the limits of legal knowledge, the language that can be used, and for what purposes. The law tells us what can be said and what can be achieved with it.[165] Like Orientalism, it aims to achieve discursive coherence.

This aspect of White's work is helpful in understanding the dynamics at play in the deployment of othering discourses in the law as it is being debated by lawmakers. It provides a more targeted set of conceptual tools for reading and understanding the legal narratives that sustain both demands for and opposition to the border wall from the perspective of legislative rhetoric. Indeed, taken together, legal debates surrounding the erection of barriers at the southern border can be understood as a form of "constitutive rhetoric" in the sense proposed by White. This entails a sort of creative process that uses pertinent cultural references to develop an argumentative discourse aimed at constituting a "rhetorical community." Constitutive rhetoric, the author explains, is the "study of the ways we constitute ourselves as individuals, as communities, and as cultures, whenever we speak."[166] As such, it calls attention to the meaning-making and identity-building qualities of the discourses deployed in favor of fencing the southern border in the first half of the twentieth century, as well as their racial and cultural specificity.

White's argument suggests that considering law from the perspective of constitutive rhetoric allows us to see the law as a participative endeavor. Instead of conceiving of law as a selfish or opportunistic practice, the law gives voice to competing views about what the language of the law should be. My application of White's argument may appear pessimistic when compared to the author's insistence on the law's promise of justice. Yet, I believe White's conception of legal rhetoric remains appropriate here. As the author notes, through legal rhetoric, our analysis of the law shifts from one concerned with the expected results of a rule to one attentive to ethics and voice. Hence, in exploring the legal debates regarding the construction of border fences, the main questions become whose voice is being heard: that of the Anglo-American, the border resident, the business community, the border officer, the Mexican American, or the Mexican national? What experience is the speaker drawing from, and how is this experience remade through written or oral text?

Paying attention to the narratives deployed by individuals and groups advocating for the fencing of the southern border, we notice the recurrent use of language framing the Mexican neighbor in totalizing negative terms and the absolute absence of a Mexican voice to contradict that discourse. The narrative deployed by INS officials, members of the cattle industry, and southwestern congressional representatives for articulating the difference between a Mexican and an Anglo-American community developed around specific themes or stereotypes characterizing Mexican people: weakness, perversion, lawlessness, and violence. Hence, the laziness and indigence of the Mexican—exemplified by his propensity for beggary, menial work, and the exploitation of US public services—was seen in stark opposition to the industriousness of Anglo-Americans.

Similarly, chaos was contrasted with an ordered and virtuous American nation. Mexico, as a source of chaos and vice, was a justification used systematically to support demands for a closed border. Mexican border towns, such as Matamoros, Tamaulipas, and Ciudad Juárez, Chihuahua, were portrayed by the INS as dangerous spaces where criminal elements from Mexico congregated before breaching into US territory to perpetrate crimes. Mexican vice was a leitmotif for prohibitionists following the passage of the National Prohibition Act in 1919, which enforced the prohibition on the production and transport of alcohol.[167] Indeed, a vice industry developed in Mexican border towns that, according to prohibitionists, threatened the moral and physical health of American customers.[168] The reasoning was that Mexico's laxity in the regulation of alcohol and other licentious activities created the conditions that permitted this industry to thrive. These concerns infiltrated debates on the erection of border fences in the late 1920s and early 1930s, as previously mentioned, when a fence was proposed in El Paso to prevent the smuggling of alcohol.

However, this narrative overshadowed the complexities of an industry built on transnational synergies conditioned by the restrictions imposed by US national law. Indeed, what was most absent from the debates were the structural conditions that made the vice industry flourish. As Kang explains, US citizens were in large part responsible for the success of the industry. Americans moved south to establish their smuggling activities;

they also owned the majority of saloons, gambling parlors, and racetracks that attracted Americans south of the border.[169] Americans were assiduous customers of these establishments. In 1920, nearly 420,000 Americans traveled to Mexico. By contrast, only 14,000 did so during the previous year.[170] Kang notes that "as Americans travelled south of the border to imbibe, Mexicans travelled north to meet their subsistence needs and find work."[171] Indeed, Mexicans were compelled to travel north of the border to buy food and household items that were scarce in Mexican border towns, which catered mostly to clients in search of entertainment.[172]

The connection between Mexican migrant women and moral corruption, sexual depravity, and prostitution was one variation on the theme of vice that came across regularly in INS documents. Like vice, the overwhelming discourse that associated undocumented migrant women with crime obscured the real conditions of these women.[173] The argument was enduring; prostitution was one justification for the erection of a fence in Nogales in 1928 and in El Paso in 1953. In reports assessing the necessity of a fence between El Paso and Ciudad Juárez in 1934 and 1956, migrant women were also perceived as a moral and health risk. This association between the illegal entry of women, prostitution, and low moral standards was common at the time; however, as historian Mae Ngai contends, it did not rest on fact.[174] While some women were forced into prostitution for survival, others were accompanying their husbands working on farms or performed domestic work.[175] Most assertions about the criminality of Mexican women rested on anecdotal claims that reiterated existing dominant narratives. It was indeed "a *well known* fact that many residents of Ciudad Juarez [*sic*] enter surreptitiously for the sole purpose of securing free medical and/or surgical treatment at public expense in El Paso," including women of the "immoral classes."[176] Yet, authoritative evidence rarely accompanied these assumptions. Much like the process described in Said's work, the language of participants in the legal discourses about the border wall and the certainty they showed in their position rested on an inherited conception of Mexican "race, character, culture, history, traditions, society, and possibilities."[177] This knowledge was not based on rationally provable facts. Instead, it was based on an experience mitigated by the imperative of explaining settler-colonial rule through an othering discourse that was already circulating at the outset of the Mexican-American War to rationalize the subjectification of Mexican culture.

Colonialism, however, demands a nuanced construction of the other to attend and adapt to political and economic exigencies.[178] This is why stereotypic representations are fluid and ambivalent. For Bhabha, a "repertoire of conflictual positions" constitutes the colonial subject, fluctuating between affection and hostility.[179] Hence, "the wide range of the stereotype, from the loyal servant to Satan, from the loved to the hated; a shifting of subject positions in the circulation of colonial power."[180] Another expression of Mexican identity, the figure of the "wetback," aptly illustrates the ambivalence Bhabha identifies. In legal discourses—and in the popular accounts feeding them—the wetback oscillates between the indolent, underprivileged, and feeble-minded laborer on the one hand, and the unredeemable deviant on the other. A 1920 *New York Times* article described the Mexican wetbacks as peaceful people "sick of earthquakes, sick of pestilence and famine, sick of the endless round of revolution"; they are "industrious, simple minded agricultural people looking for work."[181] Notwithstanding the disparaging stereotypes, the *New York Times* piece avoids associating the wetback with criminality. With the adoption of restrictive immigration laws in the 1920s, the term acquired a new meaning and came to connote violation of the law.[182] Their undocumented entry into US territory served as the foundation for the construction of the wetback as a criminal that the deviant label only reinforced.[183] This "wetback invasion" or "problem" served to associate undocumented migration with crime and social ills.[184] This association came across in a comment by an INS official who claimed that the wetback was more likely to commit crimes since they had already entered the country in violation of the law: "It is easier and sometimes appears even more necessary for him to break other laws since he considers himself to be an outcast, even an outlaw."[185] Thus, the "wetback invasion" helped justify greater control of the southern border and fed into the narrative of the Border Patrol and other US federal and local authorities demanding fences to secure the border and prevent the infiltration of criminals and individuals of "immoral" propensity.[186] The wetback had become a problem for critics of undocumented migration, and the fence a solution to that problem.[187]

The smuggler, however, remains the most constant referent of Mexican criminality. From the late 1920s until the 1950s, the smuggler repeatedly appeared in legislative debates about border fences.[188] Federal authorities proposed fences to stop all forms of smuggling activities, from alcohol and narcotics to cattle and aliens. Smugglers were a threat not only because of the merchandise and people they transported into US territory but also because of the violence they brought to the borderland, as illustrated by the numerous gun battles—sometimes deadly—between US Customs and Immigration officers and smugglers.[189] The alien nature of that violence was never in question. The American community was falling victim to foreign violence.

Storytelling operated as emotion-shaping discourses. They rendered these accounts vividly and reinforced perceptions about Mexican and American identities along a good versus bad binary. For instance, in testimony before Congress, Judge Joe G. Montague recounted the following on behalf of the Texas and Southwestern Cattle Raisers Association in 1947:

> During my service as an officer out in that area, I had two experiences where a fence would have been at lot of help to me. The first time was when a Mexican killed a boy named Ackerman at Fort Davis, Tex., and the officers got in behind him. It is a good long way from there, 90 miles, to the Rio Grande, to the point he headed for. It is closer in some places. They came up on him just as he crossed the river on the other side and came out from swimming the river. If they had had a fence there they would have caught him. He could not have cut that fence that quickly.[190]

These stories, and repeated accounts of deadly gunfire between INS agents and smugglers, formed a paradigm scenario that cast the American subject as a victim of Mexican violence. As such, the narrative accentuated the separation between the Mexican (in the role of the killer) and the Anglo-American (the boy victim, Ackerman). This distinction helped create a hierarchical ordering of morality between the innocence of the child victim on the one hand, and the nameless Mexican offender on the other.[191] In the process, the culpability of a few extended to an entire national group, facilitating an alignment of American subjects together with the exclusion of the Mexican other. In turn, these narratives contributed to not only arouse emotions of outrage, frustration, and vengeance; they also accentuated the fear of moral contamination as the violence crossed the border, which, as we will see in the next chapter, also characterizes discourses about the Secure Fence Act of 2006.

Contagious Bodies

While the invasion of vicious characters within the boundary of a virtuous American nation certainly offers one the most obvious "evidence" of the risk of physical danger and psychological contamination, other more implicit discourses reveal similar anxieties. Contagious diseases are perceived as a form of invasion that can only be prevented by creating a distance from the contagious body. One way of creating such distance is with the erection of physical barriers that prevent these diseased bodies from approaching healthy ones. When the plague erupted in southern France during the eighteenth century, walls were built around suburbs and cities to stop the spread of the disease. In some cases, it is the fear of animal contagion that sparks the desire to build walls. This was the case when, on January 29, 1947, a group of senators from the southwest introduced S. J. Res. 46. As previously discussed, S. J. Res. 46 requested funding for the erection of an international boundary fence as an emergency measure to prevent a foot-and-mouth disease outbreak in Mexico from spreading to the United States.

There were good reasons for the US authorities and the population to be anxious about the spread of the disease. Foot-and-mouth disease is a severe viral condition that affects animals with divided hooves such as cows, pigs, and sheep. Infected animals suffer from fever, excessive salivation, and lameness, and present blisters around the mouth and hooves. It is one of the most infectious viruses in livestock. It can spread directly between infected animals or indirectly by contaminated clothing, footwear, vehicles, and equipment.[192] Although animals do not usually die from the condition, from a commercial perspective, the losses remain considerable since it is not possible to consume their meat.[193] The United States had suffered outbreaks of the disease on several occasions between 1880 and 1924.[194] The last outbreak in 1924, introduced in San Francisco by ships coming from Asia, cost federal and state governments more than $20,000,000 in eradication measures. The disease eventually spread east and led to several restrictive measures at the border. Arizona even suspended human movement across the border to prevent the disease from spreading.[195]

When another foot-and-mouth outbreak erupted in 1946, the affected area was located three hundred miles south of the southern US border. Still, officials from the Bureau of Animal Industry (within the Department of Agriculture) and the IBWC argued for the construction of a fence along the border as a preventive measure. A representative of the Department of Agriculture explained that the disease was "the most infectious of all the known diseases of domesticated animals" and argued that if it were to come close to the US border, there would be a grave danger of small animals from the Mexican side of the border crossing and infecting American cattle.[196] Constituents too, especially from the cattle industry, requested an international boundary fence. The Texas and Southwestern Cattle Raisers Association called on the US government to complete an existing fence. According to the association's representative, Joe G. Montague, cattlemen in Texas, Arizona, and California were all in favor of the project. The fence, he argued, "has been an emergency for a long time" and the group had on numerous occasions urged before congressional committees the construction of the fence to stop stray animals from coming across the border.[197] Other cattle afflictions, besides foot-and-mouth disease, were mentioned to justify the fence. For instance, a fence would prevent tick fever, which had afflicted Mexican cattle and still occasionally does.[198]

Although national media reporting of the event was scarce, the few articles published echoed the purported threat the outbreak posed to the American nation. In its coverage of the issue, the *New York Times* quoted the National Wool Growers Convention, calling the outbreak "the most serious menace to the livestock industry and economic life of the United States (except the two world wars) that has existed in this country in the lifetime of any citizen."[199] Referring to a report by a mixed commission of four American and four Mexican veterinarians to the US secretary of state, the newspaper reported in February 1947 that the "disease has already become so widespread as to constitute a grave danger to the livestock industry of Mexico, the United States and other countries."[200] The article explained that the US Agriculture Department had urged the construction of a 1,905-mile fence to stop the spread of the disease.[201]

If the risk of the disease spreading north toward the United States was real, discourse in Congress at the time indicated that the motivation for the fence lay elsewhere. In fact, there were serious doubts that the fence would be a useful aid to stop the disease. As a representative of the State Department admitted in 1947 before Congress, the fence was not an absolute protection against the importation of the disease; it was simply a precautionary measure that the Bureau of Animal Industry considered useful.[202] As for the Bureau of Animal Industry, it noted that a fence at the border would not by itself keep foot-and-mouth disease in check but would merely be an aid if the outbreak ever reached the border. These doubts were still alive in July of that year when the Senate Committee on Foreign Affairs agreed to report S. J. Res. 46 to the Senate. Considering the usefulness of the fence in preventing the spread of foot-and-mouth disease, Senator Hatch stated that, while it may help, it "is rather a long-range proposition. If they [contagious animals] get up to the fence they are going to get across anyway."[203] More hope and funding were placed in collaborative actions with Mexico to eradicate the disease at the source in that country, with measures that had already been funded by Congress, as previously mentioned.[204]

Here, foot-and-mouth disease is better understood as a metaphor for fear of invasion from the southern neighbor.[205] Indeed, in discussions about a border fence, the line between animal contagion and the fear of human invasion was extremely blurred. Despite introducing S. J. Res. 46 as an emergency measure to address the outbreak of foot-and-mouth disease, immigration and smuggling resurfaced in discussions on the merits of allocating funds for the construction of the fence. When the bill was first studied by the Senate Committee on Foreign Relations in February 1947, there was confusion about the exact purpose of the international boundary project. While the State Department introduced the fence as an aid to stop animal movements, the debate rapidly moved to immigration and smuggling. The confusion was such that Republican Senator Henry C. Lodge Jr. from Massachusetts asked for clarification on the purpose of the envisaged fence: "I understood you to say that it [the fence] was to keep out the animals. Now we hear this talk about immigration and smuggling. Is that one of the purposes or not?"[206] In response, the State Department replied that the fence was for "all of those things."[207]

As it appears from congressional debates, lawmakers were reluctant to appropriate funds for the construction of a fence that would only serve to prevent the spread of diseases. This came across clearly in a comment made by Republican Senator Bourke B. Hickenlooper from Iowa, who stated during a committee session on S. J. Res. 46 that a fence for the purpose of stopping foot-and-mouth disease "would be a complete waste of money and completely useless. . . . But if it is an aid in restricting what is now the unrestricted flow back and forth of immigration and smuggling, I would be interested in the desirability of it."[208]

More telling, however, is a comment made by Democrat Senator Tom Connally from Texas when the Committee on Foreign Relations first considered S. J. Res. 46:

> This [foot-and-mouth disease] is just a particular incident that stimulated this thing. It has been a dream of the Department of State for many years to have this fence, not because of the hoof and mouth disease but for immigration and customs and smuggling and all of that sort of thing.[209]

When S. J. Res. 46 was adopted by the Senate on July 23, 1947, containing foot-and-mouth disease had become secondary to controlling immigration and crime. The fence, Senator Connally explained to Congress, would be an "aid to enforcement of our immigration laws, and it will do so very materially. It will assist in preventing smuggling. It will also help to keep out animals which may bring into the United States contagious diseases, such as the foot-and-mouth disease, and diseases of that kind."[210]

This conflation of disease, immigration, and crime reinforces the argument that the epidemic was, in fact, a metaphor for the deeper anxieties that Mexico inspired. The association between the fear of immigration and that of contagion has a long history. Health has proven to be an efficient rhetorical weapon in the battle over social values because it provides a seemingly value-neutral, rational justification for imposing restrictions that are in fact underpinned by social tensions.[211] The rhetoric of the dirty migrant, Manderson argues, is an appropriation of the concept of health to express a fear of difference.[212] Dirt, when in the right place, is simply "'soil' or 'earth' or 'land': health, strength and nationhood."[213] When "in the wrong place, it is 'filthy'" and becomes a challenge to set boundaries on.[214] Just like the disease that permeates one's body and disturbs the delicate order of the organism, the foreigner constitutes an invasion of state territory—the nation's body. The history of Mexicans being subjected to baths, health checks, and screening at US ports of entry in the late 1910s is an expression of these two ideas coming together.[215] The COVID-19 pandemic provides yet more evidence of the anxiety spurred on by a contagious foreign body. Despite little scientific evidence to support the efficiency of border control in stopping the spread of the virus, most states adopted some form of border closures to prevent COVID-19 from entering their national territory.[216] Even European states decided to restore internal border controls within the Schengen Zone. Yet, the lack of scientific support for such measures suggests that border closures and controls in response to the pandemic were symbolic acts that reflected broader anxieties about borders.[217]

This dynamic is not limited to diseases carried by human hosts. Darian-Smith explains that following the construction of the Channel Tunnel linking England and France, panic raged about a possible rabies outbreak in Britain.[218] England, which had eradicated rabies, feared that animals could infiltrate the nation's territory through the thirty-mile-long tunnel, or be smuggled in by train passengers.[219] Despite the assurance that it was unlikely any animal would travel in this underwater tunnel and the fact that travelers were just as likely to smuggle animals in through other means of transportation between the two countries, the British government forced Eurotunnel to adopt security measures to prevent those risks. These included the construction of a two-layer fence with animal-proof mesh around the terminals and the tunnel portal, as well as electrified barriers at each end of the undersea sections.[220]

The irrationality of the perceived risks that the Channel Tunnel poses to the infiltration of rabies into England illustrates the use of disease as a metaphor for the fear of invasion by foreign forces.[221] Like foreign individuals, foreign animals carrying diseases symbolize the faults or shortcomings of the community they originate from. These shortcomings do not need to be outright moral failures; negligence too is a fault that can be imputable to the foreigner or the neighbor. In the Channel Tunnel case, Darian-Smith argues that the absence of rabies in England was a mark of the nation's military and cultural superiority. This also signified the virtues of a community that abides by legal rules and applies them for the protection of the nation's border against "'third world' migration into Europe."[222]

The discourse of US authorities to explain the foot-and-mouth disease outbreak that erupted in Mexico in 1946 followed a similar rationale. Mexico's responsibility was attributed to the violation of its legal obligations under the 1928 Convention on Safeguarding Livestock Interests through the Prevention of Infectious and Contagious Diseases that it had concluded with the United States.[223] US authorities accused Mexico of having violated the convention, which prohibited the importation of ruminants from countries in which foot-and-mouth disease existed, when it imported infected bulls from Brazil in 1946. The smuggling of Mexican cattle and infected horses ridden by bootleggers into the United States was another indication of Mexico's contempt for the law.[224] Furthermore, the capacity of the United States to control this contagious disease was compared with Mexico's failure to do so. The United States had "repelled eight invasions of this disease, and since 1929 had been entirely free from it," thanks to "veterinary science."[225] We notice here a common binary of colonialist and racialized discourses that contrasts Western rationality with Mexican obscurantism. The outbreak in Mexico was a sign of its backward and chaotic management of livestock, which contrasted with a US cattle industry that applied scientific knowledge. This is illustrated in a statement from Republican Representative Charles B. Hoeven of Iowa: "They do things very differently in that republic than we do here at home. They let their cattle run at large, and there are no fences. . . . Very little has been done by the Mexican Government to educate the people about the disease, and there are few veterinarians in Mexico."[226]

The discourse about foot-and-mouth disease recalls several themes that had been deployed to justify the fence before and after 1947, when immigration and crimes were the main justifications for barricading the border (i.e., lawlessness, disorder, and backwardness). All these flaws contrasted with the rational, science-based American social order. Similarly, from the 1920s until the 1950s, references to public health were common in discourses about undocumented crossing. During those years, illegal entry raised fears that individuals afflicted with leprosy, syphilis, tuberculosis, and other contagious diseases would penetrate US territory.[227] Whether the discourse focused on human or animal invasion, crimes, or contagions, the narrative deployed marked a distinction between an American community and Mexico. The distinction is articulated through simplified generalizations that served to attribute certain moral values to Americans and Mexicans that further hierarchized the two national groups, thereby reinforcing the need for fences.

Opposition to Border Fence Projects: Imperialist Imperatives?

If the proponents of border fences relied on a demeaning articulation of Mexican identity, theirs was not the only voice heard during these early debates. The desire for containment was met by the opposition of other US citizens who ostensibly aspired for an open border. This is not to say that critics of fencing and a closed border were disinterested. As we will see, many who questioned the relevance of border barriers would benefit from it remaining open. Hence, the debate underscores the complexity of the discourse constituting Mexican identity. Notably, the stereotypes used to describe Mexican people illustrate the ambivalence Anglo-Americans feel toward them as they attempt to reconcile Mexicans' racialized foreignness with their purpose as objects at the service of imperialist ambitions.

Of all US border states, protests against border fences appear to have come mostly from residents of Texas.[228] There are a few reasons that explain this. First, Texas was the only state not covered by the Roosevelt Reservation, a presidential proclamation signed by President Theodore Roosevelt in 1907, which reserved a sixty-foot strip on all public lands along the southern border in California, Arizona, and New Mexico. Land owned by the state of Texas was excluded from the proclamation and over the years was sold to private owners, many farmers, and homeowners. The reluctance of these owners to give up a parcel of their land for the construction of the border fence—as is still the case today—helps explain why local residents in that state were more inclined to protest against its construction. However, it is the large presence of growers relying on illegal Mexican labor in Texas's Rio Grande Valley—as well as the state's temporary exclusion from the Bracero Program, a Mexican guest worker program concluded between the United States and Mexico through a series of bilateral agreements between 1942 and 1964—that explains why opposition was so strong in that state.[229]

Texas crop growers and other business leaders were particularly vocal when, as previously discussed, S. J. Res. 46 was introduced to Congress in 1947 in response to the foot-and-mouth disease emergency. During that period, the crop industry wielded substantial influence on Congress and was forcefully challenging any attempt by lawmakers or the INS to strengthen border controls that would abate the influx of cheap labor from Mexico.[230] Strong criticisms about the fence came from the fruit, vegetable, and cotton growers in the Rio Grande Valley, supported by banks and the chambers of commerce representing the business interests of the region. No doubt these protests were motivated by financial considerations. Beyond the Rio Grande Valley, growers in the Southwest were keen to ensure that agricultural wages remained low.[231] Despite the Bracero Program, the incentives for Mexican workers to choose the undocumented path, and for employers to hire them, were substantial. Stringent quotas on the number of Bracero contracts, red tape, fees, and corruption associated with the program's administration all contributed to an increase in the number of undocumented workers.[232] To avoid the Bracero Program's cumbersome restrictions, growers encouraged their former temporary Bracero employees to return to their employment illegally.[233]

It is in that context that business groups addressed letters and telegraphs to senators Connally and Vandenberg of the Senate Committee on Foreign Relations in February and March 1947 to contest the international boundary fence project. These critics denounced the project based on its cost and inadequacy in stopping the spread of contagious diseases. They also underlined the symbolism of the fence as an offending object of exclusion, referring to past experiences of physical partition. The chambers of commerce for Weslaco, Pharr, and McAllen, three cities located in the Rio Grande Valley, all sent letters to Congress to oppose the fence, voicing concerns about the impact such a fence would have on the US relationship with Mexico. The president of the Weslaco Chamber of Commerce wrote that "it is the unanimous opinion of this group and of a large segment of our citizenship as well, that the proposed fence is a needless expenditure of public funds, a direct reversal of policy as advocated by our good-neighbor policy."[234]

Walter Hurst, the president of the Chamber of Commerce in Pharr, was the most insistent on the effect the fence would have on US-Mexico relations. Noting that the fence would be a waste of money, he contended that it would not accomplish anything except

> create ill-will between ourselves and Northern Mexico, destroying the friendly attitude which all of us have been at great pains to improve during past years. . . . It would create a barrier between us and our neighbors in Northern Mexico that could not be explained away by anything our State Department might say. In a period when we are trying desperately to do away with barriers between these two nations, we definitely do not want a steel concentration-camp-type fence erected between us.[235]

A letter from the eight directors of the McAllen Chamber of Commerce also opposed the fence and made a parallel with the situation at the US-Canada border: "We feel that this will offend Mexico. Imagine a wire fence between such good neighbors as Canada and the U.S.!"[236] Texas property owners shared the fears of business groups; for instance, one noted that the "border fence between Mexico and the Rio Grande Valley is an absurd waste of funds and an insult to Mexico."[237] A resident of Houston contended that it would be unhelpful to "buil[d] an imitation 'Chinese wall' along our border at great expense," adding that "the psychological effect on the Mexican people of building such a fence would be distinctively bad and during the time it was under construction there would be no protection."[238] The view was also shared by residents of Harlingen, Texas, who were afraid that the fence was "not showing a very friendly good neighbor attitude."[239] Another resident noted that the fence "would be a direct slap-in-the-face to the policy we are trying to carry out with Mexico."[240]

Hence, these opponents to the fence project offered positive counternarratives to the discourse of closure and exclusion that permeated debates in Congress and communications between US agencies, officials, and lawmakers. This speaks to fundamental elements of discourse and rhetoric identified in previous sections. First, in these examples, we see the creative process of the law in operation, which is crucial to White's conception of legal rhetoric. That is, its potential for negotiating what constitutes the valid language of law and justice through the argumentative constitution and reconstitution of experience about "real events and actual people."[241] This involves a confrontation of competing representations or versions of concrete experiences expressed in the narrative form. The letters adopted an alternative language for understanding the relationship with Mexico that contradicted the rhetoric of fear and danger promoted by the INS and members of Congress, instead insisting on friendship and good neighborly relations.[242]

To what extent, however, these discourses were opportunistic and informed by financial interest rather than expressive of a genuine desire to open up to the Mexican neighbor is difficult to determine. If it is true that many who opposed the fences insisted on the importance of maintaining good neighborly relations, these critics did not directly challenge how the INS and other groups and individuals constructed Mexican identity. For instance, there is a Janus-faced quality to the aforementioned quote by the directors of the McAllen Chamber of Commerce and the parallel they draw between the Canadian and Mexican borders. On the one hand, the authors of the letter opposed the fence for the offense it would cause to Mexico. On the other, they implicitly recognized that the relationship between the United States and Canada was not of the same nature, that it ran deeper, and that lawmakers would never contemplate erecting a fence on the border it shares with another Anglo-Saxon country. In truth, at the time, Canadians had largely been excluded from the othering discourse that underpinned border protection at the southern border.[243] Chapter 4 will more clearly reveal the distinctions that characterized the southern and northern borders. Still, it is worth noting the tacit belief in a varying "quality" or degree of foreignness in relation to Mexican and Canadian nationals in this quote. Evelyn Ritaine notes that a country never builds a wall along a border it shares with a nation it considers to be equal, or politically and socially respectable.[244] The history of settler colonialism that informed the discursive construction of the white Anglo settler as hierarchically superior to Native Americans and other racialized populations is not explicitly apparent in the words of the directors of the McAllen Chamber of Commerce. Yet, it is manifest in the dismay of the authors at the possibility of a wall being erected between Canada and the United States: "Imagine a wire fence between such good neighbors as Canada and the U.S.!" Similarly, the Houston resident who compares the border fence to the "Chinese wall" does not challenge the conception of the border as a dangerous space when he notes that "during the time it was under construction there would be no protection."

On the contrary, the actions of crop growers opposing fencing are likely to have had a greater negative impact on Mexican identity than the construction of a fence. Their practices constructed Mexicans as objects of capitalist exploitation by promoting their illegal status and maintaining them in subservient working conditions. Instead of undermining the othering narrative, these groups helped to materialize it. That explicitly positive stereotypes may veil an implicit disavowal of the other brings us back to Bhabha's insistence on the ambivalence of the colonial discourse. Analyzing legal rhetoric in mere binary terms overshadows the complexity of the narrative that constructs the other in a relationship of power—for Bhabha's purpose, between the colonizer and the colonized. The polymorphous representation of Mexicans may be seen as an answer to the political and economic necessities of the settler-colonial process.[245]

Conclusion

The Treaty of Guadalupe Hidalgo mapped out the territorial limits of Mexican and US territories. However, the line that it drew was blurred; the text of the law was too weak by itself to affect any practical division in space where none had existed in the past. The overwhelming majority of ethnic Mexicans living on both sides of the divide challenged the legal conception of a US territory north of the new unilaterally imposed international border. With the growing presence of Anglo settlers in the border states of Texas, New Mexico, Arizona, and California in the late nineteenth and early twentieth centuries came the desire to clarify who belongs and who does not. This was not simply a spatial process but one that simultaneously relied on the construction of national identities.

Legal debates about the erection of barriers at the border between the United States and Mexico constituted one site where national identities were manufactured rhetorically. If taken at face value, these discourses supplied the demands for walls with an explanation; more importantly, they were about constituting an American community and defining its relationship with Mexico. To quote James Boyd White, legal discourses are rhetorical "process[es] by which we make ourselves [and others] by making our language."[246] The common language deployed by US federal agencies and members of Congress to demonstrate the relevance of physical partitions between the two countries assigned an identity to, and role for, the southern neighbor. It did so by constructing a Mexican identity through the language of racial and cultural differences that relied on generalizations, stereotypes, and metaphors around themes such as criminality, licentiousness, dirt, and disease, which transformed Mexico into a threat to be curtailed. Even when opponents to the fencing projects voiced their objections, they never expressly sought to undermine the association between these attributes and Mexican identity.

Importantly, this chapter showed that the racialized narratives surrounding the erection of fences at the US-Mexico border in the early twentieth century were not new. They had taken shape early on in the settler-colonial quest to justify America's territorial expansion. As Patrick Wolfe contends, colonialism precedes race, or, in his words, "race is colonialism speaking, in idioms whose diversity reflects the variety of unequal relationships into which Europeans have co-opted conquered populations."[247] Racialized discourses and practices operate to maintain colonial domination over time.[248] Race is thus a "trace of history"—a history that is specific to every distinct colonial experience.

The legal discourses deployed in Congress in support of erecting fences at the border with Mexico are inscribed in this continuing process aimed at the construction of the national territory and identity. The repeated use of othering language over time further crystallized the dominant narrative and became a frame of reference that informed the increasingly prohibitive policies applied at the US-Mexico border. Even if only a few hundred miles of fencing were built in the first half of the twentieth century, the racialized discourse remained a constrictive paradigm that made it harder to imagine alternative visions of the Mexican neighbor. This is illustrated by the fact that the desire for walls has never fully disappeared from the American consciousness. On the contrary, ever so often since the end of the 1950s, the American public, US officials, and lawmakers have demanded the construction of walls at the US-Mexico border.

Today, the southern US border remains the site where conceptions about the make-up of the nation are the most forcefully projected and challenged. As the next chapter will discuss, fences never ceased to be contemplated as an instrument for the governance of the relationship with Mexico and its people. Rather, the impetus for walling reached its apex with the adoption of the Secure Fence Act in 2006, which allowed for the building of hundreds of miles of barriers along the southern US border. This time money followed. What comes out of the analysis of the legal discourses surrounding the adoption of this act, as we will see, suggests that short of the explicit references to race that were ominous in early border fence debates, the meanings underpinning the narrative about Mexican identity in the first half of the twentieth century persist.

THREE

The Wall We Need

I walk through the hole in the fence
to the other side.
Under my fingers I feel the gritty wire
rusted by 139 years
of the salty breath of the sea.

—GLORIA ANZALDÚA, *BORDERLANDS/LA FRONTERA*,16

When reading Gloria Anzaldúa's *Borderlands/La Frontera*, we cannot ignore the continued relevance of the European settler-colonial project in the construction of the US-Mexico borderland. Writing in 1987, she tells us that the fence that stands before her, a puny fence made of steel and barbed wire, is not a novelty. No, it was erected on February 2, 1848, when the United States and Mexico signed the Treaty of Guadalupe-Hidalgo.[1] The treaty that split open a land that was once Mexican—and before that "Indian," as she reminds us—is the fence. A fence that originates from the past, extends into the present, and will most likely reach into the future. In a few lines, the epigraph above sums up one of the aims of this chapter. What I want to show in the following sections is how the wall constructed at the southern US border in the first years of our century is entangled with the history of that border, as discussed in the previous chapter.

Understanding the settler-colonial project as a process is helpful here. Settler colonialism is "temporal," "ongoing," "dynamic," and "continuous."[2] As such, its operation toward "assigning political meanings and organizing material structures driven by forces of power" to establish a specific racial order is never complete, never stable.[3] It is always, and Homi Bhabha would certainly concur, in need of reaffirmation and reiteration "implicating socioeconomic, cultural, ideological, and political practices, discourses, institutions, and actors."[4] Failing to attend to the history of American nation building as it pertains to the southern border veils the operation of the past in the construction of the wall today. Especially, it occludes the lineage of contemporary constructions about Mexican and American identities rooted in colonial conquests and imperialism.[5] This does not mean that the knowledge of the past cannot be undone. As Saidiya Hartman observes in the context of slavery, history resonates in the present, yet,

> the point isn't the impossibility of escaping the stranglehold of the past. . . . But rather that the perilous conditions of the present establish the link between our age and a previous one. . . . The past is never inert nor given. The stories we tell about *what happened then*, the correspondences we discern between today and times past, and the ethical and political stakes of these stories rebound in the present.[6]

With that in mind, this chapter calls attention to how past discourses about Mexican and Anglo-American identities "rebound" in today's debates about the US-Mexico border wall, informed by similar anxieties about "belonging, status, security, profit, power, and safety in relation to these lands," and, the racialized fears attached to these anxieties.[7]

My second purpose is to explore how the law pertaining to the border wall has evolved along with discourses about Mexican identity. Indeed, a close reading of the legal developments authorizing the erection of walls and fences at the US-Mexico border from the early 1930s to 2006 shows that if the racialized vocabulary used to justify the wall appears somewhat subdued, the law, by contrast, has become increasingly ambitious and prescriptive about the walling project. From a modest authorization buried deep within an obscure procedural act from 1935 on the division of water between the United States and Mexico, walling provisions evolved into a symbolic piece of legislation, imposing ambitious and increasingly detailed prescriptions for the closing of the border.

This in turn speaks to the need to attend to various forms of racial and identity discourses. Stuart Hall observes that ideologies about race are deployed and transmitted in complex ways.[8] Discourses may be influenced by a history of colonization, yet mute the racial considerations that ground them. A racial or colonial discourse can be inferential rather than overt. That is, it can silence its historical and ideological basis through a language that appears neutral and rational despite its subjectivity. Nonetheless, these discourses carry a buried assumption about the superiority of one's culture over another. In fact, "inferential racism," Hall contends, is more widespread and insidious than its overt variant.[9] The debates prior to and surrounding the adoption of the Secure Fence Act of 2006, as we will see, present a mixture of overt othering discourses and tacit acquiescence to a colonial or racist logic that tapped into the anxieties triggered by Mexican nationals crossing the border into the United States.

The Continued Appeal of Walls and Fences

The Tortilla Curtain and the San Diego Fence

Although this book considers two instances of wall building at the southern US border, these periods cannot be entirely severed from one another. Following Operation Wetback in the summer of 1954, the number of apprehensions of undocumented migrants at the southern border dropped sharply.[10] Apprehensions remained low throughout most of the 1960s, averaging fifty-four thousand per year, yet rose steadily from this period, reaching a peak of close to 1.7 million in 1986.[11] In parallel with increasing apprehensions, concerns over illegal immigration and border enforcement grew both nationally and locally, spurred on by a weakening economy and rapidly expanding media coverage of a border in crisis.[12]

As a site for the production and circulation of knowledge, the media's intensified attention to the border was not without consequences for how the issues of immigration and border crossings were received and understood by the American public. As Stuart Hall observes, the media are a crucial means of ideological production. They are not merely circulating preexisting knowledge but are intervening in the construction of ideas by deploying images, concepts, and premises on which we rely to "make sense" of what is unfolding. Media discourses articulate, align, join, and disjoint various concepts and images to produce and alter meanings about social events, about how we conceive of ourselves in relation to others, and ultimately inform our actions and legal practice.[13] Writing specifically on the role of the media in the construction of race, Hall observes that the media are a space where racial categories are constructed. Along with the law, and certainly informing it at times, the media offer us "a definition of what *race* is, what meaning the imagery of race carries, and what the 'problem of race' is understood to be."[14]

In the 1970s, the number of articles published annually by the *New York Times* on undocumented immigration grew more than sixfold.[15] During this period, newspapers and pundits emphasized a "threat narrative" that constructed the Mexicans as criminals—fueled by border violence and America's war on drugs[16]—and a danger to the living conditions of Americans.[17] Invasion became a popular theme to describe the situation at the southern border.[18] In 1973, a *US News & World Report* article with the evocative title "'Invasion' by Illegal Aliens and the Problems They Create" suggested that Mexican migrants were less commendable than previous waves of immigrants from Europe.[19] A few years later, the Immigration and Naturalization Service (INS) commissioner, Leonard F. Chapman, described the flow of Mexican workers as a "silent invasion," in an opinion piece titled "Illegal Aliens: Time to Call a Halt!" In the article, Chapman warned that the silent invasion "now threatens to become a national disaster" with illegal aliens "milking the US taxpayer of $13 billion annually by taking away jobs from legal residents and forcing them into unemployment; by illegally acquiring welfare benefits and public services; by avoiding taxes."[20] *Time* magazine also took up the silent invasion trope: "The US is being invaded so silently and surreptitiously that most Americans are not even aware of it. . . . No commandos or assault troops have shown more ingenuity and determination in storming a country that tries to keep them out."[21]

The threat narrative, deployed through the words and images of news stories, influenced general attitudes about immigration and informed expedient policies for the securitization of the border.[22] With the perceived failure of the federal government to achieve a solution to unauthorized immigration, in 1977, the INS asked for and received funding from Congress to build fences in El Paso, San Ysidro, and San Luis.[23] Yet, this "Tortilla Curtain" appears to have done nothing to appease anxieties over drugs and illegal immigration.[24] In fact, it did little to diminish the overall number of undocumented Mexican nationals fleeing the economic crisis of the mid-1980s.[25] The rising strategic importance of Mexico in the South American drug trade also led to an increase in drug smuggling from Mexico, reinforcing the image of the immigrant criminal.[26] Hence, in the early 1990s, demands for robust border enforcement measures grew louder; first at the local level—especially in California—and eventually in Washington, DC.[27] The US Border Patrol responded with the deployment of a series of operations to establish control over the southern border, all bearing names conveying a sense that the nation was under siege. In 1993, it deployed four hundred agents to the border in El Paso during Operation Blockade (later renamed Operation Hold the Line since the original name was considered offensive).[28] Following the same model, the US Border Patrol launched Operation Gatekeeper in San Diego and Operation Safeguard in Nogales in 1994.[29]

The movement toward robust border controls stood in sharp contrast with the rhetoric of economic integration accompanying the negotiation of the North American Free Trade Agreement (NAFTA), which was underway around the same time.[30] Still, the ostensible contradiction between border enforcement and free markets is illusory.[31] The objectives of NAFTA, entered into force in January 1994, were to liberalize markets and gradually reduce trade barriers between the United States, Mexico, and Canada. As noted by Patricia Fernández-Kelly and Douglas Massey, the treaty was never conceived for the purpose of opening labor markets across participant countries, such as in the Europe Union. On the contrary, from Mexico's perspective, the aim of the agreement was to create jobs in Mexico and increase the exportation of merchandise to the US and Canada.[32] This objective, however, never materialized. Agricultural workers in Mexico were especially hard hit by NAFTA and the economic transformations that followed, driving them to seek employment in the United States and, therefore, increasing the number of undocumented Mexican workers seeking employment north of the border.[33]

With increased undocumented border flows, the popularity of the fence as a highly visible artifact of border control rose among state and national politicians. Between 1990 and 1993, the Army Corps of Engineers and the California National Guard erected a steel wall in San Diego, where, by far, the highest number of apprehensions by the US Border Patrol were taking place. In the early 1990s, the INS would sometimes apprehend two thousand people per day in the San Diego sector alone.[34] The wall, made of landing mats used during the Vietnam War, was fourteen miles long and ran along the border from the Pacific Ocean.[35] The

INS explained that the objective of the fence was to restore order to an area characterized by lawlessness and violence. According to Gustavo De La Viña, chief of US Border Patrol for the San Diego Sector, erecting the San Diego barrier would "delineate the border . . . to show the migrants and us where the U.S. began and where Mexico ended."[36]

The fence ultimately reduced the smuggling of drugs and people in the San Diego area. It also curtailed violence against undocumented migrants in the United States.[37] Thus, the fence restored a sense of order to the area. Yet, the fence also drew sharp criticisms, not least in Mexico, where politicians and Mexican citizens interpreted it as an insult and an unfriendly act, sometimes referring to it as "the new Berlin Wall."[38] There were also doubts about the effectiveness of the fence. While it had reduced illegal flows of people and goods in the urban San Diego area, the fence had had little impact on the overall number of apprehensions, merely displacing the flow of illegal entries to other areas along the border.[39] Another unintended consequence of the fence was to bolster smuggling operations by creating the need for undocumented migrants to resort to people smugglers to guide them across the increasingly fortified border.[40]

Despite evidence of the limited efficiency of the border barrier in San Diego, fencing remained an essential element of the INS border enforcement strategy in the 1990s.[41] In 1991, the INS Office of National Drug Control Policy commissioned an analysis of the security along the US-Mexico border from Sandia National Laboratories (a federally funded multidisciplinary national laboratory and research and development center). In its report published in 1993, Sandia Laboratories qualified the situation at the border as out of control and designated undocumented travelers as a threat to the United States. It noted that there were between 150 and 200 groups involved in the majority of drug smuggling activities in the United States. These groups, mostly composed of "close-knit family members," were based in Mexico but were being increasingly infiltrated by Colombian organizations.[42] Despite singling out drug smugglers as the primary threat, the report states that it was difficult to discriminate between drug-related traffic crossings and other forms of crossing. Thus, it defined "adversaries" as drug smugglers, alien smugglers, smugglers, illegal aliens, and commuter aliens.[43] It noted that any persons from these groups could be engaged in drug smuggling. In defining the apparent neutral category of "commuter aliens," the report used language that emphasized the criminal purpose of these commutes, suggesting that people were crossing the border to break US law and commit crimes, noting that the purposes for such crossings range from illegal employment on the US side, to shopping for US services or goods, to the robbery or burglary of US property.[44]

Still, the report recognized that not all of these categories of adversaries posed the same level of risk. While the report considered that drug smugglers constituted "a severe threat to the health and social structure of the citizens of the US," as well as to the security of border agents, commuters posed the lowest level of threat. However, it noted that "their willingness to work for very low pay makes them an economic threat to US citizens and documented immigrants engaged in similar work and compounds the injustice of their continued illegal activity."[45]

The report by Sandia National Laboratories depicted the border as an out-of-control space through a narrative that compounded undocumented immigration, drug trafficking, and other crimes such as rape, robbery, and murder. What also came through in the report was a discourse that used violence committed against the migrants themselves—a point I will return to later in this chapter with regard to sexual violence against migrant women—to justify restrictive measures against them:

> It is imperative that control of the border be gained as soon as possible because of the problems caused by the uncontrolled illegal alien and drug traffic in our border communities and large inland population centers. It is also clear that we must be concerned about the inhumane treatment of these illegal aliens by alien and drug smugglers who are determined to profit from the plight of the illegal aliens. If we stop the illegal alien traffic, crimes (such as rape, robbery, and murder) being committed against illegal aliens crossing the border will also stop. If the reason to assemble on the Mexico side is eliminated, the crimes being committed there should also decrease.[46]

To stop the violence and "flagrant disregard of border law" shown by undocumented border crossers, Sandia National Laboratories proposed triple-layer fences and road checkpoints at specific segments along the border.[47] This recommendation eventually infiltrated legislative debates and influenced Congress's decision to authorize the erection of a triple-layer fence when it adopted the Illegal Immigration Reform and Immigration Responsibility Act of 1996 (hereinafter IIRIRA).

Bridging Immigration Law and the Wall

Since 1996, Section 102 of the IIRIRA authorizes the US attorney general—now the secretary of homeland security at the Department of Homeland Security (DHS)—to erect barriers along America's borders. Section 102 (a) provides the secretary of the DHS with a general authorization "to install additional physical barriers . . . in the vicinity of the United States border to deter illegal crossings in areas of high illegal entry into the United States."[48] In addition to this general authorization, as originally adopted, Section 102 (b) imposes specific requirements upon the secretary to construct a second and third fence along the existing barrier in San Diego, following the recommendations provided in the report by Sandia National Laboratories. The act was the first legislation since the Act of August 19, 1935, to explicitly grant a federal official the authority to erect fences along the border.

As in the Act of August 19, 1935, the provisions concerning fencing were only a minor aspect of the law. However, in this instance, the act substantially affected legal and undocumented immigrants. The IIRIRA constituted a fundamental overhaul of immigration law.[49] Notably, it reduced legal immigrants' access to welfare, increased the range of offenses under which they could be removed, mandated the detention of aliens ordered to be removed, and placed constraints on the judicial review of removal decisions.[50] As in the past, economic decline and the growing number of Mexican immigrants crossing the border into the United States contributed to hardening the stance against immigration. The adoption of the IIRIRA was possible due to increasing nativist attitudes in the United States in the late 1990s, which strengthened support for policies that restricted migrants' rights.[51] Events such as the recession of the early 1990s, concerns over immigration from Haiti, and the 1993 attack on the World Trade Center by suspected unauthorized immigrants all contributed to a focus on immigration and fueled the perception of a besieged nation.[52] Anti-immigration groups lent support to that discourse and were able to stir debates in Congress on the question of how to "slow the 'flood' of immigration, legal and illegal."[53]

When introducing the legislation, Republican Representative Lamar Smith from Texas used the economy, drug trafficking, violence, and the narrative of a crisis to justify measures that reframed undocumented immigration as a crime and entwined immigration with crime control. Using language reminiscent of earlier border fence debates, Smith made his case by building on one of the most potent triggers of resentment against immigration: the perception that immigrants receive more in welfare than they pay in taxes. He suggested that 40 percent of births in California's public hospitals were by illegal aliens and that the number of immigrants applying for supplemental security incomes increased by nearly sixfold from 1984 to 1996.[54] Smith referred to one study contending that immigrant families are more likely than American families to receive welfare. The study noted that the cost of legal and undocumented immigration extends to the criminal and justice sectors. For instance, it indicated that 25 percent of federal prisoners are foreign born and that illegal aliens are ten times more likely than Americans to be convicted of a federal crime. Most, the report explained, are convicted of drug trafficking, while "others, like those who bombed the World Trade Center in New York City or murdered the CIA employees in Virginia, have committed particularly heinous acts of violence."[55]

Within this broader debate, the provisions of the bill concerning the construction of fences along the border received little attention. Most of the public debate focused on the question of immigration: notably, the provisions that would prevent the children of illegal immigrants from attending public schools and other measures that would prevent federal courts (apart from the Supreme Court) from reviewing certain actions of the INS.[56] While several of these contentious proposals did not enter into law, the IIRIRA enacted some of the harshest measures ever taken against both legal and illegal immigrants. Hence provisions relating to border enforcement, including fencing, were, as one observer noted, the "most humane method" to reduce undocumented immigration when compared to some of the measures proposed in the original bill.[57]

Crime, especially drug smuggling, was the chief justification for the fence brought forward in Congress. Republican Representative Duncan Lee Hunter from California called border cities "hotbeds" for smuggling.[58] Hunter was the force behind the construction of the San Diego border fence, and also a vocal advocate for the provision of the bill that authorized the construction of fences at other segments of the border and the reinforcement of the one he had pushed for in San Diego.[59] He argued that with the deployment of more Border Patrol agents at the border, the proposed fence would help cut off smuggling corridors. Others in the House of Representatives saw the bill and fence proposal as absurd and due more to "hysteria and prejudice than to reason and fact."[60]

Republicans and Democrats did not seriously oppose the fence. What was contentious was Sandia National Laboratories' triple-layer fence design, judged to pose a risk to Border Patrol agents. The agencies most concerned with the measures—the Border Patrol, Border Patrol Union, and Department of Justice—all opposed the three-tier fence.[61] Another contentious aspect of the bill concerned the authorization to waive two environmental laws, the Endangered Species Act (ESA) and the National Environmental Policy Act (NEPA), to build fences expeditiously. Republican Representative Jim Saxton from New Jersey noted that both the Department of Justice and the Department of the Interior believed the waivers were unnecessary to complete the construction of the fence.[62] For other members, the subordination of environmental law to the construction of fences was the sticking point. Speaking about the conference report on H.R. 2202, Democrat Representative John Conyers from Michigan said, "The National Environmental Protection Act is the nation's founding charter for environmental protection, and this bill repeals that law, in effect, when it comes to border-related construction. That means when we are working on highways, roads, bridges, fences, that it is OK to ignore the environment."[63]

Although the ESA and NEPA waiver survived opposition by Congress members, the INS never used this original waiver, opting instead to comply with the ESA and NEPA. It did, however, use the extended version of this waiver, provided for in the REAL ID Act of 2005, which amended Section 102 of the IIRIRA to authorize the secretary of the DHS to "waive all legal requirements he . . . determines necessary to ensure expeditious construction of the barriers."[64] The act also limits judicial review of the secretary's decision to federal district courts. This waiver has been described by some as the most far-reaching waiver in US history.[65] It has been used to waive over eighty-six laws and regulations that would have impeded the construction of border fences.[66]

Despite the fence being secondary to the debate on the IIRIRA, Section 102 of the act marked a change in how the law engaged with border fortifications and initiated a more conscious and structured approach to border wall construction. The act signaled a more hands-on attitude by lawmakers on the issue of wall building that also heralded the growing potency of the border enforcement discourse in national law and politics. Whereas in the past, fence projects had been initiated primarily by the executive branch of government, especially the INS, this time, lawmakers in Congress were taking ownership of the issue, notably by directing the US attorney general to build a fence and setting specific obligations concerning its location, length, and design. With Section 102 of the IIRIRA, Congress unequivocally linked wall building with immigration law, moving away from the general authorization provided in the Act of August 19, 1935. Lawmakers also gave greater importance to legal provisions relevant to border walls than to other legal provisions aimed at the protection of the environment and property rights. In addition to the authorization to waive the ESA and NEPA, the IIRIRA gave the attorney general the power to exercise eminent domain toward lands that she/he deems "essential to control and guard the boundaries and borders of the United States' against violations of the IIRIRA." As mentioned in the previous chapter, Congress had contemplated a similar measure in 1947 but never adopted the bill. Most importantly, Section 102 of the IIRIRA contributed to normalizing the border wall as an instrument for regulating movement at the US-Mexico border. Hence, this paved the way for Congress's decision to build a wall running along hundreds of miles at the border with Mexico when it adopted the Secure Fence Act in 2006.

Debating the Need for Walls in the Twentieth Century

Competing Visions about Immigration Law

The Secure Fence Act, signed into law on October 26, 2006, amended Section 102 (b) of the IIRIRA by removing the provision specific to the construction of the San Diego fence. In its place, it drastically increased the minimum length of fencing the DHS was required to build by directing it to erect more than seven hundred miles of double-layer fencing along five specified segments of the southwest border around Tecate and Calexico (California), Douglas (Arizona), Columbus (New Mexico), and El Paso, Del Rio, Eagle Pass, Laredo, and Brownsville (Texas).[67] The adoption of the Secure Fence Act was not necessary for the erection of these sections of wall between the United States and Mexico. Section 102 (a) of the IIRIRA already provided a general authorization to the secretary of the DHS to erect such barriers in areas along US borders. Instead, the Secure Fence Act and the several legislative debates and hearings held before its adoption are best understood as providing the site for a contest between two competing visions of immigration law: one focusing on border enforcement and the other calling for a comprehensive reform of immigration law. Hence, this legislative exercise must be seen in the light of the broader debate over immigration reform that animated Congress ahead of the 2006 midterm elections, when all the seats of the House of Representatives and one-third of those of the Senate were contested.[68]

In that respect, the legislative debates offered a stage where legislators could deploy narratives that favored a specific understanding of what US immigration law ought to achieve as they attempted to appeal to either their social conservative or neoliberal constituencies. This episode also illustrates the ambivalence toward undocumented Mexicans crossing the border. An ambivalence that resulted, on the one hand, from a fear that a large influx of migrants of a different ethnic background—historically constructed as a "problem population"—could threaten the cultural fabric of American identity. On the other hand, it resulted from the role of Mexicans as providers of cheap labor, derived from an economic tradition of colonial economic exploitation and imperialism that endures to this day.

Proponents of the enforcement approach were guided by a protectionist and nationalist agenda. They conceived of immigration as a security risk and a threat to US sovereignty, often conflating issues of immigration, crime, and terrorism.[69] Proponents of the second approach, by contrast, recognized that immigration to the United States was driven by the demand for labor, which was largely unregulated. Their objective was to reform immigration law to make it more responsive to the US job market. The difference between the two groups was not so much the result of partisan politics, but rather the symptom of a divide within the Republican

Party between social conservatives and those defending neoliberal interests.[70] Two legislative initiatives that preceded the adoption of the Secure Fence Act reflected this tension. House Bill H.R. 4437, entitled the Border Protection, Antiterrorism, and Illegal Immigration Control Act (also referred to as the "Sensenbrenner Bill" following the name of its sponsor, Republican Representative James Sensenbrenner from Wisconsin) advocated an "enforcement first approach." It was supported mostly by Republicans and passed the House on December 16, 2005. Senate Bill S. 2611, entitled the Comprehensive Immigration Reform Act, sought—as the title suggests—a comprehensive reform of immigration, including a path to legalize undocumented immigrants in the United States. The bill was a bipartisan initiative largely influenced by Democrat Senator Ted Kennedy from Massachusetts and Republican Senator John McCain from Arizona.[71] It passed the US Senate on May 25, 2006.

The two bills deployed competing narratives about immigration. H.R. 4437 articulated the immigration debate in terms of national sovereignty and threats to national security. It hinged heavily on border security, including more fencing and resources for the protection of the southern border. Most notably, the bill made it a crime to be unlawfully present in the United States.[72] It also criminalized assistance to some undocumented migrants in the United States. According to Doris Meissner, former commissioner of the INS, what drove this approach to immigration was a rapid change in the settlement destinations of recent immigrants to the United States away from traditional destinations (i.e., New York, New Jersey, Florida, Illinois, Texas, and California). New immigrants were settling in communities less familiar with immigration, in states such as North Carolina, Georgia, and Missouri, where their visibility—coupled with the rapidity of the change—provoked anxiety and spurred calls for stronger immigration enforcement.[73] The Sensenbrenner Bill, with its focus on border enforcement, addressed this audience. Unlike the Senate bill, it provided for neither a guest worker program nor the legalization of illegal migrants. On the contrary, supporters of the Sensenbrenner Bill adamantly opposed the latter measure, which they described as a form of amnesty. Indeed, the guest worker program was unacceptable for conservative Republicans. Republican Representative Virginia Foxx from North

Carolina summarized the view of conservative Republicans on the program during a debate in Congress:

> My constituents have made it clear to me they want our borders secure, our laws enforced and the flow of illegal immigration stopped immediately. . . . The amnesty provisions contained in the Senate-passed immigration reform measure earlier this year would encourage future illegal immigration and reward those who have violated America's laws with a quick and easy path to citizenship.[74]

The Sensenbrenner Bill built on the fear that migrants inspired in these constituencies and fed mistrust by representing the undocumented as criminals and a threat to the nation to be dealt with through criminal law. As for the narratives about loss of control and invasion that had been popular in the US media during the 1970s, they were once again put forward when Representative Sensenbrenner presented his bill to the House: "Our nation has lost control of its borders, which has resulted in a sharp increase in illegal immigration and has left us vulnerable to infiltration by terrorists and criminals."[75] He also noted that estimates indicate that there were more than 10 million illegal aliens in the United States and that their numbers increased by nearly half a million each year.

The premises on which Representative Sensenbrenner built his narrative were not wrong. At the time, between 11.5 and 12 million undocumented migrants were living in the United States.[76] It was also true that between 2000 and 2005, the undocumented population had grown by an average of 500,000 each year.[77] But the way these data were interpreted and narrated by Representative Sensenbrenner construed the undocumented migrants and the situation at the border as a threat to the security of the nation. Two main themes were at play, invasion and criminality, to rationalize a set of proposed legal dispositions and practices that excluded these migrants from the American community.

By comparison, the narrative underpinning the bipartisan Senate bill painted a more conciliatory picture of immigration. The Senate bill did not reject enforcement altogether. Among other measures, it provided for an increase in US Border Patrol personnel and the procurement of border security technologies. A majority of senators aimed to bring "illegal immigration under control and achieve border security" by combining enforcement "with a realistic framework for legal immigration."[78] The bill sought to achieve this aim with the creation of a guest worker program and, under specific conditions, a path to citizenship for undocumented immigrants. It rested on the premise that undocumented crossings were a consequence of demand in the US labor market. Unsurprisingly, the bill was supported by business leaders who, as in the past, strongly opposed regulations that would increase the cost of accessing Mexican labor. The House bill was unpalatable for them, notably because it provided stricter regulations for employers to verify the legal status of their employees. Hence, the Senate bill did not necessarily undermine the power structure and economic exploitation that characterized the settler-colonial project since Mexicans access to US territory depended on the benefit of their productive labor for American subjects.

Still, to the extent that it provided a pathway to citizenship and a guest worker program, the Senate bill recognized the contribution of immigrants to the nation and the deep roots that anchor some of them in their communities, despite them having crossed the US border in contravention of the law.[79] Proponents of the bill generally subscribed to the view that although undocumented migrants may have entered the United States and worked illegally, many had resided in the country for years, paid taxes, and had strong roots in their communities, with some living in households including legal immigrants or citizens.[80] Relying on similar data to those used by Representative Sensenbrenner, Senator Kennedy, commenting on his support for the Senate bill and a path to citizenship, deployed an alternative discourse about undocumented migrants present in the United States: "How are we going to treat the 12 million individuals who are here now, the overwhelming majority of whom want to play by the rules, work hard, be part of the American process and dream, like the tradition of so many other immigrant groups?"[81]

Comparing the discourse of supporters of the Senate bill, on the one hand, with the narrative deployed by proponents of the House bill, on the other, illustrates how actors involved in the immigration debate used the same facts and events about undocumented migration and framed them differently—and sometimes antithetically—to shape narratives about immigration. This, in turn, highlights an important distinction Hall makes between language and discourse. Indeed, language is not of itself determinant. Of course, certain words carry meanings developed through history and experiences. These words may connote a particular understanding of something or someone. Yet, as Hall observes, how language is deployed gives a discourse its ideological flavor.[82] By articulating elements such as words, concepts, and images differently within the discourse, "ideological struggle takes place and ideologies are transformed."[83] By emphasizing different constructions of migrant identity—the criminal migrant as a threat to the nation or the hard-working migrant as an asset to the economic and cultural life of the country—these actors sought to stir legal approaches to immigration toward either border enforcement or a comprehensive immigration reform.

The vision of the Senate bill was supported by and reflected in the discourse of the US administration. In fact, since entering the Texas gubernatorial elections in 1994, George W. Bush had situated himself in ideological opposition to Pete Wilson—also a Republican and potential rival in a future presidential nomination, who had established himself as an "enemy of Latino immigrants."[84] Bush's solidarity with the Latino community was not entirely disinterested, according to Gary Gerstle.[85] The future US president understood the importance of the Latino vote for achieving his political ambitions. But more importantly still, Bush genuinely believed in a "religiously inflicted multiculturalism" underpinned by conservative values.[86] On May 15, 2006, President Bush delivered a prime-time Oval Office address to announce his perspective on immigration reform. During his address, he contended that "an immigration reform bill needs to be comprehensive because all elements of this problem must be addressed together, or none of them will be solved at all."[87] Still stressing that the United States must secure its borders as a national security imperative, the president conceded that there are "many people on the other side of our border who will do anything to come to America to work and build a better life. . . . This creates enormous pressure on our border that walls and patrols alone will not stop."[88] The view of the administration, like that of a majority of Senate members, was that a legal reform that addresses the root causes of undocumented immigration was the only way to achieve border security.

President Bush's depiction of undocumented migrants sought to rally public support for comprehensive reform with rhetoric that could appeal to both sides of the debate. He acknowledged the concerns of a segment of the population regarding the effect of undocumented immigration on the job market and public spending; however, the narrative integrated positive elements about migrants' identity that the other side of the debate generally lacked:

> Illegal immigration puts pressure on public schools and hospitals. . . . It strains state and local budgets . . . and brings crime to our communities. These are real problems, yet we must remember that the vast majority of illegal immigrants are decent people who work hard, support their families, practice their faith, and lead responsible lives. They are a part of American life but they are beyond the reach and protection of American law.[89]

At the time, the Bush administration hoped to merge the two bills into one comprehensive piece of immigration legislation that would become the landmark of the last two years of his presidency. On May 18, 2006, the president, who had previously opposed the construction of a wall along the border with Mexico, agreed to some fencing in critical locations to facilitate negotiation for a comprehensive reform of immigration. Just the day before, on May 17, the Senate had voted in favor of an amendment to S.B. 2611, proposed by Republican Senator Jeff Sessions of Alabama, who opposed comprehensive immigration reform, requiring the repair and construction of fences along approximately 370 miles of the border.[90] These developments occurred following growing public interest in the immigration debate. In the spring of 2006, pro-immigrant-rights demonstrations took place in more than 140 US cities in thirty-nine states to protest the Sensenbrenner Bill.[91] In response to these protests and the resistance of lawmakers to erect a border wall, proponents of fencing and stricter border enforcement launched the Send-a-Brick campaign. Under the campaign, individuals could signal to lawmakers their support for a border wall by sending a brick to the Congressional member of their choice, either directly or through the campaign organization for a $11.95 fee. Between April and May 2006, constituents sent more than ten thousand bricks to Congress. Senders were encouraged to add a message to their parcel to indicate that "the brick represented a start on building a border wall." Another standard message was "No Amnesty."[92] One brick painted with the pattern of the US flag read "Stop the Invasion, Build a Wall."[93]

Despite polls showing that a small majority of the population opposed erecting a wall, both the administration and the Senate gave in to the conservatives' demand for a border wall, hoping to gain support for a guest worker program.[94] However, for the majority of the House, the program was an unthinkable compromise. Hence, the two chambers of Congress never conducted official negotiations to reconcile the Senate and House bills.[95] Instead, on September 13, following a summer of field hearings by Republican members—an exercise primarily aimed at gathering support from constituents for the proposed fence and other border protection measures—Republican Representative Peter King of New York introduced H.R. 6061, which would become the Secure Fence Act. Explaining the bill, Representative King noted: "One issue in which there appears to be a consensus between the United States Senate and the Congress is on the issue of building a secure fence. So rather than wait, and wait for God knows how long until comprehensive legislation is enacted, there is no reason whatsoever why we should not move forward on targeted legislation which is effective and meaningful."[96]

Senate Republicans followed suit and backed away from a more holistic immigration reform. Senate majority leader, Republican Bill Frist of Tennessee claimed that H.R. 6061 was the best option to achieve some progress on the immigration reform front before the midterm elections in November. Commenting on the bill, he added, "Let's focus on a problem the American people understand . . . and that is, we have hundreds of thousands of people coming across our border every year into our country."[97]

These comments by Senator Frist underscored the symbolic nature of the Secure Fence Act; that is, the measure was not about taking action toward the effective regulation of immigration. Rather, it was about sending a simple and clear message to American voters before the 2006 midterm election that something was being done about undocumented immigration.[98] Republican members urging the president to hold a public ceremony for the signing of H.R. 6061 into law close to the November election further indicates that the measure was, above all, a performance directed at the electorate.[99] Perhaps more telling of the symbolism of the bill were the measures agreed to behind the scenes, which somewhat tempered the strict requirements of the Secure

Fence Act. For instance, when appropriating funding for the border wall required by the Secure Fence Act, legislators gave the administration flexibility over how it could use the money to build roads and other virtual infrastructure.[100] Republicans also agreed to consult with American Indian tribes, members of Congress, and local governments on the locations of the new fences.[101]

Hence, the border wall provided for in the Secure Fence Act gave the appearance of action for those who favored vigorous border enforcement, while for those who did not subscribe to that vision, the act provided a resolution of the issue at a low political cost. Fences only have a marginal impact on American constituents; very few would have their day-to-day life impacted by their construction and most would never see it with their own eyes. Consequently, lawmakers were unlikely to suffer substantial reprisals from their constituents for voting in favor of a border wall paid for with federal money.[102] As for powerful business lobbies, the fence was unlikely to have any real negative impact on their interests. In any case, it would be less damaging than another measure proposed earlier by the House to impose stricter verification requirements on employers concerning the legal status of prospective employees.

Some congressional representatives supporting a path to citizenship for undocumented immigrants hoped that their support for the erection of a fence would be interpreted as a "down payment" toward broader immigration reform.[103] Yet as Jennifer Chacón explains, this strategy failed because these members' support for a border wall reified the popular narrative of immigration enforcement being a necessary condition for public safety.[104] The administration's adherence to that narrative gave legitimacy to the misguided approach that sees "immigration as a crime and security problem to be solved rather than as a largely positive phenomenon in need of a more effective governing legal framework."[105] What remains with the adoption of the Secure Fence Act is a law focused on border enforcement, albeit a diluted version of the enforcement vision expressed in the Sensenbrenner Bill. The narrative that recognized the positive role of immigrants in American communities, found in the Senate bill, is absent from the text of the act, which frames immigration solely through the lens of criminality and the borderland as a dangerous space.

The Secure Fence Act and the Continued Salience of Race

Race did not figure overtly in legal debates leading to the adoption of the Secure Fence Act. Instead, it was substituted by an apparently racially neutral vocabulary that insisted on the threats posed by agents such as the criminal, the undocumented or illegal alien, and the terrorist. In this respect, there was continuity with the discourses deployed in support of earlier fence projects, notably the persistent presence of the criminal, especially the smuggler—although today, the product of their trade is drugs rather than alcohol. Still, compared to the narratives surveyed in chapter 2, participants in contemporary debates about the border fence sought to erase direct references to race or ethnicity from their discourse—at least until the 2016 presidential race. Indeed, overt references to racial hierarchy articulating whiteness as superior to other races largely disappeared from mainstream US politics from the 1960s to 1970s, following the civil rights movement.[106] Nonetheless, the belief in white superiority that sustained an American racial nationalism continued to travel in tropes,[107] or, in Hall's words, through "glossed and up-dated images" constructed on an ancient grammar of otherness.[108]

A similar point is made by legal scholar E. Tendayi Achiume in her analysis of legal discourses about international borders. Achiume argues that today's borders rest on a neocolonial order that enforces patterns of inclusion and exclusion along racial lines. Crucially, she observes that contemporary borders produce discriminatory outcomes through ostensibly race-neutral laws and policies.[109] This, in turn, speaks to Debra Thompson's distinction between racial amnesia and racial aphasia. Whereas *racial amnesia* refers to the "unintentional forgetting" of racial hierarchies' (continuous) role in shaping our world, *racial aphasia* is intentional.[110] The latter is also closely entwined with how discourses are constructed: "Aphasia . . . indicates a calculated forgetting, an obstruction of discourse, language and speech."[111] It is about "racial silences and evasions."[112] As such, aphasia occludes the politics of colonialism and race through a seemingly colorblind positivism that imposes "race-free discourses that keep international and domestic racial orders firmly entrenched," even today.[113]

To retain their potency without pointing to a distinguishable racialized other, narratives that promote a closing of the southern border must work through images and scenarios that have the potential to elicit a strong emotional response—a rhetoric that makes danger salient. Consequently, fear remains the emotion of choice. I say "remains" because, as we have seen in chapter 2, fear has historically pervaded discourses supporting the erection of fences at the US-Mexico border. Indeed, fear is one aspect of the colonial relationship that explains the exclusion of the colonized and the consolidation of a national identity.[114] If debates about the Secure Fence Act have elided the ethnic and racial heritage of the southern neighbor, fear continues to shape the narrative nonetheless. Hence, it is important to recognize the role of emotions and emotion-shaping discourses in the construction of legal knowledge during debates leading to the adoption of the Secure Fence Act, as well as the place of emotions in the act itself.[115] Indeed, fear is a powerful rhetorical tool that has the potential to bring communities together and divide others.[116]

When discussing fear in relation to race, Sara Ahmed notes that one response to fear is to turn away from its object and toward the object of love and protection instead, a "safe form of enclosure, or the transformation of the world into home (being-at-home)."[117] If fear moves us away from its object (the other) it also moves us toward the object of love and protection (a national community).[118] On this account, Ahmed argues that fear does not defend existing borders, but "rather fear makes those borders." While I agree with her that fear can create borders—indeed, fear is crucial to the division of people and space in the settler-colonial project—I believe that fear is also necessary for the sustenance of these divisions in time, especially when a privileged group feels that these borders are under threat of disappearing. This is why stereotypes that fix the other as an object of fear need to be repeated, as Bhabha argues.

An important point made by Ahmed is that vulnerability and fear are not commensurate. In other words, those who fear most are not necessarily the most objectively vulnerable. So, how do feelings of vulnerability take shape? Relying on Vincent Sacco and William Glackman's description of vulnerability as "feelings of susceptibility and openness to attack,"[119] we can see the salience of spatiality in the construction of vulnerability, and, more importantly, of openness as a site of danger: "Fear involves *reading* such openings as dangerous."[120] This is facilitated by narratives about who and what is threatening and who and what is not.[121] Indeed, a necessary aspect of the discourse that constructs vulnerability is the framing of the outside as inherently dangerous and the home as a safe space.[122] This is achieved through a language that intensifies threats and consequently "create[s] a distinction between those who are 'under threats' and those who threaten."[123] The process is discernible in the deployment of three main themes that led to the adoption of the Secure Fence Act: the border as a dangerous space, alien criminality, and spatialized terror.

The Southern Border as a Dangerous Space

The successful deployment of narratives suggesting that threats to the nation are most likely to enter at the border was essential to the adoption of the Secure Fence Act. Wendy Brown notes that for decades, the southern border of the United States has been constructed in discourse as the primary space where various threats to the nation, compounded into the figure of the alien, enter the territory of the United States.[124] She explains that, following the Cold War, the southern US border has been "discursively constructed as a point of entry for a variety of heterogeneous threats to the nation, threats increasingly merged into a single figure of alien danger."[125] This discourse is accompanied by the desire to prevent the dilution of dominant elements of American identity that could result from a large influx of migrants.[126] The fear of the alien, in turn, produces both a desire for containment and for impermeability. This desire, she argues, is fulfilled by walls, which provide the illusion that the nation is sealed off and that threats will therefore be stopped.[127] Above all, the wall is an act of public communication between the state and its population.[128] The Secure Fence Act and the fences that it calls for fulfill this yearning for bounded horizons juxtaposed with the geographical limits of the nation-state.

This fixation on the border partly results from its role as an instrument in the production and institutionalization of the nation-state through space.[129] Desmond Manderson illustrates how the boundary of the state holds significance as a representation of external dangers and as a marker of belonging and foreignness. He notes that the fear of border transgressions takes many forms; drugs, health, immigration, and crime can all substitute for fear of invasion. Immigration is a threat to the boundary between "us" and "them" in a community imagined as homogeneous.[130] Thus, the border is a space that triggers fears of the dilution of dominant elements of American culture by an influx of migrants. What is more, if drugs and crime penetrate the border, they too become a threat to the social order of a nation constructed as morally and culturally superior to its neighbor.

The Secure Fence Act built on this common perception of the border as a space of danger and promoted it further.[131] The legal narrative of the border as a dangerous space found its way into the Secure Fence Act through a process that prioritized claims made by government officials, legislators, and the media that articulated the narrative of a border "under siege" and "out of control."[132] Depending on the message conveyed, the image of the border moved between a thin demarcation line that marked a contrast between an orderly inside and disorderly outside, and a thick space of violence—to be sure, the danger always originated south of the border, not north of it. In the first case, the border marked a distinction between two opposites: Mexico, a nation devoid of a commitment to the rule of law, in contrast to America.[133] Mexico was represented as a lawless space, with the Mexican government as corrupted and lacking sovereign control over its territory.[134] For Republican Representative Louie Gohmert from Texas, what drove Mexican northbound immigration was the Mexican nation itself and its disrespect for the law, which again is portrayed in stark contrast with the US: "The reason that this country [the United States] has prospered, and now Mexico is forcing families to divide and some to come here in order to survive, is that they have not been a nation that enforced the laws as well across the board as we have. . . . We are the greatest nation on Earth in enforcing our laws. They have not. Corruption abounds."[135]

At the time, this representation of the Mexican state was reinforced in the media by frequent reporting on the crimes perpetrated by drug trafficking organizations. In fall 2006, the *New York Times* wrote about "an underworld war between drug gangs in Mexico, medieval in its barbarity"—a violence that included two dozen beheadings and made more than 1,700 civilian victims in 2006 alone.[136] The paper emphasized the impotence of Mexican authorities in stopping the bloodshed, either due to corruption or anticipated reprisal.

The fear in the United States was that violence would eventually find its way across the border into the United States, destabilizing an orderly society. Hence, warlike metaphors and analogies of invasions were abundant: the border became a "front line," or a space where a "flood of criminal activities" was occurring.[137] This led to the second facet of the dangerous border. Here, the narrative was slightly altered: the border was no longer the mark of a clear demarcation between disorder (to the south) and order (to the north). Instead, crime, violence, and other threats for which Mexico was held responsible became a defining feature of the US borderland. This narrative usually accompanied a discourse that cast the democratic nation as a victim and depicted the wall as an instrument for preserving the innocence of the nation.[138]

Alien Criminality

One element that contributed to creating the image of the border as a dangerous space is the familiar narrative about alien criminality. The criminal alien became the dominant figure in discourses on border fortification. As noted in the previous chapter, legal changes in the United States since the 1920s have brought immigration and illegality closer together. This process intensified in the 1980s and 1990s as the number of immigration-related crimes and crime-related grounds for deportation multiplied. In 2006, immigration law embodied so many features of criminal law that the distinction between the two was sometimes hard to trace.[139] Legal scholars commonly use the term "crimmigration" to refer to the convergence of immigration law and criminal law. For Juliet Stumpf, there is some justification for this association: while there are marked differences between criminal law and immigration law—the first seeks to prevent and redress harms, while the second determines who can enter the territory of the state—both essentially create insiders and outsiders, and both "act as gatekeepers of membership in our society."[140]

Sponsors of the Secure Fence Act tapped into the criminalization of migrants to impress upon the American public the notion that border security, in the form of walls and fences, was not an option but a necessity. A reading of the legal debates that preceded the adoption of the Secure Fence Act uncovers notable parallels between the contemporary narrative supporting the border wall and discourses held in the early twentieth century. The declaration of Republican Senator Rick Santorum from Pennsylvania during debates on the Secure Fence Act on September 29,

2006 (the day the bill was adopted by the Senate) may provide the best illustration of the resemblance between contemporary discourses about the foreigner's criminality and those of the past (as discussed in the previous chapter):

> The current immigration crisis poses an immediate threat to our communities—gang violence, drug trafficking, murders, rapes. . . . Just last week the Immigration and Customs Enforcement arrested more than 100 criminals, fugitive aliens, and other immigration status violators. . . . Among those arrested were individuals convicted of sex offenses, burglary, larceny, robbery, criminal trespass, weapons violations, narcotics violations, aggravated assault, shoplifting, fraud, and resisting arrest.[141]

A series of hearings held by the House of Representatives in 2006 played a role in legitimizing the narrative about Mexican criminality. For instance, a February 7, 2006, hearing in Washington, DC, entitled *Armed and Dangerous: Confronting the Problem of Border Incursions* was held to hear testimonies about increased violence and the problem of incursions at the southern border.[142] The hearing focused on incidents of aggression against US Border Patrol agents and other law enforcement officials, which were rising at the time. At the hearing, photographs of the violence inflicted on these officials, which one of the representatives described as disturbing, were circulated to illustrate the gravity of the violence occurring at the border. Representatives and witnesses emphasized accounts of criminal organizations adopting comparable tactics and using similar equipment to that used by the military, thus painting an image of a border that was close to a war zone. The House of Representatives held three additional hearings on related topics in the following months, all bearing titles that insisted upon the violence occurring at the border: *Outgunned and Outmanned: Local Law Enforcement Confronts Violence Along the Southern Border*, *U.S. Southern Border Security—National Security Implications and Issues for the Armed Services*, and *Criminal Activity and Violence Along the Southern Border*.[143] Most of these titles were not descriptive; instead, they were rhetorical statements that constructed the border as a space of violence. As such, they supported the purpose of the hearings, which were intended to serve as opportunities to persuade an audience of the dangers that undocumented immigration and the border pose to the

United States. This intention was unequivocal in the opening statement of Representative Michael McCaul of Texas, the chair of the fourth hearing:

> Now today we will examine the expanding crisis of violence and criminal activity on America's border with Mexico. We will hear what I expect to be sobering testimony from Federal, State and local government officials and law enforcement, as well as the victims of violence committed by those in our Nation illegally. It is my hope that this hearing and the testimony will open the eyes of America to the violence, crime, drugs and overall far-reaching impact of our unsecured borders. Today we will hear the facts and understand the true effects of illegal immigration on our society.[144]

Far-right groups further inflamed the debate, sometimes using the violence committed against immigrants to foster the construction of that space of violence.[145] Such a discourse found its symbolic expression, for instance, in the so-called rape trees of vigilante groups' lore.[146] These rape trees, where smugglers display the underwear of the female clients they have raped, appeared as a symbol of border violence in recent years. It is a very specific form of violence committed against the immigrant woman by the coyote that smuggles her into US territory. "The Botany of Illegal Immigration," a 2005 article by Mike Vanderboegh, a former leader of the Patriot movement and founder of the far-right militia movement Three Percenters, illustrates how violence against border crossers can be turned on its head to further a narrative that localizes the source of that very violence into the crosser and the border space:

> There is a new kind of tree growing out west. . . . In an era of free trade agreements . . . they represent a new Mexican export to the United States. They are called "rape trees" and they bear a strange kind of fruit. Panties. Yes, panties. . . . After the coyotes get the women across the border, safely on US soil, they gang rape them to show they have total control over them. They hang their panties in the trees as signs of the conquest. . . . And so the rape trees grow and flourish in a place where it is tough for anything else to grow. Watered by the blood of innocents, fertilized with crazed machismo and Yanqui political indifference, the rape trees continue to blossom along our border to our country's eternal shame.[147]

The space of the border thus became the receptacle of this violence against women, but a violence that, despite occurring on US soil, was perceived to be foreign to it. It is the "out-of-control" Mexican male, constructed as "hypersexual" and aggressive, that brought violence north of the boundary line.[148] In that process, sexual violence is posited as foreign through a logic of otherness that is merely an extension of colonial discourses about the sexuality and depravity of the Mexican. Here, sexuality is used metaphorically as a substitute for race. As the feminist anthropologist Miriam Ticktin observes, we mostly tend to recognize sexual violence when it attaches to other forms of alterity.[149] This is especially so in institutionalized discourses about immigration and national security. In these contexts, the narrative about violence against migrant women, such as gang rape, is woven into the politics of border control and substitutes the language of immigration in defining the limits of the nation and questions about belonging. Hence, it "perpetuates a colonially derived racist discourse that erases the role of race."[150] These discourses are not based on any common form of violence but on one that is "culturally marked" and "exoticized," such as the gang rape described above, which expresses a radical otherness that sets it in opposition to American civility.[151] In turn, this narrative justifies calls for interventions to save migrant women from a barbaric other. But there is a paradox to this neocolonial discourse. On the one hand, as Ticktin notes, it opens up a space for the victims to contest the violence they suffered. On the other hand, discourses such as these, when weaved into the debate about the border wall rationalize barring not only the perpetrators of such violence but also the women subjected to it.

The Construction of a Spatialized Terror Threat

A third pervasive narrative was deployed in 2006, which constructed the border as a space where terrorist elements were more likely to enter the state territory. As noted in chapter 2, the association between the southern border and undocumented immigration, on the one hand, and the threat to national security posed by subversive or violent ideologies, on the other, was not new. The law has historically contributed to the association between immigration and national security in times of war or national crisis, while in peacetime, restrictions on immigration have rested on economic and cultural factors.[152] The attacks of September 11, 2001, initiated a new era of crisis that had an unprecedented effect on the population's perception of vulnerability, thereby feeding support for the erection of a wall.

Initially, the national security policies adopted to address terrorism were largely unconcerned with the southern border and its fencing.[153] Reece Jones notes that America's "war on terror" was directed abroad, notably in Afghanistan.[154] Still, the feeling of vulnerability caused by the attacks in New York, Pennsylvania, and Washington, DC, the first acts of foreign terrorism to occur on US soil, heightened the perception that the nation was under threat and emphasized the potential risks of open borders.

Politicians (especially the Bush administration), US government agencies, and the media contributed to the interpretation of the terrorist attacks and helped frame the perception of a nation under threat. On September 20, 2001, in an address to Congress where he announced the creation of the DHS, President Bush warned: "Our nation has been put on notice: We are not immune from attack. We will take defensive measures against terrorism to protect Americans. . . . Terror, unanswered, can not only bring down buildings, it can threaten the stability of legitimate governments."[155]

On the same day, the *Dallas Morning News* published one of the first opinion pieces to link the attacks of September 2001 with immigration: "Those who would bring harm to our institutions and people freely roam at their pleasure within our borders. . . . [Investigations into] recent terrorist attacks are revealing that our immigration laws are too lax, the fraudulent-document business is thriving, and our national borders are not secure."[156]

The theme of terror continued to gain momentum in the media and political circles between 2001 and 2006.[157] National newspapers and news networks reported on a nation besieged. Lou Dobbs, a well-known CNN (and later Fox News) personality with strong anti-immigration views, made regular inflammatory comments on immigration.[158] In his response to President Bush's address about immigration amid the 2006 immigration debate, Dobbs reported: "Not only are millions of illegal aliens entering the United States each year across that border, but so are illegal drugs. . . . If it is necessary to send 20,000 to 30,000 National Guard troops to the border with Mexico to preserve our national sovereignty and protect the American people from rampant drug trafficking, illegal immigration and the threat of terrorists, then I cannot imagine why this president and this Congress would hesitate to do so."[159]

This rhetoric benefited politicians favoring extensive security enforcement measures.[160] During the February 7, 2006, hearing by the Subcommittee of the Committee on Homeland Security of the House of Representatives, mentioned previously above, Representative McCaul linked the attacks of September 11, 2001, to the immigration debate: "We know that al-Qa'ida would like to exploit our borders and we know that they are vulnerable, and I have often stated that in the post-9/11 world, this is no longer just an immigration issue, it is one of national security."[161]

Other House hearings on border security and immigration held in 2006 conveyed comparable messages, insisting on the existence of a terrorist threat at the southern border. Again, they bore suggestive titles, such as *Checking Terrorism at the Border* and *Border Vulnerabilities and International Terrorism*.[162] Members of Congress and witnesses at those hearings explained how, in their view, illegal immigration could facilitate the incursion of terrorist militants, allowing the latter to use the same smuggling and transportation networks used by illegal aliens to cross the border and smuggle biological or chemical weapons through the southern border.[163] Republican Representative Edward R. Royce from California insisted: "No one is eager to devote more resources to border security, frankly, or build border fences. . . . But we live in an age where dedicated terrorists want to hit us as hard as they can. They want to knock us out. So we need to be responsible."[164]

The same discourse served as a justification when Representative King introduced H.R. 6061 on September 14, 2006. According to Republican Representative David Dreier from California, documents had been discovered that indicated Al-Qaeda had planned to infiltrate militants through the southern border. He then noted how the fence was essential to fighting that threat: "I hate the idea of our having to put up a fence. The fact of the matter is we have no choice. We have no choice because this week, as we marked the fifth anniversary of September 11, we are in the midst of a global war on terror. We face the threat of someone who would like to do us in coming across our border."[165]

This construction of a spatialized terror threat located at the southern border, in conjunction with othering discourses targeted at the southern neighbor in political, media, and popular discourses, generated a feeling of vulnerability that produced the desire for enclosure and made the adoption of the Secure Fence Act possible. Yet, this dominant narrative occluded contending facts about crime and terrorism that, if considered, would have discredited the wall as a desirable policy for the regulation of undocumented migration. Indeed, despite the importance of the September 2001 attacks in the framing of the southern border as a security risk, there is no correlation between the alleged porosity of that border and those terrorist events. None of the perpetrators of the attacks entered the country through that border. Rather, all individuals involved in the September 2001 attacks came to the United States legally on temporary visas, making the argument in favor of a border wall less credible. Just as perplexing, while there have been no reported cases of suspected terrorists attempting to enter the United States through the southern border, there have been instances of individuals allegedly determined to commit acts of political violence entering the US-Canada border.[166] These events should have directed attention to the northern border as a priority. Yet, no walls are prescribed for the northern border in the Secure Fence Act. Instead, the insistence on walling the southern border contributed to locating the "war on terrorism" at the boundary between the United States and Mexico.

As discussed below and in the next chapter, this hints at the salience of race in the treatment of the two US land borders. It speaks directly to claims by race theorists that today's borders are racial borders. That is, they are not only the product of colonial interventions; they are equally instrumental in perpetuating the long-established hierarchies that privilege whiteness, notably in allocating mobility rights between a constructed white north and a black south,[167] which find its expression in the text of the Secure Fence Act itself.

Normative Content and Precedents Set by the Secure Fence Act

In chapter 1, we saw that legal texts have normative power. They have the potential to communicate values and ideologies and regulate social relations. This is especially true of immigration and criminal law, whose roles are to define the contours of social categories, distinguishing between insiders and outsiders. The Secure Fence Act, which weaves together these two legal disciplines, falls under a group of legal texts that structure knowledge about belonging and exclusion. Two elements are crucial for understanding the importance and normative significance of the Secure Fence Act: first, the substance of the narrative embedded in the text of the law and, second, the kind of precedent that the act sets.

Narratives Embedded in the Secure Fence Act

Written law can tell us about how lawmakers perceive groups of people and whether they are trying to bring them into the fold of the community they represent or exclude them. Similarly, legal texts can provide clues about how space is imagined by legislators. Although national territory is one example of a space constructed by law, the law can give significance and meaning to other spatialities. These intentions and beliefs can be more or less obvious in the text of the law. Legal texts sometimes appear neutral at first sight. By contrast, others deploy a language that leaves little doubt about the ideologies that have underpinned their adoption.

The Secure Fence Act is one of those legal texts that reproduces rather faithfully the beliefs and narratives of its strongest advocates: the lawmakers in favor of a border enforcement approach to immigration law. In doing so, it produces a normative content that transmits a specific form of knowledge about the social relations that the United States ought to entertain with Mexico and its people and the meanings American lawmakers have attached to the southern border. The three themes upon which this security narrative was forged during the 2006 immigration debate—alien criminality, the threat of terrorism, and the southern border as a dangerous space—are manifested in the act. These themes are apparent in the aesthetics of the text, its language, and its structure, which attribute certain qualities to the border and those crossing it.

The discourse of the Secure Fence Act is essential to the construction of Mexico as a threat to the United States. This is most evident in the definition that the act provides for "'operational control' [as] the prevention of all unlawful entries into the United States, including entries by alleged terrorists, other unlawful aliens, instruments of terrorism, narcotics, and other contraband."[168] There is a paradox in this section of the act. In one way, the absence of a reference to undocumented workers and other benign forms of crossing could be interpreted as an attempt to deflect attention away from them. Yet, a number of insidious consequences emerge from this language, which compounds all flows not related to terrorism and drug trafficking to "other unlawful aliens." One is to deny the individuality—even the humanity—of the individuals that make up that category; there are only unlawful aliens. Representing Mexican nationals in this manner objectifies them and makes it difficult to conceive of them as anything other than a menace to the community as it brings into the totalizing unit of the lawbreaker all people entering outside ports of entry. This representation, which generalizes the criminality of undocumented crossings, leaves little room for considering the many circumstances and experiences that bring people to cross the border undocumented. Notably, in this legal construction, the commuter that crosses into the United States to shop or visit family—and even the more controversial figure of the hard-working undocumented worker—are lost. Criminality is all that remains.

The criminality attached to undocumented migrants is intensified by its alignment with terror and drug-related crimes, both symbolic crimes often associated with barbarous violence The United States has waged "wars" on both drugs and terrorism.[169] The war metaphor is indicative of the intensity of the reactions these crimes provoke within the American imagination, which is also reflected in the harsh penalties associated with them. The alignment of the undocumented migrant with the figure of the terrorist in particular intensifies feelings against the former. The language of the act may appear dispassionate, but emotions are aroused nonetheless by the figure of the terrorist in the text. Unlike the migrant, the terrorist tends to stir up unambiguous feelings of anger, hate and fear. The strength of these feelings against terrorism was such that following the attacks of September 11, 2001, the terrorist became the unlawful combatant, unworthy of the protection of the law.

The Secure Fence Act introduces a rapprochement between the vague figure of the unlawful entrant and the terrorist, the unlawful combatant. Through this "metonymic slide," to use Ahmed's words, the negative emotional response to the terrorist is extended to the undefined unlawful entrants and constitutes the two characters as a common threat.[170] Such movement from one figure to the other is only possible, according to Ahmed, because of certain associations between the two that are already in place.[171] If we pay attention to the narratives that supported the adoption of the Secure Fence Act, these associations become apparent. Both the undocumented migrant and the terrorist are imagined as an invasion of the nation's territory, a danger that comes from outside. Both are read as a material threat, a precursor to economic decline and physical violence. Both threats are racialized. Both are constructed as a danger to the social and cultural fabric of the nation. As the figure of the unlawful migrant becomes entwined with terror, the perception of the degree of threat they pose to the American community is intensified and gives the state grounds to respond through hostile measures such as walls. Indeed, the events of September 11, 2001, have given prominence to the "spatial and bodily politics of fears"[172] that feed on existing meanings of foreignness. This explains why the terrorist threat attaches more readily to some groups and some spaces.

The Secure Fence Act is molded by an emotional portrait of the southern border and constructs it as *the* dangerous space, in opposition to any other border. This representation may be less explicitly articulated in the Secure Fence Act than it was during the 2006 immigration debate. The legal text is not a format that can accommodate narration. Technicality, legal jargon, impersonal style, and pragmatism are some of its distinctive lexical features.[173] It is not amenable to anecdotal stories; it cannot reproduce graphic images of the violence that is occurring at the borderland. Nonetheless, the message is implicitly present in the law's structure and content. From the outset, the subtitle of the act identifies the objective of the law as "An act to establish operational control over the international land and maritime borders of the United States." This introduction to the legal text suggests that control must be established, that the measure prescribed, the fence—the purpose and method of the act, as the title suggests—will (in the future) achieve operational control of the border, which implies a lack of it in the immediate. In turn, the absence of control, defined as a vulnerability to external threats, establishes the border as a space of inherent danger, which is then further spatially circumscribed by Section 3 of the act, which makes fences mandatory only at the southern land border. The insistence on this boundary exclusively distinguishes it from the other US land border it shares with Canada. The exclusion of the latter from the remedy of the law not only reflects a biased appreciation for the two borders by lawmakers, but it is also constitutive of a normative difference between these borders that communicates knowledge about how the law should engage with each neighbor in the future.

The Secure Fence Act as a Legal Precedent

In both common law and civil law traditions, legal precedents refer to previous court decisions that will guide judgments in future similar cases. We do not speak of written law as a precedent. That said, legal texts operate similarly to legal decisions and the doctrine of legal precedent, which, by nature, "requires the denying of competing narratives, historical incongruities, and the wider contextual considerations in which the original case was determined."[174] Like court judgments, legal texts take one set of facts, or one version of a story, and elevate it to the status of validated truth.[175] They are authoritative because the legislative process that underpins their adoption gives them validity and is seen by people as a guarantee that legal outcomes reflect superior information about the issues they regulate.[176] Consequently, acts and statutes may influence the beliefs of the public and officials about what constitutes appropriate behaviors and informs future actions.[177]

Following this reasoning, the Secure Fence Act, adopted by Congress at the outset of a year-long debate when two competing narratives of immigration law were disputed, constitutes a legal precedent. The resulting three-page legal text built on an othering narrative of Mexican identity that silenced alternative discourses about immigration put forward by proponents of a comprehensive reform of immigration law. For better or worse, it also excluded the many alternative remedies to address undocumented immigration proposed in bills H.R. 4437 and S. 2611. As with any form of legal precedent, the act simplified facts about illegal immigration and summed them up into one principle, border enforcement, for which the wall became a symbol. The act produced "an official version of the truth,"[178] which conceived of the southern border as a danger and the fence as the only valid remedy to that threat.

As a discourse that conveys a vision of illegal immigration at the southern border in terms of criminal law and border enforcement, the Secure Fence Act provides a normative canvas that has structured meanings and informed later actions on immigration. The act constitutes a crucial "discourse-altering" legislation that has intensified Mexican and American feelings about the southern border.[179] Like the walls built under its authority, the act has produced "a collective ethos and subjectivity that is defensive, parochial, nationalistic, and militarized," feeding xenophobic attitudes and the rise of an "us" versus "them" mentality.[180] Hence, the discourse of the Secure Fence Act has set the tone for the issue of undocumented immigration by committing the US government to divisive and punitive strategies, thereby constraining opportunities for more compassionate options. This is illustrated by the failure to achieve comprehensive immigration reform in 2013 and the rise of an "enforcement first" philosophy in which nearly all measures considered to regulate illegal immigration have since focused on enforcement.

The most significant consequence of the Secure Fence Act is to have naturalized the wall as a legal remedy to undocumented migration and unlawful crossings and, therefore, intensified demands for its construction. Since the adoption of the Secure Fence Act in 2006, more than forty-five bills have been introduced in the House of Representatives and Senate to fund the border wall or demand more fencing (e.g., Fund and Complete the Border Wall Act, Finish the Wall Act, Solving the Border Crisis Act, Close Biden's Open Border Act, WALL Act of 2023). This trend was particularly acute under President Trump's administration from 2016 to 2020, following his promise to build a wall at the US-Mexico border. By contrast, only a handful of bills were introduced to rescind the DHS's waiver authority or redirect border wall money for other purposes.[181] The demand for walls has not abated since President Joe Biden took office in 2020. More people were supportive of building a wall in December 2023 than in 2019.[182] And despite President Biden's termination of the declaration of a national emergency at the southern border, Congress refused to rescind the funding already appropriated for the wall under the Trump administration to other projects.[183]

The adoption of the Secure Fence Act has also emboldened people to take action when their demands for walls are refused by the government. For instance, in 2011, the State of Arizona attempted to compel the DHS to complete the construction of the fences provided for in the Secure Fence Act.[184] In a counterclaim against the United States brought before the District Court of Arizona by the State of Arizona and Governor

Janice K. Brewer, the counterclaimants argued that the Secure Fence Act requires the DHS to achieve operational control of the border and build at least seven hundred miles of fencing. It further argued that this obligation could not be unreasonably withheld or delayed and therefore sought an injunctive, declaratory, and mandamus relief against the United States and the DHS to complete it and take temporary measures to protect Arizona. Although the court dismissed the claim and found that it could not compel the DHS to erect specific sections of fencing, this incident demonstrates how central the wall has become as a symbol of border enforcement in the imaginations of public officials following the adoption of the Secure Fence Act. It also highlights how, due to the definition of operational control in the act and the identification of the fence as the path to achieving it, the failure to build a wall can be interpreted as a breach of the State's responsibility to protect its population.

It is a similar sentiment that inspired private donors to contribute more than $25 million to the "We Build the Wall" initiative. The now-defunct nonprofit organization convicted of defrauding its donors was founded in 2018 to raise funding for and manage the construction of private walls at the border with Mexico. After pointing to the failure of the government to build President Trump's wall, the organization's website stated "We the People Can Build the Wall." It then described its mission as to "unite private citizens that share a common belief in providing national security for our southern border through the construction, administration, and maintenance of physical barriers inhibiting illegal entry into the United States."[185] The group, founded by Brian Kolfage, an Air Force veteran, and chaired by Stephen Bannon, a former White House chief strategist in President Trump's administration, completed its first border wall project at Sunland Park, just west of El Paso, in New Mexico, in June 2019. Then it built a second wall in the Rio Grande Valley, in Texas.

More recently, then Arizona Republican governor Doug Ducey responded to what he considers to be President Joe Biden's weak border policies with an executive order providing for the construction of a wall made of shipping containers at its border with Mexico.[186] The executive order stressed that the "federal government has intentionally neglected Arizona's southern border as it installed barriers on the border with Mexico from California to Texas" and noted the "lack of action by the federal government" and its delay "to close the gaps in the border wall." In the end, the four-mile-long shipping container wall, built by the state at the cost of $82 million, was dismantled in late 2022 and early 2023 following a lawsuit filed by the Department of Justice claiming that the wall was unlawfully built on federal land.[187] These examples, albeit largely unsuccessful, show that nearly two decades following its adoption, the narrative of the Secure Fence Act still resonates strongly among certain national and state legislators and the general population.

Conclusion

Reviewing the debates surrounding the Secure Fence Act of 2006 in light of similar discussions about a border fence that occurred in the first half of the twentieth century offers a fresh perspective on the US-Mexico border wall. From this analysis, the claim that settler colonialism is a process that is never really over takes on its full meaning. If the vocabulary of race has somewhat disappeared, the structural order that sustained the settler-colonial project remains intact. Moreover, when we examine the legal framework that has governed the erection of physical walls at the US-Mexico border, we see a progression in the form that these laws have taken and how each new iteration of the legal authorization to build border walls is becoming increasingly explicit and ambitious. The Act of August 19, 1935, was a procedural piece of legislation that merely provided authorization to the State Department to erect fences at the border with Mexico. It can be likened to a "private communication" between the legislator and the executive, the "agent" who ought to carry out the law.[188] The 1996 IIRIRA still addressed in priority US officials, but it reframed the issue of wall building from a question governed by administrative law to one firmly in the domain of immigration law. This shift was ushered in by local and national politicians, keen to entice voters concerned about the alleged threat of a porous southern border and, therefore, sympathetic to dramatic policies that appeared to seal the border from the danger beyond. In subsequent years, the perception that the nation was vulnerable grew stronger, supported by growing media attention to the southern border. This, in turn, contributed to transforming the border wall into an issue of national rather than local significance.

Exacerbated by the terror attacks of September 11, 2001, this perception pervaded the 2006 immigration debate as the site of two competing visions about immigration. The first focused on border enforcement, while the second advocated for a comprehensive approach to immigration that considered both economic and enforcement needs. The Secure Fence Act attests to the success of the "border enforcement" discourse over the more conciliatory understanding of southern immigration and sets a precedent for future actions. Had it not been for the persistence and intensification of othering narratives about the southern neighbor and the representation of the border as a dangerous space, it is unlikely the act would have been adopted in its current form. In a fundamental departure from previous provisions regulating the erection of walls at the southern border, the Secure Fence Act introduces into the law an implicit othering narrative that had justified closing the border for more than a century but had not previously been reflected in the law itself. This, I argue, establishes a new precedent for how we think about and regulate immigration and movements at the southern border—a precedent that firmly weaves together the issues of race, immigration, and crime and thus commands the construction of walls as remedies to undocumented northbound flows. The audience of the law is also broadened; the act is no longer simply a communication between the legislator and the agents of the law. Now, it addresses the population as the subject and object of the law and calls upon citizens to subscribe to its message.

FOUR

The Wall as Law

1,950 mile-long open wound
dividing a *pueblo*, a culture,
running down the length of my body,
staking fence rods in my flesh,
splits me   splits me
me raja   *me raja*

This is my home
this thin edge of
barbwire.

—GLORIA ANZALDÚA, *BORDERLANDS/LA FRONTERA*, 16

I have so far emphasized the textual and oral qualities of the legal discourses surrounding the US-Mexico border wall. Yet, as I have advanced in chapter 1, discourses are not limited to written or spoken words. Textuality, orality, and materiality are all media through which knowledge, including knowledge about national identity, circulates.[1] At the beginning of this book, I made the case for an understanding of the law as material. I will return to this point in the section that follows, but before, I wish to acknowledge more specifically the role of materiality in the ongoing process of settler inclusion and exclusion as meanings about certain identities become inscribed into the matter and then conveyed to the body through representations and the senses.

When speaking about US settler colonialism, Kevin Bruyneel notes that functions and practices of collective memory—that is, the stories we tell about what happened in the past—contribute to creating, mobilizing, and reconstituting a nation, race, or settler group.[2] These stories are not necessarily recounted in words. In the ongoing process that is settler colonialism, stories can be told by "forms of networking" and "lived assemblages."[3] This gives settler-colonial discourses a material quality that cannot be captured by the Saussurean model, which sets discourses in binary opposition with material "nondiscursive" representations and practices.[4] I place the word within quotation marks because this chapter seeks to undo this distinction between discourse and matter. We must recognize that material narratives, through the built environment, for instance, have a unique potential to "make a space a place" and "speak to a collectivity's relationship to land and legacy that threads together a sense of identity and meaning over time."[5] In this respect, connections exist between the work of postcolonial and race theorists on the one hand and the work of scholars in the field of legal geography, sociolegal studies, and legal materiality on the other. All recognize the role of materiality in shaping understandings about identities through representations and the senses.

In the context of the US-Mexico border, there is no account more vivid of the effect of the walled landscape on the body and consciousness of people of Mexican descent than Gloria Anzaldúa's aforementioned words; of how the legal text—be it the Treaty of the Guadalupe Hidalgo or the Secure Fence Act—comes to mark the Mexican body through a material translation. For Anzaldúa, the border is a painful, open wound for Mexicans on both sides of the divide. The staking rods that hold the fence split the body in ways that words alone cannot. As it marks the landscape, the reality of the barbed wire fence becomes part of the everyday experiences of the inhabitants of the borderland. It becomes their home.[6]

This chapter aims to highlight the importance of the border wall's materiality in making "real" the ideational norms that legal texts communicate—in this instance, the Secure Fence Act. It also seeks to contextualize the wall's normative power by reflecting on the experiences of the people confronted with the walled landscape. In the first part, I argue that the border wall between the United States and Mexico constitutes a form of legal discourse communicated through the experiences provided by the walled landscape. On the one hand, this is imparted through symbols associated with the wall, and on the other, from the constraints it imposes on bodies. With this in mind, in the following part, I briefly reflect on the symbolic meanings that the wall embodies and explore how these have influenced our current understanding of walls. The third part more specifically considers the physical constraints imposed by the walled landscape. I compare the aesthetic experience lived at the walled border between Mexico and the United States with that of the relatively unobstructed land border between the United States and Canada. This allows me to contemplate how walled and open landscapes affect border communities differently and how these communities perform and conceive of their relationship with each other. The primary argument of this chapter is that by materializing norms of national and social order, the walled landscape is, like the text of the law, a source of legal normativity that shapes understandings about territory, identity, and belonging. More specifically, I posit that the walled US-Mexico border embodies the narrative of exclusion underpinning the Secure Fence Act and makes it a reality of everyday life.

The Wall as a Normative Object

As outlined in chapter 1, traditional legal theory conceives of law as immaterial. Accordingly, through a purely positivist lens, the border wall has no legal status. It stands merely to reaffirm the limits of two state territories already delimited by law. From this perspective, walls are not conceived *as* law but rather as "signals or markers of law."[7] This positivist account of the relationship between the law and the border wall relies on a conception of the law as a set of immaterial and ideational norms transmitted through language—written or oral—rather than as something material out there in the physical world. Yet, law understood as a discourse that operates through language does not stand in opposition to the materiality of the law. On the contrary, we should view the material world as a continuation of the legal discourses that shaped and are found within the text of the law. As Goodrich explains, the material rendering of the law is what gives it its sensory force and makes the law more readily knowable to those unfamiliar with the legal text.[8] The wall, like any statute, communicates the law. It is this very potential of the law to materialize the "power of its imagery" and the "aesthetic of its reception" that those in favor of the Secure Fence Act were striving for when they voted for its adoption. Indeed, the imagery of a wall running hundreds of miles along the border is a potent way of reaching out to a population to convey the impression that something is being done to protect it and its interests.[9]

Legal materiality's claim goes further than simply conceiving the material as a "representation" of the legal norm. A central argument of legal materiality is that law necessarily possesses a material dimension that is more than just a consequence of state law or its physical representation. Instead, matter in all its forms—human, object, environment—is seen as holding normative potential because the way people experience and interpret the material environment influences their behaviors, social relations, and understanding of the world. The idea that the law and physical objects are intertwined and co-constitutive of each other underpins legal materiality. Indeed, Margaret Davies argues that law emerges from networks of actions, practices, and interactions that are material:

> There is in fact no law and no idea of legality that is not thoroughly imbricated with physicality and the relationality of things—"things" in this context can refer to textual and digital forms, human bodies and brains, landscapes and objects, and the whole sphere of perceptible things. . . . Law is visible and material, not abstract and reified, and it cannot exist without this materiality.[10]

Desmond Manderson underlines the circular relationship that exists between law and the material and that structures our understanding of space.[11] If "law makes assumptions about the normative significance of space: a property, a land, a territory, a people,"[12] the materiality of space and the aesthetic experiences lived through it remains just as powerful at conveying normative meanings about these same concepts. A space, with its streets, buildings, monuments, and arts, can communicate meanings; it can structure and locate social events, restrict them, or facilitate them.

One useful way of approaching the issue of material normativity and the walled US-Mexico border is through the concept of the landscape, understood as a constructed or encoded social space and an experimental process.[13] There is a strong visual dimension to the landscape. For Sarah Keenen, it is primarily a way of observing different sections of space.[14] The works of Donald Meinig, W. J. T. Mitchell, and Eve Darian-Smith recognize the representational facet of the landscape, —often mediated by sight.[15] But sight is not the only sense through which we experience the landscape; our experience of it also implicates touch, smell, and hearing. The landscape is a cultural and material practice that is seen, lived through, and felt by human bodies. It brings together a wide range of senses that are interpellated in the material experience of a space. Thus, the landscape is not a mere representation. It is not "an object to be seen or a text to be read"; it is "a process by which social and subjective identities are formed."[16] Through this sensorial and emotive experience, the landscape may encourage, promote, or force specific conducts and movements and, in doing so, reinforce or create new meanings.

In her ethnography of the Channel Tunnel between England and France, Darian-Smith elaborates on the meaning of the landscape.[17] She explains how the landscape intervenes in the construction of meanings about space—e.g., state territory—and identities. The landscape, she argues, influences how people think about social relations, about how they relate to each other. The characteristics of specific landscapes make them particularly propitious for conveying ideologies, values, and "mythologized collective visions," with the potential to articulate national identities and become icons of nationalism.[18] In this sense, the landscape may be a strategy for imposing social order for the state.[19] It can reify identities created in law by making them tangible through the organization of space.[20] This is a point that Keenan makes, that law, by regulating the landscape and its fixtures, and the activities and ways of life taking place within it, "produces social and physical spaces in which some subjects belong and others do not," and in doing so, laws that dictate "*where* subjects can be, also affect *who* they can be."[21]

Other legal scholars have used a variation of the concept of the landscape to express the conjunction of law and space. Andreas Philippopoulos-Mihalopoulos speaks about the "lawscape" as a space where law and the material intertwine and where the law is made visible to varying degrees.[22] In certain landscapes, the law will be more obvious than in others. At home, the law is almost invisible, albeit always present, while at the airport, it is made obvious to reassure or intimidate people, making them feel as though they are under scrutiny.[23] David Delaney uses the term "nomoscape" to describe spaces that reflect the "spatio-legal expression and the socio-material realization of ideologies, values, pervasive power orders and social projects."[24] The walled borderland is an effective landscape in that respect. The material environment of the border, with the wall at its center, is filled with symbolic meaning about who belongs and who does not. In parallel, its materiality provides cues about the permitted and the forbidden, facilitating or preventing the movement and location of bodies in space. What this implies is that the material and discursive qualities of the walled landscape can never be completely severed.

Discussing territorial jurisdiction, legal scholar Richard Ford notes that it is constituted by three essential elements—material technologies, the built environment, and a discursive intervention—none being subordinated to the other, all being equally important, which suggests a particular understanding of the social world.[25] Ford argues that "we must reject the way of thinking that neatly severs fact from representation or 'the material' from 'the discursive.'"[26] The rules of jurisdiction are both discourses and acts that provide people with a model about how to "perform themselves."[27] They are a "set of social practices" or a "code" that needs to be learned and communicated through the representations of approved behaviors and their performance.[28] Territorial jurisdiction is the law since it encourages and discourages certain behaviors to influence how people think of themselves. Comparing jurisdiction to a tango, Ford claims that it is simultaneously a diagram that tells people where to step and the product of their actual movement:

> Jurisdiction is a function of its graphical and verbal descriptions; it is a set of practices that are performed by individuals and groups who learn to "dance the jurisdiction" by reading descriptions of jurisdictions and by looking at maps. This does not mean that jurisdiction is "mere ideology," that the lines between various nations, cities and districts "aren't real." Of course the lines are real, but they are real because they are constantly being made real, by county assessors levying property taxes, by police pounding the beat (and stopping at the city limits), by registrars of voters checking identification for proof of residence. Without these practices the lines would not "be real"—the lines don't preexist the practices.[29]

The walled landscape operates like Ford's tango. With its barriers made of concrete and barbed wire, checkpoints, and Border Patrol agents, it is a materially engineered space that seeks to enforce US territorial sovereignty and turn it into a "material force."[30] It is a physical map that induces certain performances. Through representations and induced experiences, the walled landscape is an attempt to make the line between the United States and Mexico real. And indeed, the wall is a response to repeated practices that challenge the sovereign and jurisdictional limits established by treaty and law. It embodies and creates law through an altered experience of the space that affects how communities on both sides of the divide relate, live together, and understand each other.

The experience of the walled landscape is both direct and mediated by symbols. Manderson and Yi-Fu Tuan similarly underline the dual nature of the aesthetic experience, the sensorial and symbolic.[31] It is direct as it hails our senses of touch and sight—even hearing and smell. These modes of experiencing are always arbitrated by emotions and thoughts. What our bodies experience from primary senses is processed as pleasurable or painful, enjoyable or unpleasant, and triggers feelings. Feeling "on the one hand designates qualities felt *on* things, *on* people, *on* the world, and on the other hand, manifests and reveals the way in which the self is inwardly affected."[32] As Lakota writer and poet Layli Long Soldier wrote in her essay "Layli Long Soldier on Wounded Knee and the Murder of George Floyd," "From our senses, we remember what's stored within us already. Maybe, sometimes, I/we cannot put words to it, but we feel something."[33] Physical experiences and their related thoughts are ways of knowing and constructing the world around us. Repeated sensorial experiences form memories that prompt anticipation, apprehension, and other feelings that, over time, may attach to a place or an object, endowing it with symbolic meaning. Thus, there is a circularity between symbols and the sensorial experience because if experience creates symbols, then symbols, when attached to an object or place, contribute to affect our experience of a place. The same occurs in the walled landscape.

In the remainder of this chapter, I further develop the analysis of these two facets of the normativity of the walled landscape: the representational aspect, which emerges through the preexisting meanings that the wall embodies (its symbolism, acquired through its functions, as well as its role in historical sociopolitical events), as well as its material/performative aspect.

Reading into Walls

Representation and symbolism are recurrent themes in the literature on border walls, including the wall between the United States and Mexico. The conceptualization of borders and walls in schools of thought such as postmodernism, constructivism, and critical studies is subjective rather than based on the walls' physical qualities.[34] For constructivists especially, a wall's significance is subordinate to its meaning. Recourse to disciplines such as constructivist studies, the sociology of knowledge, and border studies can help us understand how practices and "discursive repertoires" participate in attributing meanings to walls.[35] Constructivists are interested in the social construction of problems. Christine Leuenberger explains that such construction can be supported by references to material objects such as walls to "evoke powerful images of social ills"[36] or, conversely, social agreement, cohesion, and cooperation. Most importantly, the wall as an object symbolizes different things to different people. Indeed, walls "are only obstacles to some bodies."[37] Some bodies come up against a wall, while others do not even see it.[38] Often, the connotation of the wall fluctuates between protection on the one hand and division and exclusion on the other, depending on where one stands in relation to it.

We can trace the association between walls and protection back to the securing walls of the dwelling space. For the historian Claude Quétel, these represent the "first separation between men" and mark the beginning of the defensive function of the wall, which protects against the elements, animals, and other humans.[39] Suffice to look around us at home to understand and feel the sense of security that the walls of our house offer. The walls of the home not only protect against external threats but also contribute to shaping identity and creating a sense of containment and belonging. Iris Marion Young departs from an understanding of the home as a mere shelter. In this regard, she notes that at home "(1) my belongings are arranged in space as an extension of my bodily habits and as support for my routines, and (2) many of the things in the home, as well as the space itself, carry sedimented personal meaning as retainers of personal narrative."[40] Within the walls of the home, space is organized to support the habits and routines of those who inhabit it, and the disposition of objects "provides pathways for habits."[41] Mary Douglas also conceived of the home as more than a protective shell and approaches the idea of the home as an "embryonic community."[42] She explains the importance of the home as "a kind of space" that fosters solidarity for the achievement of the collective good of its inhabitants.[43] This concept implies control over a delimited space and a regularity to its outlook and the people that constitute it or "flow through" it.[44] The walls of the home provide a sense of boundedness associated with safety and familiarity that echoes the concept of the nation.

The alternate side of the wall, as a symbol of protection, is exclusion: if the wall contains and protects from what lies beyond its bounds, it is necessarily through a more or less coercive form of exclusion that seeks to prevent unwanted incursions. Even the seemingly peaceful idea of a home is underpinned by an act of division. Feminist scholars have argued that the home, as a symbol of security, rests on the repression of difference and of exclusion based on class and race. For instance, the exclusion of nonwhites and whites of lower economic status from wealthy suburbs contributes to the experience of security that is felt by more privileged white Americans.[45]

Margaret Davies explores the normative complexity of the idea of the home when transposed to the political sphere.[46] She explains that the wall is a useful metaphor because everyone is hailed by the image of the home as a container of normative values and "normalities, and familiarities associated with family, status, ethnicity, culture and nation."[47] However, as a corollary, when the concept of the home is transposed to the state, it almost inevitably involves "a rejection of those who allegedly do not belong or were not invited."[48] Walls, when erected at the border of the state, are a vivid illustration of the infiltration of the home metaphor in politics: here, the border walls substitute for the walls of the home. The wall at the US-Mexico border, Pratheepan Gulasekaram explains, introduces elements of private property law, such as trespass and nuisance, into immigration and public international law. This he argues creates the perception that the territory is owned by each and every US citizen; it personalizes the act of transgression from the citizen's perspective, and therefore, oversimplifies the issue of undocumented presence in the state territory while normalizing the fence itself.[49]

In *Walled States, Waning Sovereignty*, Wendy Brown highlights the performative function of border walls, notably as a theatrical stage for the expression of state power and national unity.[50] For the author, the popularity of the US-Mexico border wall as a protective mechanism springs from the visual reassurance it provides in mitigating psychological anxieties about the erosion of nation-states' sovereignty through cross-border movement and other transnational threats.[51] The wall is built to project an image of national strength in the face of the growing inability of the state to confront security challenges that are transnational, diffused, and often imperceptible.[52] The wall achieves this through a "theatricalized and spectacularized performance of sovereign power at aspirational or actual national borders."[53] Crucially, it produces "a spatially demarcated 'us'" at a time when it is difficult to discern a homogeneous nation-state identity.[54] The visual image of the wall, its most crucial performative element, stands as a warning against the dangers that await those who dare go up against it, while its monumentality signifies protection and security for those inside.[55] The sight of the wall deploys a narrative of territorial control that makes the concept of territorial sovereignty tangible.[56] One particular comment made by a participant I interviewed during a visit to Washington, DC, in 2016 is telling in this regard. The man explained to me that the border wall between the two countries is a declaration that the United States is the one who decides who and how many are going to be let in and on which basis: "It's an assertion of our determination to defend our own sovereignty. . . . In a sense, even if the fence didn't do anything, I want a fence. Just as a symbolic assertion that this is ours and that's yours, and this is not yours, this is ours."[57]

As a symbol of political exclusion, the wall also draws from a long genealogy of defensive ramparts and military fortifications that were built to protect against potential aggressors and other threats.[58] These walls, built to exclude barbarian invasions—like the Great Wall of China or the Roman *limes*—still capture the collective imagination today. The popular enthusiasm for historic walls built to divide is reflected in the continuous artistic and tourist interest that they attract.[59] We cannot discuss the wall as a symbol of exclusion without mentioning the walls of prisons, which represent an amalgam of walls and cages that operate to exclude the criminal from a law-abiding population. Or, the walls of ghettos—whose connotations contrast sharply with the idealized historic walls—which uniquely and unequivocally evoke the violent exclusion of a minority discriminated against.

It is often in association with pain and violence, or through the threat of these outcomes, that the wall excludes. At the political level, the wall cannot be separated from its martial past as an instrument used in the bloody repression of invasions. Discussing the medieval walled city, geographer Gregory Ashworth and historian and urban planner David Bruce remind us that the aesthetically pleasing forms and materials of city fortifications were designed to maximize human suffering and facilitate the destruction of the enemy.[60] The arch-shaped machicolation, an opening from which stones, boiling water, or other material could be dropped on the enemy, as well as the glacis, an erected slope that ricocheted missiles onto attacking forces, were both embellishing structural elements of fortresses that were designed to efficiently deliver projectiles into "vulnerable human bodies."[61] Still, the violence that walls connote does not solely derive from their military applications. The violence of the dehumanizing treatment suffered by those encircled by the walls of Nazi concentration camps also tainted the history of the wall.

Barbed wire, when present, adds another symbolic layer to the wall. The symbolic power of barbed wire developed through a politic aimed at regulating movement through the painful application of force against bodies.[62] Indeed, the ubiquitous presence of barbed wire in World War II camps, as well as its role in a sequence of brutal historical events—the domination of indigenous populations in North America and the brutality of trench warfare in both world wars—have helped render barbed wire a universal symbol of violent oppression that implicates the border wall equipped with it.[63] Philosopher Alain Brossat explains the evocative power of barbed wire by "its capacity to unite memory and pain—memories of apocalypses, of crimes, memories of the most unreasonable presumptions of our modernity. . . . It is one of the numerous channels through which violence is signalled."[64] By its physical appearance alone, barbed wire signals the deprivation of liberty. Its physical form, "a thorny, aggressive strike" in space, evokes its "violent and oppressive vocation."[65] Its power is metaphysical in that it has come to symbolize "all that separates human beings from one another and that pits them against each other."[66]

The Berlin Wall is perhaps the most vivid example of repression made possible by the merging of the monumental strength of concrete and the slender construction of barbed wire. Because of its proximity to us in time and its continuous commemoration, the Berlin Wall continues to be a referent for understanding other walls separating populations.[67] Albane Geslin writes that since the 1960s, using the term *wall* in a geopolitical context immediately evokes the Berlin Wall. The wall between the United States and Mexico does not escape comparison with the Berlin Wall. When Congress adopted the Secure Fence Act in 2006, Mexico's then president-elect, Felipe Calderón, made the parallel between the Cold War wall and the US-Mexico border wall: "Humanity committed a grave error by constructing the Berlin Wall, and I am sure that today the United States is committing a grave error in constructing a wall along our northern border."[68]

The potency of the symbolism attached to barbed wire and the wall it supports is so heavily loaded with the violence of past performances and practices associated with it that it has become a "metaphor for violence."[69] It crystallizes into a visual symbol of the heterogeneous, yet always violent and exclusionary practices associated with it.[70] For those outside, the wall signify distrust and embody repression, humiliation, and domination. It represents asymmetrical violence of a material, political, and emotional nature.[71] This holds significant consequences for the normative influence that the wall may have in shaping the lives of the divided communities, especially if we accept Leuenberger's argument, as I do, that the meanings embodied in each wall are eventually enacted in the everyday lives of those facing them.[72]

Sensing and Feeling the Walled Landscape

Experiencing (Un)Friendly Landscapes

The fences erected following the adoption of the Secure Fence Act, and their supporting mechanisms, have altered the landscape of the southern border in radical ways. To better grasp the implications of the walled landscape on border communities, it is useful to compare its effect with that of the mostly open land border that the United States shares with Canada. A comparison of the experiences of visitors at two binational "friendship" parks—the International Peace Garden straddling the border between Manitoba, Canada, and North Dakota, United States, and Friendship Park, located entirely in the United States but abutting Tijuana in Mexico—helps us understand the ways in which the built environment affects how people read and perform national territorial divisions. The contrast between these two parks underlines how the walled borderland in one case and the open border space in the other affect the experiences of visitors in what should be a space of communal contact between two friendly nations. Similarly, a comparison of two urban sites along the US-Canada border (Stanstead, Canada, and Derby Line, United States) and the US-Mexico border (Nogales, Mexico, and Nogales, United States) demonstrates how the material and symbolic natures of the borderland environment affect the long-term community ties between residents and understandings of territoriality and identity. Crucially, by juxtaposing these specific segments of the border, we can see how the structures of settler-colonial history are being reproduced in the landscape to form distinct border arrangements contingent on culture, ethnicity, and race.

Friendship Park and the International Peace Garden

The International Peace Garden in Manitoba and North Dakota and Friendship Park in California illustrate how different the landscapes are at America's northern and southern borders. Each park is presented as a celebration of the friendship that spans the US-Canadian and US-Mexican international boundaries, respectively. Despite having been inspired by similar visions, each offers a very different experience to their visitors. The International Peace Garden seems to have lived up to the expectations of its founders and provides a welcoming and peaceful retreat to those who cross its gates. By contrast, Friendship Park has evolved into a symbol that contradicts what its founders had in mind: a representation of the division between Mexico and the United States.

The International Peace Garden

The International Peace Garden was created in 1931 to commemorate the friendship and peace between the United States and Canada. The park extends across US and Canadian territories, into the province of Manitoba in Canada and the state of North Dakota in the United States. It was created by a joint act of the US Congress and the Canadian Parliament following the donation of close to six square miles of land by Manitoba and North Dakota for the development of the park.[73] Its management by a binational staff of Americans and Canadians is regulated by a treaty between the two countries.[74] The International Peace Garden is one of the most popular attractions in the area.

The boundary line that slices through the park for 1.5 miles, and its regulation, is one of the most distinctive characteristics of the park. The park entrance is located in a 650-foot-wide space between the US and the Canadian ports of entry.[75] Visitors entering the park drive past either of these two ports to get to the park's entry gate, technically located on the Canadian side of the border. Once past the entry gate, as the park's website explains, "you are no longer in either of these two countries."[76] Visitors can stroll from one country to the other freely as long as they remain within the park. People only need to register once they leave the park, at the customs office of the country they are entering. Passports are not mandatory; a government-issued identification card with a birth certificate is accepted.[77] A number of treaty waivers and concessions contribute to the perception that the border is nonexistent here. For instance, goods bought inside the park have tax-free status.[78] The restaurant and gift shop accept both Canadian and US currency, as is the case within the rest of the park.[79] Notably, the Canadian–American International Boundary Commission authorized the International Peace Garden to erect a Peace Chapel and other structures directly above the boundary line.[80]

While the process of crossing a border can feel uncomfortable to travelers,[81] the border at the Peace Garden does not seem to have this effect. In a survey about their experiences when visiting the park, most respondents indicated they felt safe crossing the border. Only a few were unsettled by the lack of helpfulness and "rude behavior" of border officials, especially when asked to answer questions about tourism.[82] In fact, border officials reported a notable lack of awareness of the border among travelers, whereas "many assume that because the IPG [International Peace Garden] lies within this so-called 'no-man's land', they do not have to pass through border formalities."[83]

The atmosphere created by the International Peace Garden, accentuated by it being a neutral territorial space, works to erase the perception of visitors of crossing an international border—or at least prevents them from experiencing it as an obstacle.[84] The design of the park contributes to a sense of comfort and unity.[85] The park immerses its visitors in an inviting natural environment, originally conceived by the horticulturist Henry J. Moore in 1928.[86] Moore's objective in designing the park was to create a landscape that expresses peaceful coexistence. Since its inception, the gardens have been a significant element of the park.[87] Today, the park is adorned with water cascades and ponds, such as the Sunken Garden facing the Interpretative Center and the eighteen-foot-wide Floral Clock made up of between two thousand and five thousand flowers and plants, depending on the design that changes every year. One of the floral designs most illustrative of the unity of the two countries is the Floral Flags, representing the national flags of the United States and Canada, each facing the other. As one scholar notes, the intention of those who imagined and conceived the garden was to create "a garden which symbolizes humanities [*sic*] greatest ambitions and highest ideals," with its principal organizing element being the international boundary line.[88]

Besides the one hundred and fifty thousand flowers that embellish the garden grounds, the approximately one thousand-hectare site offers picnic areas, camping grounds, canoeing activities, hiking trails, and bike paths. It is also a wildlife refuge where deer and moose can be spotted. The park holds regular events; in recent years these have included a Mother's Day celebration, a quilt show, the Kotz Artz Festival, the Country Gospel, and a 9/11 memorial celebration. In the winter, the park offers a 3.3-mile cross-country skiing course.[89] Several monuments are scattered throughout the park, such as the Carillon Bell Tower, the Peace Chapel, the Historic Lodge, and the 9/11 Memorial. A cairn was also erected directly on the borderline, reading, "We two nations dedicate this garden and pledge ourselves that as long as men shall live we will not take up arms against one another."[90]

Friendship Park

Established in 1971, Friendship Park is a small plaza (less than half of one hectare) within the 150 hectares of Border Field State Park, a California State Park located at Imperial Beach, fifteen miles south of San Diego. Border Field State Park was created through the efforts of the South Bay Historical Society, a group of local business leaders and philanthropists who, for ten years, lobbied for the establishment of a binational park celebrating the relationship between the United States and Mexico.[91] The park follows the US-Mexico border that abuts Playas de Tijuana in Mexico and is symbolically located at the starting point of the first boundary survey following the Mexican-American War.

The values and objectives that guided the development of the park are similar to those of the International Peace Garden: internationalism and shared public space between San Diego and Tijuana. While entirely located on the US side of the border, the South Bay Historical Society and its president, Sidney Cornell, envisioned that people from both sides of the border would be able to freely access the park.[92] For Cornell, the park would be a space bridging the United States and Latin America, where people could meet and take advantage of the existing recreational facilities, including picnic facilities, a campground, unique flora, and access to the beach and estuaries.[93] The performance of First Lady Patricia Nixon, who, on the day of the park's inauguration on August 18, 1971, ordered that a small barbed wire fence within the park be cut while wishing that "there won't be a fence here too long," reinforced this hope.[94] Mrs. Nixon's actions suggested that the park would transcend borders and unite the San Diego and Tijuana regions, in line with the park's founders' vision.

These hopes were never fully realized. While US Border Patrol officers allowed Mexican families to cross over into the United States to enjoy the park with their American neighbors in the early days of the park, a lack of funding and growing concerns over immigration and crime soon got in the way. The fact that, unlike the International Peace Garden, Border Field State Park is located entirely on US soil facilitated a sense of American ownership over the space, sometimes developing into nationalism and nativism in the face of a strong Mexican presence.[95] For instance, negative and racialized headlines in local newspapers reported on the "illegal" presence of families from Mexico in the park, presenting them as "uninvited guests" littering the space.[96] By the end of the 1970s, the park became associated with criminal activities and smuggling, and, in 1979, the thin barbed wire that was already present at the inauguration of the park was replaced by a solid fence.[97] The situation was exacerbated in the 1980s and 1990s when the park became one of the main stages for the government's fight against narcotics—a space compared to a war zone by the media.[98] The park's landscape suffered a major setback in May 1995 when, during the course of Operation Gatekeeper, a fence almost ten feet tall was erected at Friendship Park, with its mesh so tightly woven that it was impossible to hold hands through it. A former Border Patrol officer explained that while the fence had had some measure of success at stopping undocumented crossings, it also turned people away who had met friends and families there for generations.[99]

The park's poor management also contributed to creating an uninviting atmosphere that drove visitors away. Kathryn Balint, a reporter who visited the park in 1995, noted that the entry gates of the park sometimes were "trick-locked" to dissuade visitors, or, when the park was opened, the sign at the gate would indicate that it was closed.[100] At other times, the gate would be open but there was no state park employee to collect the entry fee, or the public restrooms were chained shut. The space, she explained, offered a dreary sight. The unwelcoming atmosphere, according to State Parks district superintendent Ed Navarro, was a disingenuous tactic by the US Border Patrol to deter visitors. Nonetheless, the park remained a popular place in the late 1990s and early 2000s for families from both sides of the border who had no other option for where to meet and share a meal other than across the fence.[101]

This changed with the construction of new fences under the authority of the Secure Fence Act and with increased border enforcement regulations. In fall 2008, a second fence was erected, complemented by a ninety-foot-wide US federal patrol zone with roads and security lights extending down to the sea.[102] Since then, an interdiction to access that space within the US patrol zone effectively prevents casual meetings at the fence. Since Friendship Park itself is now within that US federal patrol zone, its access is restricted and under the control of the US Border Patrol. Visitors wishing to access Friendship Park must present an identification document that proves legal residence in the US, even if they are not permitted to cross the border.[103] Visits are limited to Saturdays and Sundays, from 10:00 a.m. to 2:00 p.m., and new rules adopted in February 2018 limit the length of any meeting to thirty minutes. Recent rules have also reduced the number of people allowed in the park at any one time from twenty-five to ten and prohibit people from taking photos in the Binational Garden.[104]

During a visit to the park in 2016, I was left with a similar, if not worse, impression to that described by Balint. The park was a desolate sight. The space was empty, with very few visitors taking advantage of the beach. The beach itself was littered with garbage washed up from the ocean. There was no lifeguard; indeed, swimming was discouraged due to the poor quality of the water. There were observation towers atop the main plaza and constant patrolling by Border Patrol agents in Chevy Tahoe SUVs. Unlike at the International Peace Garden, there was no embellishment at Border Field State Park to distract visitors from the existence of the territorial boundary and the presence of border enforcement authorities. While there was a garden at the time of my visit, the Binational Friendship Garden of Native Plants, given its location within the gates of Friendship Park, it was inaccessible.[105] Anybody approaching the fence was hailed to move back. Visiting the park itself made me feel as if my presence alone was reprehensible—a feeling accentuated by the interdiction and warning signs common throughout the park.

The emotion I recall when visiting the park is certainly felt more acutely by the Mexican families meeting there. Visitors have noted the carceral atmosphere that dominates the space, comparing meetings across the fence to a prison visit, which "leave families feeling like they have entered a maximum-security prison on visiting day."[106] In 2018, all

FIGURE 4.1: Littering at Border Field State Park, California, 2016. By the author.

FIGURE 4.2: Debris swept by the sea at Border Field State Park, California, 2016. By the author.

visitors had to wait outside the border wall to be escorted through by a Border Patrol agent and into Friendship Park, within the "security zone." Inside, another barrier kept park visitors four feet away from the main fence, making it impossible to get close and touch family and friends on the other side of the divide. Janet Fernandez, a woman who regularly visits her mother at Friendship Park, explained how she feels about the rules: "I don't like it at all. . . . They're treating us like we're bad people, bad families that are going to do something. All we want to do is see our family."[107] Despite how uncomfortable these visits might have been, they allowed families to meet. However, these meetings have stopped since the 2020 COVID-19 outbreak and the decision by US officials to close the US side of Friendship Park to visitors. Despite the reopening of international borders following the outset of the pandemic, the park remains closed. This, along with the construction of a doubled-layer thirty-foot-tall steel wall in 2023, are the latest setbacks in achieving a space of binational unity.[108]

FIGURE 4.3: Gate of Friendship Park, located within Border Field State Park, California, 2016. By the author.

Ambos Nogales

Twelve twin cities are spread along the border between the United States and Mexico. Despite being divided by the international border, these sister cities often share historical, cultural, economic, and social ties; even families may be spread across the international divide.[109] Of these pairs of twin towns, Nogales (Sonora, Mexico) and Nogales (Arizona, United States) are among those that have been most closely connected—to the point that the term *Ambos Nogales* (both Nogales) has emerged to refer to the community made up of the two cities. Passage between the two cities takes place mostly at two major ports of entry: the Dennis DeConcini Port of Entry in the downtown area of Ambos Nogales, and the Mariposa Port of Entry, the fourth largest port of entry along the US-Mexico border, slightly outside the city center and primarily dedicated to freight traffic.[110]

Ambos Nogales has witnessed substantial changes to its landscape since its establishment in the nineteenth century. Originally, the border between

Nogales, Sonora, and Nogales, Arizona, passed through the center of Calle International, a wide road with no impediment to crossing from one side to the other. Only a boundary monument signaled the existence of the border. The extent of the spatial integration of the two cities was such that certain buildings, for instance, the railroad depot, straddled the border.[111] The border slowly materialized, starting in 1880 with the construction of a trading post and the formal separation of Nogales, Sonora, and Nogales, Arizona, by an international agreement.[112] Then, in the first half of the twentieth century, chain-link fences were put up. The first one was erected in 1915 at the request of the Mexican governor Jose M. Matoreyna. Then, in 1918, US authorities constructed a more permanent barrier, two miles long and six feet high, to contain tensions arising from the Mexican Revolution of 1910.[113] Yet, the sentiments that these chain-link fences may have provoked did not alter the sense of community that characterized Ambos Nogales—at least not to the extent of the wall that divides the two towns today. Describing these twin cities in 1928, R. M. Cousar, the inspector in charge at the Nogales office of the Immigration Service, wrote that they form "practically one community," as a daily average of between twelve thousand and thirteen thousand people entered the United States through the cities' two ports of entry.[114] Anthropologist Randall McGuire notes that today's residents of Nogales think back to this fence with nostalgia, a barrier more akin to a "picket fence between neighbors."[115]

For most of the twentieth century, the towns developed in tandem. In 1950, the economies of the twin cities were deeply intertwined. Businesses were often run by families with ties on either side of the border. Americans would cross into Nogales, Sonora, for day trips, while Mexicans would shop in Nogales, Arizona, where they could find better quality goods at lower prices. The community leaders in both towns possessed an awareness of the binational and bicultural identity of the cities.[116] Until the early 1990s, Ambos Nogales was considered the easiest place to cross the border without documents;[117] someone could simply walk to the neighboring city without undergoing stringent identity checks.[118] The two cities were one in many ways; they shared services such as a sewage treatment plant, and there was close cooperation between their police departments and fire brigades. A spring parade took place every year for the Fiesta de Mayo, starting in Nogales, Sonora, and ending in Arizona.[119]

In 1996, the erection of an eight-foot-high green steel wall made from surplus corrugated steel landing mats severely impaired this ease of movement.[120] Regular car and helicopter patrols along the wall, the installation of towers equipped with cameras and motion sensors, mobile observation towers, and checkpoints within twenty-five miles of the border gave the space an increasingly military atmosphere. The fence, complemented by steel mesh anticlimb guards, severely undermined the sense of community between the two towns. Many shared activities and services were made difficult or halted because of it, including the Fiesta de Mayo parade. Fire trucks could no longer go through the main gate, impeding collaboration between the two fire brigades.[121]

The border between the two cities was further reinforced in 2011 when an impressive bollard-style steel wall, equipped with surveillance towers and cameras, was substituted for the earlier structure made of landing mats.[122] The new wall spans a little over 2.8 miles, ranging in height from twenty-three to thirty feet. Its main body is composed of steel tubes filled with concrete to prevent them from being cut, and metal sheets have been fixed atop the wall to prevent climbing. Its foundation runs about six feet deep to make digging tunnels difficult. The controls that are now imposed have drastically reduced the ability of residents to move freely between the two cities, especially affecting Mexican nationals. The two-way movement that used to be the norm between the two cities is now mostly one-way.[123] Crossing from the United States into Mexico is easy for drivers and pedestrians, while Mexican nationals face waits of several hours, car and body searches, and thorough examinations of their identification papers when seeking entry into the United States.[124] These obstacles to entry have had consequences on socioeconomic exchanges between the two communities. Notably, this has resulted in a 30 percent decline in the number of people entering the United States through the main Nogales port of entry between 2002 and 2011 (the year the reinforced wall was erected), with an equivalent reduction in business activities.[125] The increased militarization of the border has also disturbed families now divided by the fence. One resident explains how the new wall has undermined cross-border relations in Ambos Nogales:

> You know, when I was a boy, this border wasn't a wall. . . . My family crossed all the time to visit relatives and friends. When I was a *chamaco* [a youngster],

> we would sneak back and forth to buy Mexican sweets or American candy. Later, I had a girlfriend on *el otra lado* [the other side] and I would crawl under the fence to take her to the movies. She is my wife now and we live in Nogales, Arizona, but we still have family and friends in Nogales, Sonora. This new wall replaces that old ugly green thing but it is still hideous because it separates us from *nuestros queridos* [our loved ones].[126]

Hence, it is not only the physical constraints imposed by the wall that challenge the unity of Ambos Nogales; the striking sight of this new wall also defeats any idea of shared space between the twin cities. It imparts division. The way it scrolls through the hills of Ambos Nogales is an insistent reminder of a legal divide that can be traced back to nearly two centuries ago when the Treaty of Guadalupe Hidalgo was signed; but it goes further, giving the landscape of Ambos Nogales a prison-like atmosphere. Like at Friendship Park, the landscape magnifies feelings of exclusion for those standing south of the wall. It clearly says that *we don't want you here.* As Anzaldúa writes, whether you are Chicano, Indian, or Black does not matter; "the only 'legitimate' inhabitants [of the borderland] are those in power, the whites and those who align themselves with the whites."[127]

Yet, even those with the proper documents for crossing the border find its sight disturbing. For author Paul Theroux, the experience of standing before the wall was a confronting one. The wall that he describes as "more formal than the Berlin Wall" and "more brutal than the Great Wall of China" transforms what was a routine action of walking across the line only a few decades ago into a pondered decision as to whether cross it or stay home.[128] The atmosphere of duress and hostility that it creates makes the border "inimical to inhabitation."[129] It transforms the landscape into one of suspicion and control.

This is even more so since the Trump administration affixed conspicuous concertina wires to the wall. For those on both sides of it, the wall visually reinforces the "sense of its being 'my side' of the vexed circumstance."[130] Each side becomes the victim of the other side; each side is on "the side of the right itself."[131] The wall arouses strong emotions that affect how residents experience and understand the border and those found on the other side. Philosopher Edward Casey and psychologist Mary Watkins explain how the wall between the two cities splits ambivalence "into outright hatred or love, envy or admiration, just as it converts openness of mind into settled opinion and rightful hesitation into precipitous action."[132] Through both the symbolic and material oppression of the wall, "rigidity sets in and a destructive antagonism replaces a more sensitive multilateralism of approach. . . . Instead of admitting the intrinsic ambiguity of the border, a descent into dogmatic self-righteousness looms."[133] As a material object, the wall is not only a *marker* of demographic, economic, and political differences that cast a shadow on any trace of shared culture and history; it also actively participates in the production of a distinction between two nations.

Derby Line–Stanstead

At the border between the towns of Stanstead in Quebec, Canada, and Derby Line in Vermont, United States, one could be forgiven for not knowing in which country they stand. There is no wall to mark the border. There are a few chain-link fences here and there, to be sure, but the contrast between the visual outlook of that segment of the border and that of Ambos Nogales is remarkable. This explains why, in recent years, the two towns have been singled out by the media to illustrate the dissimilarity of the two US land borders.

Both Stanstead—created in 1995 by the merger of three villages (Stanstead Plain, Rock Island, and Beebe Plain)—and Derby Line are small communities. The former had a population of 2,824 inhabitants in 2021, while the latter barely reached 687 at the census of 2020.[134] The Webster-Ashburton Treaty of 1842 established the border that divides the towns.[135] However, despite the international boundary, a strong sense of community and unity has characterized these two border towns since their incorporation. For most of the first half of the twentieth century, Canadian and US residents crossed the border without hurdles.

As between the two cities of Nogales, shopping across the border was common in the past. Depending on exchange rates, Canadians would cross south for their petrol or groceries and vice-versa. Canadian-owned businesses in the United States and Americans crossed daily into the more developed Canadian towns to work in factories. The largest employer in the area in the late 1970s and early 1980s was Butterfield, an industrial cutting tool manufacturer that hired close to 600 employees at that time, half of them Americans and the other half Canadians.[136] The factory itself was built directly on the border. This situation allowed Butterfield to operate two corporations at the same premises: one American (buying American raw products that it transformed and sold to American consumers) and the other Canadian (buying and selling products in Canada).[137]

Utilities and social infrastructure also overlapped national boundaries. For instance, the International Water Company, established in 1906, continues to treat and store drinking water for the two towns. Water is pumped in Canada, stored in the United States, and distributed to residents on both sides of the border.[138] Stanstead and Derby Line also share sewage facilities and a fire department, while the paramedics of the towns are linked so that they can second one another if necessary. The shared telephone service was another peculiarity of the area: residents on either side of the border could call each other and be spared the international long-distance fee by dialing the 819 area code.[139] The Boundary Rotary Club, with members from both Stanstead and Derby Line, was the first international Rotary Club in the world.[140]

Today, many public and private facilities are used or attended by residents on both sides of the border. Canadians and Americans alike frequent the Stanstead United Church and volunteer at its community events. The church remains a visual symbol of cross-border unity,[141] much like the Haskell Free Library and Opera House that caters to residents of both countries. Stanstead College, also on the Canadian side of the border, is a private school attended by a large number of American students who live only a short distance from the border. This and other schools in the city regularly organize binational sports games.[142] These shared initiatives have contributed to strengthening a singular cross-border identity.

The built environment is one of the most unique aspects of the place. Despite the events of September 11, 2001, this segment of the border remains distinctively open. Upon viewing the area from above, Stanstead and Derby Line appear as one united city; the main street of Derby Line seamlessly becomes Dufferin Street, the main street in Stanstead. Canusa Street, a contraction of "Canada" and "United States of America," illustrates how entwined the two towns on each side of the border are. Besides its name, another peculiarity of that street is that the border divides part of it down its middle: eastbound traffic drives in the United States and westbound traffic drives in Canada. Houses on the south side of the street are located in US territory, while those on the north side are in Canada, creating a strange situation where foreign residents become front-door neighbors. Until the early 2000s, residents visiting neighbors across the street were spared the requirement to report to the customs office. A resident on the US side of the street explained that in the 1980s, all of her friends were living in Canada. According to her, most residents thought of the place as "one big country."[143]

Because the Canadian and US ports of entry are some distance away from the official borderline at crossings in Derby Line and Stanstead and Beebe Plain and Stanstead, there remains a "neutral zone" that residents cross without thought. In the past, several residents built their houses in this zone, and, in some instances, these buildings straddle the border. Today, a regulation prohibits new buildings within ten feet of the border; but those already standing cannot be demolished.[144] Several of these houses still stand. They have both a US and Canadian civic address and their owners pay property taxes in both countries.

The Haskell Free Library and Opera House is the most prominent building straddling the border between the two towns. The library, founded in 1901, occupies a parcel of land that Martha Haskell, a US citizen of Derby Line, donated to the towns of Derby Line and Rock Island (now Stanstead) in memory of her husband, Carlos Haskell, a Canadian. Her conditions were to build the library directly on the border so that it could be used by residents of both countries.[145] The binational nature of the building is uncommon. The entry to the library is located in the United States, while the circulation desk and books are in Canada and the reading room is international.[146] On the second floor, most of the four hundred seats of the Opera House are in the United States, while the stage is in Canada.[147]

In the past, the building's location has led to events that tested the concept of territorial sovereignty. For instance, it was used to evade stringent US censorship laws: patrons could access books banned in the United States that were part of the library's book collection on the Canadian side of the building.[148] On a few occasions, the library has transformed into a courtroom for rogatory commissions—an out-of-court hearing to take a witness's deposition when that witness is outside the territorial jurisdiction of the court—circumventing a law providing that foreign witnesses cannot be legally forced to appear in trials in the United States.[149] In the 1970s, the members of the Beatles also considered the site for a meeting. John Lennon, living in the United States at the time, feared that he would not be allowed to return if he left the United States, and George Harrison and Paul McCartney were not permitted to enter the United States, where they were considered "undesirable aliens" because of convictions for the use of drugs in the United Kingdom. The group made arrangements with the Haskell Free Library to meet but eventually abandoned the plan after it became public.[150] The Beatles' idea was recently taken up by families divided as a result of President Donald Trump's Executive Order 13780, on March 6, 2017, which banned nationals of certain countries from entering the United States.[151] For citizens of these countries already in the United States under a single-entry visa, the library was one of the rare spaces where they could meet with their relatives without fear of being prevented from reentering the United States. As of November 2018, a dozen Iranian families had met at the library, some traveling from Iran to see their relatives in the United States.[152] As these meetings grew increasingly popular, however, the library decided to ban them.[153]

Despite a built environment that promotes movement and the maintenance of friendship and family relationships across the border, since the terrorist attacks of September 11, 2001, free crossings between Derby Line and Stanstead have been restricted. Lee and Ball streets, two previously unguarded road crossings, were closed.[154] Then, in 2008, the Western Hemisphere Travel Initiative (WHTI)—a joint US Department of State and DHS plan that implemented recommendations by the 9/11 Commission and the requirements provided for in the Intelligence Reform and Terrorism Prevention Act of 2004—put an additional burden on Canadians crossing the border into the United States.[155] With the implementation of the WHTI, Canadian citizens must now show a passport or an enhanced identification card when crossing south of the border, or otherwise face arrest. While these new restrictions certainly strained the unity of the cross-border community, their impact has no common measure with the controls imposed at the US-Mexico border and the material landscape of that borderland. As geographers Victor Konrad and Heather Nicol observe, the events of 9/11 have certainly made the border between Canada and the United States more visible. Nonetheless, the vision of a

FIGURE 4.4: Line of petunias marking the border between Stanstead, Canada, and Derby Line, United States, 2016. By the author.

cooperative border relationship prevails through the cultural enactment of the borderland.[156] Most processes aimed at securing the border rely on technological screening mechanisms that are invisible to the eye, leaving the borderland relatively unaltered.[157] The most vivid illustration of this is the choice of boundary markers used to signal the limits of US and Canadian territories on Church Street, a street intersection that connects the two countries. Here, it is not a fence that delimits the space between the two jurisdictions but a line of aesthetically pleasing potted petunias.[158]

Performing the Walled Landscape

The vignettes presented in the previous section illustrate that the normativity of the wall rests strongly on its impact on how people may perform, or act, within the border landscape. The wall constrains people's movement and therefore the ability of communities to relate to each other. It also exacerbates mistrust, fear, and hostility.[159] By contrast, open borders facilitate interaction and nurture kinship. The concept of pathways explored by Davina Cooper and Margaret Davis is useful here.[160] We can think of pathways as the trajectory followed by one individual or a group of individuals repeating movement in time and space. The idea of pathways is relevant in the context of the walled border because the wall stands in the "way." It disturbs existing pathways and creates new ones. Cooper distinguishes between de jure and de facto pathways. The latter are like customary law; they are created through a reiteration of practice, out of routine and habits—the "multiple trampling of the same soil."[161] De jure pathways are imposed within a logic of governance, for instance, state governance. We can conceive of the wall as a de jure pathway, a boundary imposed on communities from above to foreclose previous de facto pathways that have been traced through the free-flowing practices of these same communities. The wall and other coercive fixtures of the environment disturb the neighborly habits that are used to link communities. This physical environment dictates where people can walk, cross, and stand; that is, where they can be and who they can interact with, hence achieving a crucial aim of territoriality, which is to regulate the movement of bodies in space so as to shape and articulate social relations within that space.[162]

The wall's normativity depends on its ability to communicate meanings through bodily senses, reinforced by its symbolic power. Touch is one of the senses the wall hails. As Cooper reminds us, touch can emphasize certain relations and downplay others: "Touch foregrounds propinquity (and distance), reciprocity (although not necessarily symmetry), texture, embodied depth, and the quality of connections or interactions. Thus, it goes to the heart of thinking about state/society relations and boundaries."[163] Touch is an essential mode of communication in the walled landscape, where "the body, the skin, the nerves, and the nervous system are immediately enrolled in regimes of spatial prohibition."[164] We see how the wall, as a fixture of the Ambos Nogales landscape, forecloses existing paths or connections to create an artificial distance between two communities that used to live almost like one.[165] Cinco de Mayo celebrations, shared community services, and cross-border commerce have all suffered from the physical division the wall creates. By contrast, the openness of the US-Canadian border has allowed interactions between Stanstead and Derby Line to subsist.

The same holds in the case of Friendship Park. Here again, the walled landscape diminishes the possibility for contact and erodes the strength of existing relationships. Limits on the number of people allowed to visit at any time, restrictions on binational projects such as the binational garden, and strict rules regulating access to the space constitute further impediments to fostering ties between the two communities. The carceral environment of Friendship Park—in sharp contrast to the blissful landscape of the International Peace Garden—humiliates visitors, especially those of Mexican descent, who report feeling like criminals when they find their bodies constrained by the bollards that separate them from family members on the other side of the divide.

The material used for the construction of physical barriers contributes to feelings of exclusion and humiliation among those they constrain.[166] Indeed, the physical features of the fence, what it looks like and what it feels like are essential to—if not constitutive of—the kind of division the builder wants to enact.[167] The metaphorical, Anzaldúa observes, precedes rational thinking because "images are more direct, more immediate than words."[168] Images have the power to cut through the skin and reach the unconscious in ways that words cannot. The bystander always reads the choice of material as a clue to the meaning of the partition.[169] The barbed wire reads "as a vicious . . . alien element."[170] The barbed wire splits open the flesh. It has no place in neighborhoods where natural and unobtrusive fencing material is preferred. The "narrative the community has chosen for itself" usually determines the kind of material used in one space.[171] The openness of the view, as is the case at the US-Canada border, suggests an openness to the neighbor. It can be read as an invitation to come in, to mingle, to interact. Chain-link fences such as those found along some segments of the border between the United States and Mexico are usually prohibited within a "good" neighborhood and are only accepted at the outer limits of the community.[172] The height and opacity of a wall also affect its reception. Low fences tend to simply delineate land in a conflict-free space where communities do not feel the need for more exclusionary barriers.[173] This is the type of fencing, where there exists any at all, that divides Stanstead and Derby Line. By contrast, high fences (above the average adult body height), such as those found in most urban areas along the border between the United States and Mexico, express a desire for protection against encroachment and trespass.[174] They also express distrust for those beyond, impeding their movement much more severely than those of their neighbors to the north, who are usually spared the long lines and stringent security checks at crossing gates.

Evelyne Ritaine notes that "the monumentality of the barrier that reassures and comforts identity for those inside is also profoundly humiliating for outsiders."[175] The stature of the wall is indeed integral to its emotional economy. The "massive, weighty, and untouchable" qualities of a place, such as the walled landscape, as opposed to an active and "lived-in" space, contribute to creating the feeling of interdiction that "one should not go near."[176] But the awe-inspiring landscape goes further by expressing superiority. Nussbaum underlines the conceptual distinction between awe and wonder. While both may provoke amazement, awe, unlike wonder, implies a "hierarchical emotion."[177] This helps us understand the causality between the monumentality of the wall and the feeling of humiliation that Ritaine and other scholars have associated with it. Humiliation is the "public face of shame," which is itself a painful emotion triggered by the feeling of inadequacy or a failure to embody certain valued characteristics.[178] These standards may align with what society judges as desirable, but they can also be personal benchmarks or expectations. By contrast, humiliation, Nussbaum observes, comes from outside oneself; it involves "the hostile infliction of shame on others."[179] As she notes, the failure to meet self-imposed ideals does not cause humiliation. Rather, it is the "combination of publicity with hostility" that turns shame into humiliation.[180] The wall is a highly public translation of the othering discourses of the law into a material form, out there for the world to see. The shame stirred up by the wall is not only personal; in fact, most standing against it will disagree with what the wall says about them. Yet, it remains a shameful offense to dignity that "spread to include identity itself."[181]

Racialized groups are more likely to be the target of humiliation-generating practices, as the comparison of the southern and northern US land border illustrates. However, even at the southern border, not everyone is affected by the walled landscape in the same manner. Again, some will come up against a wall and feel a "visceral encounter," while others will experience it as air.[182] The walled landscape is felt more or less solidly depending on who you are. For the mestiza, Anzaldúa writes,

"The borders and walls . . . are entrenched habits and patterns of behavior [de jure pathways]" that constitute "the enemy within." She has to fight these imposed Western patterns of exclusion to maintain a more inclusive perspective of herself and her surroundings as she juggles between Indian, Mexican, and Anglo identities.[183]

In this account, the connections between race, space, and habits become even clearer. In *A Phenomenology of Whiteness*, Ahmed furthers this reflection as she highlights the co-constitutive relationship between the sensual experience and past traces of racialization (historic-racial schema).[184] One question she asks in this piece is how whiteness is maintained. Her answer is through habits: "a bodily and spatial form of inheritance" passed down from a history of colonialism that "makes the world 'white.'"[185] She is not so much interested in how spaces shape bodies as she is about how bodies shape spaces.[186] Nonetheless, her comments shed light on how the touch between a body and a surface can be lived as a "social experience of restriction" or a phenomenology of "being stopped," that she opposes to one of motility experienced more readily by white people.[187] Crucially, within an inherited "white world," white people enjoy greater spatial freedom and access. Reflecting on the work of phenomenologists such as Husserl and Merleau-Ponty, Ahmed considers how whites inhabit a space that already fits their bodies, made for them through the "accumulation of past decisions" that have shaped it.[188] If space is so comfortable for some, it is because it has been "impressed upon by the shape of such bodies."[189] Ahmed uses an analogy similar to Cooper's "multiple trampling of the same soil" when she observes that space, "'record[s]' the repetition of acts, and the 'passing by' of some and not others."[190] Hence, whites "inhabit spaces that extend their shape."[191] By contrast, in a white world, nonwhites feel pressure on their bodily surfaces. This experience is one of negation and restriction where "your body feels the pressure point, as a restriction in what it can do."[192] Let us consider how Anzaldúa illustrates this tension felt by Chicanos and Chicanas[193] at the US-Mexico borderland:

> In the fields, *la migra* [immigration/border patrol]. My aunt saying, "*No corran*, don't run. They'll think you're *del otro lao* [from the other side]." In the confusion, Pedro ran, terrified of being caught. He couldn't speak English, couldn't tell them he was fifth generation American. *Sin papeles* [without papers]—he did not carry his birth certificate to work in the fields.

> *La migra* took him away while we watched. *Se lo llevaron* [they took him]. He tried to smile when he looked back at us, to raise his fist. But I saw the shame pushing his head down, I saw the terrible weight of shame hunch his shoulders. They deported him to Guadalajara by plane. The furthest he'd ever been to Mexico was Reynosa, a small border town opposite Hidalgo, Texas, not far from McAllen.[194]

In this story, skin color dictates how the body can and cannot move. What is the most revealing are the reactions of Pedro and the author's aunt. Why is Pedro terrified at the sight of the Border Patrol, and why is he ashamed? What about the aunt's response? Why is it that her first reaction is a warning not to move: "Don't run!" I argue that the answer lies in the normativity of the walled landscape, as I have previously described. The aunt knows that a Mexican-looking man running at the border gets caught. He gets deported. Her knowledge of how a brown male can move within the borderland has been assimilated through repeated experiences of the space. She has integrated ways of performing within that space to avoid being visible and exposed. Over time, this has become a habit of the mind. The fear and shame felt by Pedro also reveal the normative force of the walled landscape. In the white space that is the borderland, Pedro feels that his Mexican identity is out of place. He is conscious that his outlook makes him suspicious of the white gaze of the Border Patrol. That is the danger with a borderland that is becoming increasingly restrictive. Habits of suspicion and fear settle in. Not only for people of Mexican descent but for white Americans too, who *read* a built environment that abjectifies those on the other side of the wall and those that resemble them, conveying the impression that they stand outside the pale of civilization and governable politics.[195] For those who are the object of this narrative, humiliation wells up. Under the judging gaze of the wall, Pedro's body shrivels; he bows down his head and hunches his shoulders.

Yet, if the walled landscape embodies a demeaning asymmetry between two nations, two cultures, two identities, and interdicts performances that foster unity while enforcing practices of exclusion, not all audiences agree with the divisive narrative. In Nogales and at other segments along the US-Mexico border, the wall has become the canvas for a "projection of political intentionality" that works performatively to impose an image of the closed border that border artists seek to deflect.[196] The US-Mexico border, political geographer Anne-Laure Amilhat Szary explains, must be understood as a resistance scene of shifting narratives that creates opportunities for protesting against policies of division.[197]

Several advocacy groups and artists have answered the call and staged performances at the border that question and challenge the border wall's discourse of exclusion. On various occasions, the prison-like atmosphere of Friendship Park has been transformed into a space for binational salsa dancing lessons, yoga classes, language exchanges, and sign language classes organized by advocacy groups such as the Border Meetup Group and the Border Angels.[198] During the Fiesta Binacional in April of every year from 1979 to 2007, the towns of Naco, Arizona, and Naco, Sonora, organized a competition of "wallyball" where the wall became a volleyball net.[199]

These types of performances by border communities would not be acknowledged as law creating in a traditional account of what the law is. Nonetheless, they challenge the norms set by state law and the walled landscape and hold the potential for a reconceptualization of the border and border communities.[200] Law, including state law, is enacted, transgressed, and made through the performances—discourses—of plural subjects, not only by legal experts and politicians in Congress.[201] As Manderson notes, "Law is not manufactured by 'a multiplicity of closed discourses' precisely because it is only realised through the actions of particular human beings who exist simultaneously in several discourses and who are, therefore, themselves plural."[202]

The performances of these communities, the way they appropriate the wall for themselves to transform the divisive walled landscape into a space of binational unity, is itself a discourse that challenges the narrative of the Secure Fence Act of 2006, encourages questions about its legitimacy, and highlights the indeterminacy of the formal discourse. These performances also illustrate the point that sources of normativity are plural, emerging not only from state institutions but also from how people engage with their physical environment.

Conclusion

Too often, the distinction between the law and discourse, on the one hand, and the material world, on the other, is taken for granted. This chapter has challenged this assumption by arguing that the wall built by the United States at its border with Mexico constitutes a form of legal discourse in the same way that the Secure Fence Act and other legal texts are. Both operate to regulate patterns of living and performing in the borderland; hence, both are normative. Certainly, the ways in which legal texts and the material environment communicate differ. The wall is a legal discourse whose narrative is inflicted by the symbols attached to it through past experiences of partition. The wall means different things to different people. At the sight of the wall, a person, depending on their position in space and legal status, will read protection, containment, or (violent) exclusion. The sensual experience of the walled space mediates this reading—hence the importance of considering the physical effect of the border wall on those confronted by it.

The comparison between America's southern and northern land borders illustrates how the materiality of the walled landscape, its texture and shapes, informs meanings about territoriality and identity and conditions the prospects for cross-border interaction or, to the contrary, inhibits it. The open border between the United States and Canada and the ease with which people can cross to the other side reinforce ties between the two neighbors and contribute to erasing the national boundary from their minds. It is a space where law retreats, where movement is fluid, allowing bodies to expand. By contrast, the monumentality of the barriers built at the southern border evokes violence and oppression and sends one clear message: *Keep out! We don't want you here.* The physical constraints that the wall imposes with its supportive control mechanisms are another crucial feature of the normative power of the walled landscape. Here, the law is made obvious. It takes up space and applies pressure on bodies, forcing them to retract; disappear even. In the walled borderland, residents and other passers-by learn the territorial dance described by Ford. Or, to use Cooper's analogy, it forces them into de jure pathways, making contact between the neighbors more difficult, if not impossible. Yet, these de jure pathways are not emerging out of nothing. They are the traces of a history of settler-colonial division. Indeed, the walled landscape is the last iteration in a suite of institutional decisions that have shaped the borderland to regulate who can inhabit that space and how, depending on where one is positioned within that colonial history. The wall without the Secure Fence Act that authorizes it is illegitimate, but without the wall, the legal text is impotent. The wall becomes the law's most powerful voice.

CONCLUSION

Looking Back to the Future

In *Building Walls, Constructing Identities*, I have argued that we gain from understanding the wall as a legal object. It is an object of the law because it is the product of the legal discourses deployed to justify it. But it is also a legal object in a material sense—the wall is the law. The wall just like the text of the law holds a normative force and conveys legal knowledge about questions of territoriality and national identity that inform attitudes and practices in relation to the border and the people who encounter it. Arriving at this conclusion requires one to relinquish the myth of the law as necessarily rational, objective, or abstract. The law and its discourses cannot be severed from our experiences of the world, which are both physical and ideational. The law has multiple sources, involves a plurality of actors, and deploys in many forms beyond the legal text or the rulings of a judge. To think of the wall and the law as such allows us to pay attention to the dominant voices in the law-making process, the cultural biases that may influence legal outcomes, and the existing knowledge that informs a decision. If we recognize this, then it makes sense to consider how the (legal) history of the US-Mexico border has shaped recent decisions to build a wall along its length.

The Importance of the Past in Understanding the Present

The wall has become a steady feature of American politics in recent decades. Yet, as *Building Walls, Constructing Identities* has shown, we can trace the idea of a wall at the US-Mexico border much farther back in time. As I discovered the existence of plans to wall the border in the first half of the twentieth century, I was tempted to probe the connections (or their absence) between contemporary and early walling projects at the US-Mexico border. I started this journey in the mid-nineteenth century when the Treaty of Guadalupe Hidalgo defined the spatial limits of the American and Mexican nations, which approximately correspond to today's boundary. We saw that there was nothing natural about this new land border: the treaty transferred a large portion of the space that used to be under Mexico's jurisdiction to the United States, and along with it, the population that inhabited these territories. The new border became the open wound that, to this day, Gloria Anzaldúa reminds us, continues to split a people and culture.[1] When drawing the line, however, US officials ensured that the new border would only encompass the most sparsely populated territories to limit the number of Mexican people coming under US jurisdiction. America's deliberate decision to limit its territorial expansion to sustain the European Anglo-Protestant makeup of the country is telling of the importance accorded to race and culture as elements of national identity.

The endurance of the territorial remapping of North America illustrates the power of the law to reorder spatial and social relations and thus "generate subjective affiliations and national identities."[2] At the same time, the dynamic that characterized the US-Mexico borderland shows the partial failure of the law to impose the territorial and national vision envisioned in the Treaty of Guadalupe Hidalgo. From the time of the treaty's adoption, populations on both sides of the border regularly challenged its existence through the mundane routines of their daily lives. They crossed the border to visit friends and family, shop, and work. Meanwhile, the value of legal citizenship that benefited Americans of Mexican descent was regularly undermined by a racialized conception of national identity and belonging that excluded them. As the state centralized and consolidated its power in Washington, DC, its resolve and capacity to secure and control movement at its southern land border expanded. A range of legal innovations supported this goal: the creation of the Border Patrol, the criminalization of undocumented entry into US territory, and the adoption of legal provisions granting enhanced powers to arrest aliens entering in contravention of the prescriptions of state law. The appearance of the border wall in legal discourses coincided with these developments and, with them, shaped subjective interpretations about the southern border and neighbor articulated through a colonial discourse that created a hierarchy of otherness.

Colonial discourses, as we saw in chapter 2, justified the partial conquest of Mexico but also established the structures for administering the colonized-colonizer relationship, of which the wall is one aspect.[3] The endurance of the colonial narrative that had influenced the decision about the location of the border is apparent in debates prior to and following the Act of August 19, 1935. The racial and cultural hierarchy established during the Mexican-American War remains alive in the stereotypes used to draw the contours of Mexican identity and what was in many ways understood as its opposite: American identity, conceived as peaceful, civilized, and respectful of the law. Despite attempting to capture Mexican identity as a heterogenous degenerative whole, fault lines occasionally appeared that showed the ambivalence of white Anglo settlers toward them. An exploration of the narratives in support of or against the wall allows us to see just how crucial the selection of facts and their interpretation within that negotiation process were in orienting understandings about national identities and race in one way or another. This was particularly evident in the contest that opposed the crop and livestock industries in the mid-1900s. With the former seeking access to Mexican labor and the latter set on curtailing smuggling, the image of the Mexican shifted from the lazy indigent to the hard worker to accommodate a specific vision of their character. The same ambivalence was apparent during the 2006 debate preceding the adoption of the Secure Fence Act when Congress debated two visions of immigration law: one focused on the enforcement of the border and the other promoting a comprehensive approach to immigration.

This rhetorical process highlights the indeterminacy of the law and supports the claim that legal rules are the outcome of a choice between a range of possibilities debated in political institutions and beyond. This approach to the law challenges the positivist view that conceives of the law as a set of value-free and neutral rules. As sociolegal and critical legal scholars have argued, we can gain useful insights from recognizing the law as a form of language that emerges through a rhetorical process. Marianne Constable notes that thinking of law as language allows us to move beyond a restrictive assessment of a legal text or action in terms of its impact. As we become aware of how "law is said and unsaid, heard and unheard, in claims and counterclaims made by persons who participate in the law," its assumed static and atemporal character unravels.[4]

If one finding of *Building Walls, Constructing Identities* is that Mexican identity and race were discursively produced in opposition to American identity—aided by an association of the former with indigeneity—another is that these discourses have not disappeared. Instead, they have provided the "organizing grammar" for delimiting an American national distinctiveness that persists to this day.[5] The juxtaposition of two walling episodes in US history—the adoption of the Act of August 19, 1935, and the Secure Fence Act of 2006—underlines the ongoing nature of the settler-colonial project described by Rita Dhamoon and Kevin Bruyneel. For Bruyneel, Donald Trump's obsession with undocumented migrants echoes President Andrew Jackson's campaign of Indian removal.[6] He notes that Trump's white settler nationalism, for which the wall has become the emblematic symbol, is deeply entrenched in and maintained by America's colonial history: "Trump's candidacy and presidency, and the intense devotion of his supporters to him, are driven by white settler imperatives, grievances, identifications, and policies that manifest in implicit and explicit assertions of racial superiority, settler masculinity, and the often violent desire for territorial, bodily, and political domination."[7] It is true that, with the exception of Trump's rather explicit racialization of discourses about the southern border, race as a criterion for differentiation is not as prevalent today as it was in the early 1900s when racial identity, based on biological referents, overtly supported the construction of national identities. In recent decades, proponents of the wall have usually avoided formulations that would bring awareness to the racial premises that underpin their statements. Still, the endurance of the stereotypes that construct the social and moral attributes fixing Mexican identity in binary opposition to American identity are traces of the colonial history that grounds them. As such, they signal the continued relevance of settler-colonial discourses in shaping understandings about the US-Mexico border that promote a specific racial and cultural hierarchy.

This brings me to the idea of precedent of injustice articulated by Eve Darian-Smith to further develop the role of the law in the construction of the border wall. In chapter 3, I discussed the concept of the legal precedent of injustice and its application beyond the framework of case law. I argued that it is useful to think about the legal discourses found in legislative debates and legal texts as setting precedents akin to a court case since, in both instances, the outcome is the result of a process that denies competing narratives and obscures history and context.[8] My point is that we can conceive of the Secure Fence Act of 2006 as a form of legal precedent that may inform future practices at the border. But the notion of precedent of injustice is also helpful for understanding how the law, molded by a history of settler colonialism, has facilitated the construction of US-Mexico border walls during both the twentieth and twenty-first centuries. Developing the idea of precedents of injustice—instances of lawlessness silenced in legal records but essential to establishing the rationale of a legal case and creating the conditions for applying that rationale in the future—Darian-Smith notes that ignoring these precedents "precludes us from seeing the larger structural inequalities and political contexts . . . [and] from fully understanding law in the United States for what it is—a site of constant struggle and negotiation over what constitutes 'legitimate' social, cultural, political, and economic interests at any one moment in time."[9]

Racially motivated precedents that arise from a selection of facts, narratives, and experiences are difficult to identify because they are usually excluded from the text of the law.[10] Still, it is important to recognize these precedents of injustice because they incorporate into law values and language, which in turn "create opportunities and constraints on later interpretation and mobilization of law by both state and societal actors."[11] The notion of precedent of injustice proposed by Darian-Smith resonates with the argument made by critical legal scholars and critical race theorists about the importance of attending to what is absent from a discourse, the "said and unsaid."[12] More to the point of this book, Darian-Smith reminds us that "throughout the 19th and 20th centuries, certain narratives of American exceptionalism, frontier romanticism, and triumphant capitalism [the very narratives on which the American nation was constructed] were privileged over other narratives such as racial discrimination and economic exploitation of minorities and women."[13] In other words, our laws tend to develop through narratives that silence past violence and injustices. In turn, these absences or omissions are constitutive of the "'stories we tell about what happened then' and help reproduce a form of collective memory that shields white Americans from coming to terms with the nation's racist history and present."[14] By muting the settler-colonial circumstances that have and continue to inform divisive border practices, the law has contributed to them being forgotten. In this respect, the idea of precedent of injustice speaks to Debra Thompson's notion of racial aphasia—the willful forgetting or silencing of racial hierarchies that inform decisions and practices.[15] Race as a legal *non-dit* is nonetheless shaping today's approach to the southern border.

To become influential, narratives do not necessarily need to be readily apparent in the text of the law. Unjust precedents are often absent from legal texts but are nonetheless essential in the development of future laws.[16] The Act of August 19, 1935, is a case in point. Even in a statute that is as technical and free of justification for the wall, we can read a desire to differentiate, categorize, and visually express a hierarchy of otherness in the authorization to unilaterally build fences along the US-Mexico border. By authorizing the erection of fences, the act underwrote the adoption of a divisive and punitive strategy for the regulation of undocumented flows that has contributed to shaping not only the future legal framework for the erection of a border wall at the southern border but also the development of immigration law more generally.

As noted in chapter 3, since then, each new act authorizing the construction of a border wall has become increasingly explicit and ambitious in both its form and content. This development was facilitated by precedents that discursively constructed the southern "other" and the border as a threat. The audience that the law addresses has also widened. While the Act of August 19, 1935, was an obscure, procedural act that consisted of a close conversation between the legislator and US federal agencies and was drafted in an opaque technical language, the message of the Secure Fence Act is a widely diffused piece of symbolic legislation. The othering message is clear and leaves little room for interpretation. The act provides an explicit narrative of the meaning it attaches to the US-Mexico border and those attempting to cross it. Through language, the act reifies existing legal categories that developed along racial fault lines—notably the undocumented immigrant and the criminal. The act also casts the border as an area that is out of control, a theater where drug smuggling, violent crime, and terrorism flourish. It is, therefore, a space where "operational control" must be regained. To convince of the validity of the vision it conveys, the act appeals to the emotions of the reader: it reinforces an association between fear and anger on the one hand, and the border and those crossing it on the other. These narratives are not only justifications for the wall; they also create the need for the wall as the story of a border in crisis spreads in the authoritative form of the legal text and gains credence among constituents. The legal text creates a common language that consists not only of set terms but also of "a set of intellectual and social activities" through which "culture and community and character are constituted and transformed."[17]

These precedents then facilitate the adoption of increasingly restrictive measures for the enforcement of the southern border and against migrants seeking to cross into the United States. Relying on the Secure Fence Act, on January 25, 2017, President Donald Trump issued Executive Order 13767, ordering the construction of a new, sturdier wall at the border.[18] Then, on February 15, 2019, he issued a presidential proclamation declaring a national emergency at the southern border to redirect funds already appropriated by Congress toward the construction of the wall.[19] On the other side of the debate, Nancy Pelosi, the speaker of the US House of Representatives, called the wall "an immorality. It's not who we are as a nation."[20] Nonetheless, between 2017 and 2020, Congress provided $4.5 billion in appropriation for the border wall, nearly $2 billion more than the amount authorized between 2007 and 2016.[21] And again, in 2023, despite President Joe Biden's promise not to build more walls, another twenty miles of border fences were erected, requiring the waiving of twenty federal laws and regulations.[22]

The Law in All Its Forms

Another question that *Building Walls, Constructing Identities* has attended to is how the physical wall and its surrounding environment operate as a legal discourse. I identified the normative power of the physical wall as one modality of the law's participation in the construction of American national identity. Instead of understanding border walls as instruments that support the enforcement of the law, I recognize their legal nature; they are the law. As such, I depart from a definition of the law as a system of state rules and align more closely with the works of critical legal scholars, including those whose work engages directly or indirectly with legal materialism. I defend an expansive understanding of the law—one that recognizes a concrete relationship between the law and the material world and considers connections between people and between people and objects as sources of law. Following this conception of the law, the distinction between discourse and matter unravels and allows us to recognize the power of the physical environment in creating and transmitting legal meanings. Chapter 4 instantiates this argument, suggesting that the walled landscape can be understood as a legal discourse that participates in the creation of norms that regulate meanings about the border and the communities it divides. The walled landscape embodies and materializes notions of national and social order and authority that it communicates through an aesthetic discourse resting on symbolism and physical experiences of the space.

Building Walls, Constructing Identities confirms the importance of symbolism in the study of border walls, a point that scholars interested in the issue of physical partitions have repeatedly noted.[23] While symbolism may appear disconnected from the law, critical legal scholarship reminds us that symbols permeate the law and help signal its authority.[24] Any form of social order, including law, relies on material artifacts to impart a sense of legitimacy and authority. The robe and gavel of the judge and the statue of Lady Justice are symbolic objects that immediately come to mind, but the built environment too can be symbolic and alert us to laws that would otherwise escape us and our senses.[25] One way in which the wall communicates the law is by translating sovereign order into the border landscape. The walled landscape symbolizes the power and the right of the state to control its territory and to decide who it admits. But more than that, as discussed in chapter 4, the wall is also a symbol of division and distrust; it signals danger.[26] In this sense, the wall translates into material form the language that the Secure Fence Act uses to define the southern border and those that cross it. It is a visual discourse that transmits the values, ideas, and emotions found in the text of the act. As such, the wall is a visible sign that represents the "invisible presence" of the law.[27]

It is not only as a representation that the wall communicates; its sheer materiality induces and forces certain actions and movements upon those confronted by it. Directed at all the senses, the walled landscape can prevent or promote movement across the international boundary line. The walls straddling the border at Friendship Park and Ambos Nogales obstruct movement between the two countries. This imposes physical resistance upon bodies that used to cross (more) freely. In doing so, the built environment of the US-Mexico border contributes to the making of a "white space" on the US side of the divide. It is a space that fits comfortably around white bodies, extending as they move, while it applies pressure against nonwhites to varying degrees, depending on where they situate themselves within a hierarchy of otherness inherited from a settler-colonial past that endures into the present. By contrast, the border between Derby Line and Stanstead as well as at the International Peace Garden straddling the international border between Manitoba and North Dakota are designed to foster a sense of shared identity by facilitating movement and obscuring the existence of an international legal boundary.

The distinct material environments of the southern and northern US land borders substantiates the argument that today's borders are "racial borders" that bear traces of settler-colonial history.[28] E. Tendayi Achiume observes that the contemporary international order is constituted of national borders that are "inherently racial."[29] That is, today's borders enforce territorial exclusion along racial lines, benefiting certain nations or racial groups over others. These racial borders, according to Achiume, have emerged through a legal architecture that builds on imperialist and colonialist structures and, therefore, reproduces an attribution of mobility privileges that favor whiteness. The governance of the two land borders illustrates Achiume's point. The walled US-Mexico borderland imprints into the landscape the "algebra of inequality"[30] derived from the settler-colonial context. Moreover, the built environment constricts movement, especially for nonwhites. This contrasts sharply with the open land border between the United States and Canada. In this case, the divide between these two white nations barely exhibits the legal mark of territorial sovereignty. The security imperative is carefully balanced with a desire to maintain the openness of the space to spare border residents the strain of a closed border, which risks being read as a sign of difference and exclusion. This is not to say that Canada and the United States have relinquished enforcing the border; however, in that space, the law's operation is invisible. Recall Evelyne Ritaine's observation: We do not erect border walls against equals.[31] A wall embodies asymmetry. It is a unilateral decision made with disregard and often contempt for the neighboring state. Instead, bilateral collaboration underpins the governance of borders between "coequals" such as the United States and Canada. The Safe Third Country Agreement concluded between the United States and Canada in 2002 and expanded in 2023 is one instance of a regime of border control that leaves the borderland intact and has little to no effect on Canadian and US nationals. This agreement does not enforce the border against white bodies; it regulates the movements of asylum seekers from Latin America and beyond, who must make their claims in the first safe country they reach or otherwise be returned to that country. As such, the agreement is not about controlling the movement of Canadians into the United States and vice versa. Rather, it is a coordinated effort between the two countries to regulate the movement of racialized others. It creates an invisible wall through a legal fiction that screens the movement of people from the Global South. If border walls signal asymmetry, an exploration of the walls that run along international borders today suggests that colonization and race are constitutive of that asymmetry. The walls standing at the territorial limits of Europe are further evidence of the salience of race in the decision to erect physical partitions between states. This reminds us that walls, material or otherwise, are only concrete for some.

• • •

As law becomes more prescriptive about the need for walls, physical barriers along the southern border are becoming longer, higher, and sturdier. From a few hundred miles of fencing in the first half of the twentieth century, the wall has now grown to cover approximately one-third of the border in 2024. With this material expansion, pathways that once connected the two communities on either side of the border are obstructed and new ones are formed that engrave a specific racial and cultural hierarchy onto the landscape. These de jure pathways imposed by state law force the repetition of movement and performances that alter the experience of the border from one of openness to one of division. It is true that transgressive paths can also appear that undermine the exclusionary discourse that the wall conveys.[32] Yet, as the wall grows longer and taller, the possibility for transgressive pathways to emerge diminishes. With time, division is learned and becomes normal. Margaret Davies's proposition that the law is made up of *processes* of exclusion finds an application here. For Davies, the law is in many respects "a large-scale exercise in social line-drawing" concerned with the question of where to draw the line between inclusion and exclusion.[33] There are few instances in which the law provides a more literal answer to this question than in relation to the drawing of a national border and its further crystallization with the erection of a wall. With these material changes, it becomes almost impossible to imagine a space undivided.

APPENDIX

A Tour of the US-Mexico Borderland

As of 2024 the wall at the border between the United States and Mexico covers approximately one-third of the border. It is a discontinuous series of fences and walls that varies in design and material. Despite often being referred to as a wall, at most points along the border, the structures are more akin to a fence, made of steel rather than concrete. The most well known are the pedestrian fences that stop foot traffic. Some of the older walls built in the 1990s are rather puny, sometimes barely standing. By contrast, recent walls built following the adoption of the Secure Fence Act are considerably more imposing. And since 2017, bollard-style walls replacing old, dilapidated fences have reached imposing heights. For instance, the wall erected at Friendship Park in 2023 to replace the previous fence is thirty feet high. There used to be three hundred miles of vehicle fences: Normandy barriers, named after the barriers used on Normandy beaches during the Second World War and made of iron rails welded in standing x shapes, and low bollard-style barriers that stop vehicles but have little impact on those crossing by foot. The government stopped erecting that type of fence in 2017 and since then has started to replace them with forbidding pedestrian walls.

From the east, the wall begins abruptly in the form of a twenty-foot steel bollard wall near the city of Brownsville, Texas.[1] In that area and at other points of the border in Texas, the wall is often built miles away from the border that follows the Rio Grande River. This is because the winding waterway creates geographical and topographical conditions that complicate the construction of a wall along the national boundary. As a result, US citizens and their properties are sometimes walled out on the southern side of the fence.[2]

West of Brownsville, the wall intermittently stops and starts until McAllen, Texas. However, as of July 24, 2023, the US government had concluded contracts to build fences at many of these opened segments. From McAllen to El Paso, the border is still mostly unfenced. In this area, the Rio Grande River wanders through farmlands and rugged terrain. It crosses Big Bend National Park where the Chisos Mountain range and the Chihuahuan Desert stretch.[3] The topography of the national park that runs along 120 miles of the border makes crossing extremely arduous, with canyons featuring cliffs of over 1,500 feet and what seem to be endless deserts.[4] Still, in 2019, the US Customs and Border Patrol noted a sharp increase in the number of undocumented migrants trying to cross in that region to evade more heavily fenced and patrolled

FIGURE A.1: Gap by design in the fence at Sabal Palm Sanctuary along the Rio Grande, Brownsville, Texas, 2014. Library of Congress, Prints & Photographs Division, photograph by Carol M. Highsmith [reproduction number LC-DIG-highsm-26281].

FIGURE A.2: **Border fence in El Paso, Texas, 2016. By the author.**

segments of the border.[5] This unfenced section of the border used to end about fifty miles east of El Paso, but in October 11, 2022, there were plans to build a new border wall extending fifty-seven miles out of the city. In the city itself, the wall's design varies between corrugated metal fences, mesh metal fences sitting in concrete footings, and see-through steel bollard walls.[6]

West of El Paso, the border follows almost a straight line to the Pacific Ocean. From there, pedestrian fencing used to give way to vehicle barriers, but these are slowly being replaced by new bollard walls, similar to those found in Nogales, for the majority of the border between New Mexico and Mexico. Vehicle barriers were also prominent in Arizona, where the border crosses isolated deserts along the Tohono O'odham Indian Reservation, the Organ Pipe Cactus National Monument, and the Barry M. Goldwater Air Force Range. The terrain, which provides little shade and where water is scarce, makes it one of the harshest places to cross the border. There too, Customs and Border Protection is replacing old structures with more imposing bollard-style walls.

FIGURE A.3: **Border fence cutting through Ambos Nogales, 2016. By the author.**

In the urban areas of Douglas and Nogales, steel bollard walls stand to stop people who try to cross by foot. The sight of the wall crossing the densely populated hills of the twin cities of Nogales, Mexico, and Nogales, Arizona, is one of the most striking the border offers. From afar, as it blends through the waving landscape and lush vegetation, the wall seems to lose some of its sinister feel. But a closer look at it reminds us of its coercive purpose, giving to the place a prison-like atmosphere that only intensified in 2019 with the installation of miles of concertina wire to the wall structure.

In California, pedestrian fencing covers most of the border's length. The fifty-five-mile-long and six-mile-wide area of sand dunes between Yuma and Calexico is another spectacular but potentially deadly section of the border. There, the sand produced by the ancient Lake Cahuilla shifts according to opposing seasonal winds and makes the construction of a fixed wall like those found at other segments of the border impossible.[7]

FIGURE A.4: Border fence near Yuma, Arizona, 2016. By the author.

FIGURE A.5: Border fence stopping abruptly near Yuma, Arizona, 2016. By the author.

Therefore, the wall in that area, sometimes called the "Sand Dragon," is a floating, fifteen-foot-high fence built over the sand dunes that can be lifted to adjust to the movement of the sand.[8] The desert landscape eventually gives way to the agricultural lands of Imperial Valley and at its center the border cities of El Centro, California, and Mexicali, from where hundreds of Mexican workers cross the border every day to work on US fruit and vegetable farms. Yet, it is not long before the deadly Yuma desert takes over.

Moving farther west, the current fence east of San Diego was approximately eight feet tall and in a derelict condition when I visited in 2016. It was made from army surplus carbon steel landing mats used during the Vietnam War. During my visit to that stretch of the border, a young boy, no more than twelve years old, was showing off to us, jumping back and forth over the fence, crossing from Mexico to the United States and vice versa in a few seconds with no difficulty. On the Mexican side of the border, houses abutted the fence, their roofs higher than the barrier. These

FIGURE A.6: The US-Mexico border fence (the "Sand Dragon") snakes through sand dunes in the Imperial Sand Dunes recreation center, California, 2016. By John Moore via Getty Images.

FIGURE A.7: The border fence built southeast of San Diego in the 1990s still stands in 2016. By the author.

FIGURE A.8: Border fence at Border Field State Park, California, going into the Pacific Ocean, 2016. By the author.

fences have also been replaced by bollard walls. Finally, at the westernmost point of the border, at Border Field State Park, south of San Diego, the wall is a triple fence that serves to control entry to Friendship Park, a space where for decades families and friends divided by the border have been meeting. Past Friendship Park, the wall becomes a single bollard barrier that disappears into the Pacific Ocean.

Notes

Introduction

1. US Government Accountability Office, *Southwest Border: Additional Actions Needed to Address Cultural and Natural Resource Impacts from Barrier Construction* (September 2023).

2. Claude Quétel, *Histoire des murs* (Paris: Perrin, 2012).

3. Andréanne Bissonette and Élisabeth Vallet, eds., *Borders and Border Walls: In-security, Symbolism, Vulnerabilities* (Abingdon, UK: Routledge, 2021), 1.

4. Tim Marshall, *The Age of Walls: How Barriers Between Nations Are Changing Our World* (New York: Scribner, 2018), 2; Samuel Granados et al., "Raising Barriers: A New Age of Walls," *Washington Post*, October 12, 2016, https://www.washingtonpost.com/graphics/world/border-barriers/global-illegal-immigration-prevention/?hpid=hp_no-name_graphic-story-b%3Ahomepage%2Fstory.

5. I recognize that the wall between the United States and Mexico affects various groups of people beyond Mexicans, Mexican Americans, and white Anglo-Americans. Some scholars have considered the effects of the wall crossing the Tohono O'odham Indian Reservation on indigenous people. These are important contributions to which I refer; however, in this book, I emphasize the role of legal discourses surrounding the border wall in shaping American and Mexican national identities. See Kenneth D. Madsen, "A Basis for Bordering: Land, Migration, and Inter-Tohono O'odham Distinction Along the US-Mexico Line," in *Placing the Border in Everyday Life*, ed. Reece Jones and Corey Johnson (Abingdon, UK: Routledge, 2016), 93–116.

6. See James Boyd White, "Law as Rhetoric, Rhetoric as Law: The Arts of Cultural and Communal Life," *University of Chicago Law Review* 52, no. 3 (1985); Peter Brooks and Paul Gewirtz, eds., *Law's Stories: Narrative and Rhetoric in the Law* (New Haven, CT: Yale University Press, 1996); Desmond Manderson, *Songs without Music: Aesthetic Dimensions of Law and Justice* (Berkeley: University of California Press, 2000); Marianne Constable, *Our Word Is Our Bond: How Legal Speech Acts* (Stanford, CA: Stanford University Press, 2014); Heather Conway and John Stannard, eds., *The*

Emotional Dynamics of Law and Legal Discourse (Oxford: Hart, 2016); E. Tendayi Achiume, "Racial Borders," *Georgetown Law Journal* 110, no. 3 (2022).

7. See Ronen Shamir, "Without Borders? Notes on Globalization as a Mobility Regime," *Sociological Theory* 23, no. 2 (2005); Élisabeth Vallet and Charles-Philippe David, "Introduction: The (Re) Building of the Wall in International Relations," *Journal of Borderlands Studies* 27, no. 2 (2012); Wendy Brown, *Walled States, Waning Sovereignty*, 2 ed. (New York: Zone Books, 2017).

8. S. Deborah Kang, *The INS on the Line: Making Immigration Law on the US-Mexico Border, 1917–1954* (New York: Oxford University Press, 2017); Oscar J. Martínez, "Border Conflict, Border Fences, and the "Tortilla Curtain" Incident of 1978–1979," *Journal of the Southwest* 50, no. 3 (2008).

9. The earliest record I found debating the construction of a fence is dated May 2, 1930, but records mention earlier plans including a bill for the construction of a fence at Cordova Island, El Paso, Texas, and Ciudad Juárez, Mexico, in 1928.

10. Patrick Wolfe, "Settler Colonialism and the Elimination of the Native," *Journal of Genocide Research* 8, no. 4 (2006).

11. Lorenzo Veracini, "Introducing: Settler Colonial Studies," *Settler Colonial Studies* 1, no. 1 (2011).

12. Veracini, "Introducing: Settler Colonial Studies," 2–3.

13. In that sense, Veracini argues, the two are not only different, they contradict each other: "Introducing: Settler Colonial Studies," 3.

14. Patrick Wolfe, *Settler Colonialism and the Transformation of Anthropology: The Politics and Poetics of an Ethnographic Event* (London: Cassell, 1999), 3; See also Veracini, "Settler Colonial Studies," 2; Evelyn Nakano Glenn, "Settler Colonialism as Structure: A Framework for Comparative Studies of U.S. Race and Gender Formation," *Sociology of Race and Ethnicity* 1, no. 1 (2015): 55.

15. Rita Dhamoon, "A Feminist Approach to Decolonizing Anti-Racism: Rethinking Transnationalism, Intersectionality, and Settler Colonialism," *Feral Feminisms* 4 (Summer 2015): 32.

16. Glenn, "Settler Colonialism as Structure," 52.

17. See also Richard Slotkin, *The Fatal Environment: The Myth of the Frontier in the Age of Industrialization, 1800–1890* (New York: Atheneum, 1985), 173–90; Peter Guardino, *The Dead March: A History of the Mexican-American War* (Cambridge, MA: Harvard University Press, 2017), 324; Hannah Gordon, "Cowboys and Indians: Settler Colonialism and the Dog Whistle in U.S. Immigration Policy," *University of Miami Law Review* 74, no. 2 (2020): 520.

18. Gloria Anzaldúa, *Borderlands/La Frontera: The New Mestiza*, 5th ed. (San Francisco: Aunt Lute Books, 2022), 19.

19. Anzaldúa, *Borderlands*, 69–70.

20. Achiume, "Racial Borders," 445.

21. Achiume, "Racial Borders," 455.

22. Methodologically, I depart from most of the current scholarship in that field, given my reliance primarily on textual sources rather than extensive ethnographic

work. That said, I substantiate the insights I draw from written sources with my own experience of the border during multisite fieldwork I carried out in July 2017 in Texas, New Mexico, Arizona, and California.

23. Brown, *Walled States, Waning Sovereignty.*

24. Peter Goodrich, "Specula Laws: Image, Aesthetic and Common Law," *Law and Critique* 2, no. 2 (1991): 235.

25. Yi-Fu Tuan, *Space and Place: The Perspective of Experience* (Minneapolis: University of Minnesota Press, 1977); Davina Cooper, "Talmudic Territory? Space, Law, and Modernist Discourse," *Journal of Law and Society* 23, no. 4 (1996); Davina Cooper, "Against the Current: Social Pathways and the Pursuit of Enduring Change," *Feminist Legal Studies* 9, no. 2 (2001); Desmond Manderson, "Interstices: New Work on Legal Spaces," *Law, Text, Culture* 9 (2005); David Delaney, *The Spatial, the Legal and the Pragmatics of World-Making: Nomospheric Investigations* (New York: Routledge, 2010); Sarah Keenan, *Subversive Property: Law and the Production of Spaces of Belonging* (Abingdon, UK: Routledge, 2014); Margaret Davies, *Law Unlimited: Materialism, Pluralism, and Legal Theory* (Abingdon, UK: Routledge, 2017).

26. Albane Geslin, "Sémantique, sémiotique et matérialité des murs," in *Les murs en droit international*, ed. Jean-Marc Sorel (Paris: Pedone, 2010), 47–74.

27. Geslin, "Sémantique, sémiotique et matérialité des murs."

28. Geslin, "Sémantique, sémiotique et matérialité des murs."

29. Stéphane Rosière and Reece Jones, "Teichopolitics: Re-considering Globalisation through the Role of Walls and Fences," *Geopolitics* 17, no. 1 (2012): 225.

30. Exec. Order No. 13767, 82 C.F.R. 8793 (2017). The executive order calls for "secur[ing] the southern border of the United States through the immediate construction of a physical wall on the southern border."

31. Rosière and Jones, "Teichopolitics," 225.

32. Geslin, "Sémantique, sémiotique et matérialité des murs," 54.

33. Rosière and Jones, "Teichopolitics," 226.

Chapter 1

1. See David Newman and Anssi Paasi, "Fences and Neighbours in the Postmodern World: Boundary Narratives in Political Geography," *Progress in Human Geography* 22, no. 2 (1998); Emmanuel Brunet-Jailly, "Special Section: Borders, Borderlands and Theory: An Introduction," *Geopolitics* 16, no. 1 (2011); Christine Leuenberger, "Technologies, Practices and the Reproduction of Conflict: The Impact of the West Bank Barrier on Peace Building," in *Borders, Fences and Walls: State of Insecurity?*, ed. Élisabeth Vallet (Farnham, UK: Routledge, 2014), 223–42.

2. See Wendy Brown, *Walled States, Waning Sovereignty*, 2nd ed. (New York: Zone Books, 2017); Evelyne Ritaine, "La barrière et le checkpoint: mise en politique de l'asymétrie," *Cultures & Conflits* 73 (Spring 2009); Reece Jones, *Border Walls: Security and the War on Terror in the United States, India and Israel* (London: Zed Books, 2012); Élisabeth Vallet, ed., *Borders, Fences and Walls: State of Insecurity?* (Farnham, UK: Routledge, 2014); Matthew Longo, *The Politics of Borders: Sovereignty, Security,*

and the Citizen after 9/11 (Cambridge: Cambridge University Press, 2017); Andréanne Bissonette and Élisabeth Vallet, eds., *Borders and Border Walls: In-security, Symbolism, Vulnerabilities* (Abingdon, UK: Routledge, 2021). Work on border walls in other disciplines includes Robert Lee Maril, *The Fence: National Security, Public Safety, and Illegal Immigration along the U.S.-Mexico Border* (Lubbock: Texas Tech University Press, 2011); Mohammad A. Chaichian, *Empires and Walls: Globalization, Migration, and Colonial Domination* (Chicago: Haymarket Books, 2014); Elisa Ganivet, *Esthétique du mur géopolitique* (Québec: Presses de l'Université du Québec, 2015); Massimiliano Demata, *Discourses of Borders and the Nation in the USA: A Discourse-Historical Analysis* (London: Routledge, 2023).

3. Some notable exceptions include a number of contributions in Jean-Marc Sorel's edited collection *Les murs et le droit international*. See also Pratheepan Gulasekaram, "Why a Wall?," *UC Irvine Law Review* 2, no. 1 (2012). Gulasekaram asks why the US government is building a wall despite evidence showing its inadequacy at stopping migration flows. The answer, he argues, lies in the symbolism of the wall and the contrast between the invisibility of the law and the "visceral power of a fence." Law, he says, lacks emotive force; the fence is replete with it. For an analysis of the border wall as part of a "mobility regime" consisting of "epistemological, technical, and institutional" interventions by governments over populations from the Global South, see Ronen Shamir, "Without Borders? Notes on Globalization as a Mobility Regime," *Sociological Theory* 23, no. 2 (2005). Shamir argues that with globalization reducing distance between people, a paradigm of suspicion, built on the amalgamation of threats of terrorism, crime, and immigration, has developed and informed policies and regulations relevant to mobility.

4. Sorel, *Les murs et le droit international*; Jean-Marc Sorel, "Is the Wall Soluble into International Law?," in *Borders, Fences and Walls: State of Insecurity?*, ed. Élisabeth Vallet (Farnham, UK: Routledge, 2014), 133–41. Many contributions have focused on the Israel-Palestinian wall and the International Court of Justice's advisory opinion in *Legal Consequences of the Construction of a Wall in the Occupied Palestinian Territory* (Advisory Opinion) [2004] ICJ Rep 2004 136.

5. See for instance Christian Tomuschat, "Murs et responsibilité des états," in *Les murs en droit international*, ed. Jean-Marc Sorel (Paris: Pedone, 2010), 176–78; Hélène Ruiz Fabri, "Murs, accessibilité et libre circulation," in *Les murs en droit international*, ed. Jean-Marc Sorel (Paris: Pedone, 2010), 156; Moria Paz, "Between the Kingdom and the Desert Sun: Human Rights, Immigration, and Border Walls," *Berkeley Journal of International Law* 34, no. 1 (2016).

6. See Robert Neustadt, "Intervention II: Borders: Strangers and Neighbors: The Tohono O'odham and the Myth of 'Us versus Them' on the US/Mexico Border," *Cross Currents* 67, no. 3 (2017).

7. Keegan C. Tasker, "Waived: The Detrimental Implications of U.S. Immigration and Border Security Measures on Southern Border Tribes; An Analysis of the Impact of President Trump's Border Wall on the Tohono O'odham Nation," *American Indian Law Journal* 8, no. 1 (2019).

8. Kenneth D. Madsen, "Institutionalising the Exception: Homeland Security Section 102(c) Waivers and the Construction of Border Barriers," *Geopolitics* 28, no. 5 (2023). See also David Fisher, "The U.S.-Mexico Border Wall and the Case for "Environmental Rights," *Texas International Law Journal* 50, no. 1 (2015). The waiving of these federal laws, David Fischer argues, has reduced the protection of border populations from environmental damages caused by the US federal government, therefore violating the principle of equal protection under the law.

9. See Simon Harrall, "The Federal Government's Power of Eminent Domain Over State Lands Regarding the U.S.-Mexico Border Wall," *Houston Law Review* 56, no. 3 (2019).

10. Ruiz Fabri, "Murs, accessibilité et libre circulation," 156.

11. Margaret Davies, *Law Unlimited: Materialism, Pluralism, and Legal Theory* (Abingdon, UK: Routledge, 2017), 136.

12. See Margaret Davies, *Asking the Law Question*, 3rd ed. (Pyrmont, Australia: Thomson Legal & Regulatory, 2008), 100; Eve Darian-Smith, *Laws and Societies in Global Contexts: Contemporary Approaches* (New York: Cambridge University Press, 2013).

13. Darian-Smith, *Laws and Societies*, 100–101.

14. Davies, *Law Unlimited*, ch. 3.

15. James Boyd White, "Law as Rhetoric, Rhetoric as Law: The Arts of Cultural and Communal Life," *University of Chicago Law Review* 52, no. 3 (1985): 686.

16. White, "Law as Rhetoric, Rhetoric as Law."

17. Darian-Smith, *Laws and Societies*, 98.

18. See for instance Martha-Marie Kleinhans and Roderick A. Macdonald, "What Is a Critical Legal Pluralism?," *Canadian Journal of Law and Society* 12, no. 2 (1997): 38; Desmond Manderson, "Interstices: New Work on Legal Spaces," *Law, Text, Culture* 9 (2005): 1; Darian-Smith, *Laws and Societies*, ch. 3; Andreas Philippopoulos-Mihalopoulos, *Spatial Justice: Body, Lawscape, Atmosphere* (Abingdon, UK: Routledge, 2015); Davies, *Law Unlimited*, 70; Emilie Cloatre and Dave Cowan, "Legalities and Materialities," in *Routledge Handbook of Law and Theory*, ed. Andreas Philippopoulos-Mihalopoulos (London: Routledge, 2019), 438.

19. Davies, *Law Unlimited*, 72–73.

20. Darian-Smith, *Laws and Societies*, 101.

21. See for instance Marianne Constable, *Our Word Is Our Bond: How Legal Speech Acts* (Stanford, CA: Stanford University Press, 2014).

22. White, "Law as Rhetoric," 684. Although White is interested in the performance of lawyers in the courtroom, his analysis is relevant to the way legal texts are created through legislative debates.

23. White, "Law as Rhetoric," 690.

24. White, "Law as Rhetoric," 689–90.

25. White, "Law as Rhetoric," 691–92.

26. Davies, *Law Unlimited*, 41.

27. Joshua Fishman quoted in Michelle L. Burgis, *Boundaries of Discourse in the International Court of Justice: Mapping Arguments in Arab Territorial Disputes* (Leiden: Martinus Nijhoff, 2009), 34.

28. Burgis, *Boundaries of Discourse*, 35.

29. Martti Martti Koskenniemi, "Letter to the Editors of the Symposium," *American Journal of International Law* 93, no. 2 (1999): 361.

30. David Feldman, "Beginning at the Beginning: The Relationships between Politics and Law," in *Law in Politics, Politics in Law*, ed. David Feldman (Oxford: Hart, 2013), 7.

31. Teemu Ruskola, *Legal Orientalism: China, the United States, and Modern Law* (Cambridge, MA: Harvard University Press, 2013), 2.

32. Robert M. Cover, "The Supreme Court, 1982 Term; Foreword: Nomos and Narrative," *Harvard Law Review* 97, no. 1 (1983): 4.

33. See also Cover, "The Supreme Court, 1982 Term," 9; Peter Brooks, "The Law as Narrative and Rhetoric " in *Law's Stories: Narrative and Rhetoric in the Law*, ed. Peter Brooks and Paul Gewirtz (New Haven, CT: Yale University Press, 1996). 14. Although Brooks is mostly interested in the analysis of case law, his remarks are also relevant to legal texts.

34. Some legal discourses are more explicitly normative than others; procedural and administrative law, for instance, has a limited audience, usually state officials, and little to no normative ambitions. See Desmond Manderson, *Songs without Music: Aesthetic Dimensions of Law and Justice* (Berkeley: University of California Press, 2000), 59.

35. Kitty Calavita, *Kitty Calavita, Invitation to Law & Society: An Introduction to the Study of Real Law* (Chicago: Chicago University Press, 2010).

36. Calavita, *Kitty Calavita*, 35. See also Nicholas K. Blomley, *Law, Space, and the Geographies of Power* (New York: Guilford, 1994), 12.

37. Brooks, "Law's Stories," 17.

38. Margaret Davies, "Exclusion and the Identity of Law," *Macquarie Law Journal* 5 (2005): 17.

39. See Edward W. Said, Moustafa Bayoumi, and Andrew Rubin, *The Edward Said Reader* (New York: Vintage Books, 2000).

40. James Boyd White, "Rhetoric and Law: The Arts of Cultural and Communal Life," in *The Rhetoric of the Human Sciences: Language and Argument in Scholarship and Public Affairs*, ed. John S. Nelson, Allan Megill, and Donald N. McCloskey (Madison: University of Wisconsin Press, 1987), 304.

41. Edward W. Said, *Orientalism* (New York: Vintage Books, 1979).

42. Ruskola, *Legal Orientalism*.

43. Ruskola, *Legal Orientalism*, 197.

44. Cover, "Nomos and Narrative." The Greek word *nomos* has a complicated etymology, and its meaning, although much debated, is usually associated with "custom" or "law," or in terms that suggest order and convention, such as "the normal order of things," "the way men live," "linguistic usage," "religious norm," "normal

behavior," "legal and political rule," and "statute"; see Julia H. Chryssostalis, "Reading Arendt 'Reading' Schmitt: Reading Nomos Otherwise?," in *Feminist Encounters with Legal Philosophy*, ed. Maria Drakopoulou (Abingdon, UK: Routledge, 2013), 162. In the present context, I follow Robert Cover's understanding of *nomos*, which consists of "bodies of rule and doctrine" that form the universe we "live in," the "formal institutions of the law," and the "conventions of social order" as well as the narratives that explain, justify and give meanings to these norms and institutions.

45. Cover, "Nomos and Narrative," 8.

46. Cover, "Nomos and Narrative," 8–9.

47. Eve Darian-Smith, "Precedents of Injustice: Thinking About History in Law and Society Scholarship," in *Studies in Law, Politics and Society*, vol. 41, ed. Austin Sarat (Bingley, UK: Emerald Group, 2007), 61–81.

48. E. Tendayi Achiume, "Racial Borders," *Georgetown Law Journal* 110, no. 3 (2022).

49. Achiume, "Racial Borders," 500.

50. Manderson, *Songs without Music*, 99.

51. Manderson, *Songs without Music*, 56.

52. Manderson, *Songs without Music*, 57.

53. Sara Ahmed, "Collective Feelings: Or, the Impressions Left by Others," *Theory, Culture & Society* 21, no. 2 (2004): 25; See also Martha C. Nussbaum, *Political Emotions: Why Love Matters for Justice* (Cambridge, MA: Harvard University Press, 2013).

54. Ahmed, "Collective Feelings," 25–26. The text Ahmed refers to reads as follows: "The depths of Love are rooted and very deep in a real White Nationalist's soul and spirit, no form of 'hate' could even begin to compare. At least not a hate motivated by ungrounded reasoning. It is not hate that makes the average White man look upon a mixed race couple with a scowl on his face and loathing in his heart. It is not hate that makes the White housewife throw down the daily jewspaper [*sic*] in repulsion and anger after reading of yet another child-molester or rapist sentenced by corrupt courts to a couple of short years in prison or parole. It is not hate that makes the White workingman curse about the latest boatload of aliens dumped on our shores to be given job preferences over the White citizen who built this land. It is not hate that brings rage into the heart of a White Christian farmer when he reads of billions loaned or given away as 'aid' to foreigners when he can't get the smallest break from an unmerciful government to save his failing farm. No, it's not hate, It is Love."

55. Ahmed, "Collective Feelings," 25–26.

56. Nussbaum, *Political Emotions*, ch. 10.

57. Davies, *Law Unlimited*, 42.

58. Karen Barad, "Posthumanist Performativity: Toward an Understanding of How Matter Comes to Matter," *Signs: Journal of Women in Culture and Society* 28, no. 3 (2003): 801.

59. Barad, "Posthumanist Performativity," 822. Barad's account of the inseparability of discourse and materiality, based on the work of physicist Niels Bohr, goes beyond the inseparability of meaning and matter. A key concept in her work

is agential realism, which develops the idea that matter is always constituting and reconstituting itself in an intra-active way, that objects do not preexist the interaction of matter. However, for the purpose of the book, what I retain from her work is the idea that materiality is discursive and, therefore, has an impact of its own in shaping realities, including social realities. That is, practices and objects, like language, are forms of discourses that may carry normative content.

60. Ernesto Laclau and Chantal Mouffe, *Hegemony and Socialist Strategy: Towards a Radical Democratic Politics*, 2nd ed. (London: Verso, 2014), 108.

61. Benno Herzog, *Discourse Analysis as Social Critique Discursive and Non-Discursive Realities in Critical Social Research.* (London: Palgrave Macmillan UK, 2016), ch. 2.

62. Stuart Hall, "Race—The Sliding Signifier," in *The Fateful Triangle* (Cambridge, MA: Harvard University Press, 2017), 46.

63. Peter Goodrich, "Specula Laws: Image, Aesthetic and Common Law," *Law and Critique* 2, no. 2 (1991): 235.

64. Goodrich, "Specula Laws," 235.

65. Goodrich, "Specula Laws," 236; Manderson, *Songs without Music*, 11.

66. Goodrich, "Specula Laws," 238.

67. Manderson, *Songs without Music*, 74.

68. Manderson, *Songs without Music*, 103; Darian-Smith, *Laws and Societies*.

69. Pierre Schlag, "The Aesthetics of American Law," *Harvard Law Review* 115, no. 4 (2002): 1049. Other legal scholars have adopted a similar definition of aesthetics, see Manderson, *Songs without Music*; Darian-Smith, *Laws and Societies*, 103.

70. Darian-Smith, *Laws and Societies*, 103.

71. Manderson, *Songs without Music*, 19.

72. Manderson, *Songs without Music*, 21.

73. Yi-Fu Tuan, *Space and Place: The Perspective of Experience* (Minneapolis: University of Minnesota Press, 1977).

74. Tuan, *Space and Place*, 6.

75. This is how, eventually, symbolic associations between objects and space develop. See Tuan, *Space and Place*, 9.

76. Tuan, *Space and Place*, 8. In practice, the symbolic/direct nature of our experience of the material world cannot be rigidly severed. In fact, symbolic associations emerge out of how we feel about the world. As Manderson notes, both dimensions influence meaning: Manderson, *Songs without Music*, 19.

77. Tuan, *The Perspective of Experience*, 102.

78. Tuan, *The Perspective of Experience*, 107.

79. Tuan, *The Perspective of Experience*, 107.

80. Tuan, *The Perspective of Experience*, 114.

81. Tuan, *The Perspective of Experience*, 12.

82. See Tuan, *The Perspective of Experience*, 34–50.

83. Yi-Fu Tuan, "Space and Place: Humanistic Perspective," in *Philosophy in Geography*, ed. Stephen Gale and Gunnar Olsson (Dordrecht, The Netherlands: D. Reidel, 1979), 390.

84. Antoine de Saint-Exupéry, *Wind, Sand and Stars* [Terre des Hommes], trans. Lewis Galantière (New York: Reynal & Hitchcock, 1939), 114.

85. In addition to scholars already discussed, see Bruno Latour, *The Making of Law: An Ethnography of the Conseil d'Etat* (Cambridge: Polity Press, 2010).

86. See Blomley, *Law, Space*, 29–30.

87. Blomley, *Law, Space*, 29–37.

88. Blomley, *Law, Space*, 28, 46.

89. Nicholas Blomley, "From 'What?' to 'So What?': Law and Geography in Retrospect," in *Law and Geography*, ed. Jane Holder and Carolyn Harrison (Oxford: Oxford University Press, 2003), 29.

90. Philippopoulos-Mihalopoulos, *Spatial Justice*, 3.

91. Philippopoulos-Mihalopoulos, *Spatial Justice*, 38.

92. Philippopoulos-Mihalopoulos, *Spatial Justice*, 34–36.

93. Davies, *Law Unlimited*, 69–70.

94. Eve Darian-Smith, *Bridging Divides: The Channel Tunnel and English Legal Identity in the New Europe* (Berkeley: University of California Press, 1999).

95. Darian-Smith, *Bridging Divides*, 21. Rob Shields defines the operation of implicitly giving meaning to space "social spatialization": "In social spatialization, spaces are not only overcoded, but physical space itself is 'produced' via classification schemes with various (ideological) divisions as good and bad areas . . . ours and theirs. . . . This 'production' of space also concerns social and cultural reproduction." Rob Shields, "Spatial Stress and Resistance: Social Meanings of Spatialization," in *Space & Social Theory: Interpreting Modernity and Postmodernity*, ed. Georges Benko and Ulf Strohmayer (Oxford: Wiley-Blackwell, 1997), 192.

96. Darian-Smith, *Bridging Divides*, 21.

97. See Darian-Smith, *Bridging Divides*.

98. Irus Braverman, *Planted Flags: Trees, Land, and Law in Israel/Palestine* (New York: Cambridge University Press, 2009).

99. Interestingly, Braverman notes that the most common reason that was given for uprooting olive groves in the West Bank was the construction of the Israel-Palestine wall: Braverman, *Planted Flags*, 131.

100. Davina Cooper, "Against the Current: Social Pathways and the Pursuit of Enduring Change," *Feminist Legal Studies* 9, no. 2 (2001): 129.

Chapter 2

1. Benedict Anderson, *Imagined Communities: Reflections on the Origin and Spread of Nationalism*, rev. ed. (London: Verso, 2016), 324.

2. Ernest Gellner, *Thought and Change* (London: Weidenfeld and Nicolson, 1964), quoted in Anderson, *Imagined Communities*, 6.

3. John Agnew, "The Territorial Trap: The Geographical Assumptions of International Relations Theory," *Review of International Political Economy* 1, no. 1 (1994): 55.

4. Patrick Wolfe, "Settler Colonialism and the Elimination of the Native," *Journal of Genocide Research* 8, no. 4 (2006): 388. Various modes of territorial appropriation

can be deployed depending on the context, including the imposition of a private property regime, the adoption of rules regulating ownership rights, and the mapping and drawings of territorial boundaries.

5. Wolfe, "Settler Colonialism."

6. See Wolfe, "Settler Colonialism"; Patrick Wolfe, *Traces of History: Elementary Structures of Race* (London: Verso, 2016); Kevin Bruyneel, *Settler Memory: The Disavowal of Indigeneity and the Politics of Race in the United States* (Chapel Hill: University of North Carolina Press, 2021).

7. Gloria Anzaldúa, *Borderlands/La Frontera: The New Mestiza*, 5th ed. (San Francisco: Aunt Lute Books, 2022), 17.

8. A few notable exceptions are the work of historians Oscar J. Martínez and Deborah Kang: Oscar J. Martínez , "Border Conflict, Border Fences, and the 'Tortilla Curtain' Incident of 1978–1979," *Journal of the Southwest* 50, no. 3 (2008); S. Deborah Kang, *The INS on the Line: Making Immigration Law on the US-Mexico Border, 1917–1954* (New York: Oxford University Press, 2017). See also Michael J. Dear, *Why Walls Won't Work: Repairing the US-Mexico Divide* (New York: Oxford University Press, 2013).

9. Rita Dhamoon, "A Feminist Approach to Decolonizing Anti-Racism: Rethinking Transnationalism, Intersectionality, and Settler Colonialism," *Feral Feminisms* 4 (Summer 2015): 32; Evelyn Nakano Glenn, "Settler Colonialism as Structure: A Framework for Comparative Studies of U.S. Race and Gender Formation," *Sociology of Race and Ethnicity* 1, no. 1 (2015): 55.

10. Act of August 19, 1935, 49 Stat 660 (1935).

11. Joseph Nevins, *Operation Gatekeeper and Beyond: The War on Illegals and the Remaking of the U.S.-Mexico Boundary*, 2nd ed. (New York: Routledge, 2010), 23.

12. Treaty of Peace, Friendship, Limits, and Settlement with the Republic of Mexico (Treaty of Guadalupe Hidalgo), signed February 2, 1848, TS 207 (entered into force May 30, 1948).

13. Unless otherwise stated, when using the terms *America* and *American community/identity*, I refer not only to the United States as a territorial political identity and its population, but also to the set of economic, social and cultural claims it makes as a nation-state.

14. Peter Guardino, *The Dead March: A History of the Mexican-American War* (Cambridge, MA: Harvard University Press, 2017), 323.

15. Guardino, *The Dead March*, 324. See also Matthew Frye Jacobson, *Whiteness of a Different Color: European Immigrants and the Alchemy of Race* (Cambridge, MA: Harvard University Press, 1998), 210; Richard Slotkin, *The Fatal Environment: The Myth of the Frontier in the Age of Industrialization, 1800–1890* (New York: Atheneum, 1985), 183.

16. Slotkin, *Fatal Environment*, 180–90.

17. See Slotkin, *Fatal Environment*, 173; Hannah Gordon, "Cowboys and Indians: Settler Colonialism and the Dog Whistle in U.S. Immigration Policy," *University of Miami Law Review* 74, no. 2 (2020).

18. Quoted in Jacobson, *Whiteness of a Different Color*, 210. The *Democratic Review* was primarily dedicated to the promotion of the Democratic Party's ideology. It is in this periodical in 1845 that O'Sullivan articulated the idea of America's "manifest destiny" to spread democracy through the expansion of its dominion westward and into Mexican territory.

19. Jacobson, *Whiteness of a Different Color*, 210.

20. Slotkin, *Fatal Environment*, 184; Guardino, *The Dead March*, 324.

21. Slotkin, *Fatal Environment*, 184.

22. Guardino, *The Dead March*, 324.

23. Guardino, *The Dead March*, 324.

24. Guardino, *The Dead March*, 324.

25. Treaty of Guadalupe Hidalgo, art. VIII.

26. During the negotiations, Mexico had attempted to safeguard the rights of the populations in transferred territories. Especially it sought to introduce into the treaty specific protections for property and the practice of Catholicism. Congress eventually wrote off or watered down these provisions. This included the removal of Article X of the draft treaty that would have recognized the property rights flowing from Mexican land grants, including communal land holdings. This in turn prioritized claims by settlers over previously recognized Mexicans' communal rights: Adam Dalh, *Empire of the People: Settler Colonialism and the Foundations of Modern Democratic Thought* (Lawrence: University Press of Kansas, 2018), 117; See also Neil Foley, *Mexicans in the Making of America* (Cambridge, MA: Harvard University Press, 2014), ch. 1.

27. Dear, *Why Walls Won't Work*, 38; See also Andrés Reséndez, *Changing National Identities at the Frontier: Texas and New Mexico, 1800–1850* (Cambridge: Cambridge University Press, 2004), 2.

28. For a detailed discussion of the dynamic between Mexico's northern provinces and Mexico's central government in the years preceding the Mexican-American War, see Andrés Reséndez, "National Identity on a Shifting Border: Texas and New Mexico in the Age of Transition, 1821–1848," *Journal of American History* 86, no. 2 (1999).

29. Nevins, *Operation Gatekeeper and Beyond*, 25–27.

30. See Dear, *Why Walls Won't Work*, 38.

31. Dear, *Why Walls Won't Work*, 37; Nevins, *Operation Gatekeeper and Beyond*, 23–29.

32. Reséndez, "National Identity on a Shifting Border."; Dear, *Why Walls Won't Work*, 37–39.

33. Dear, *Why Walls Won't Work*, 37–45.

34. Dear, *Why Walls Won't Work*, 43.

35. Nevins, *Operation Gatekeeper and Beyond*, 56.

36. Linda Gordon, *The Great Arizona Orphan Abduction* (Cambridge, MA: Harvard University Press, 1999), 59; Gordon makes this comment in relation to circular migrant labor from Mexico. She notes, however, that the relationship between

Mexican workers and Anglo Americans followed a colonial model of segregation, notably with regard to labor standards and rights: Gordon, *The Great Arizona Orphan Abduction*, 221.

37. Foley, *Mexicans in the Making of America*, 34.

38. For example, courts in the territory of New Mexico did not recognize community property rights; therefore, they did not uphold titles for lands held in common by Mexicans. Mexican landowners, whose titles to the land were often based on communal knowledge, were also disadvantaged by the California Land Act of 1851 that required proof of land ownership: Foley, *Mexicans in the Making of America*, 32.

39. Foley, *Mexicans in the Making of America*, 32.

40. Foley, *Mexicans in the Making of America*, 36. Foley remarks, however, that a revived interest for Spanish culture by Anglo Americans at the turn of the twentieth century advantaged a small number of Mexican Americans, mostly light-skinned Mexicans whose physical features were more akin to European Spaniards. Foley explains that light-skinned, English-speaking Mexicans took advantage of the fascination with Spanish heritage to identify themselves as Hispanos, or Spanish Americans, tracing their descendance to Spain to "escape the stigma of being 'Mexican'—poor, uneducated, and racially mixed." These Spanish Americans came to form an elite class with rights comparable to those of Anglo-Americans.

41. Nevins, *Operation Gatekeeper and Beyond*, 70.

42. Nevins, *Operation Gatekeeper and Beyond*, 27.

43. Rachel C. St. John, *Line in the Sand: A History of the Western U.S.-Mexico Border* (Princeton, NJ: Princeton University Press, 2011), 119.

44. St. John, *Line in the Sand*, 119.

45. St. John, *Line in the Sand*, 138–39; Kang, *The INS on the Line*, 11.

46. Kang, *The INS on the Line*, 17–18; St. John, *Line in the Sand*, 179.

47. Kang, *The INS on the Line*, 17–18.

48. Dorothee Schneider, *Crossing Borders: Migration and Citizenship in the Twentieth-Century United States* (Cambridge, MA: Harvard University Press, 2011), 97; Kang, *The INS on the Line*, 16.

49. Kang, *The INS on the Line*, 18.

50. For instance, officials of the Bureau of Immigration implemented an agricultural labor program, literacy test waivers, and a border crossing card program; see Kang, *The INS on the Line*, 20.

51. Kang, *The INS on the Line*, 32.

52. David Gutiérrez, *Walls and Mirrors: Mexican Americans, Mexican Immigrants, and the Politics of Ethnicity* (Berkeley: University of California Press, 1995), 72.

53. Gilberto Cárdenas, "United States Immigration Policy toward Mexico: An Historical Perspective," *Chicano-Latino Law Review* 2 (1975): 90.

54. Nevins, *Operation Gatekeeper and Beyond*, 136.

55. Gutiérrez, *Walls and Mirrors*, 72; Nevins, *Operation Gatekeeper and Beyond*, 42–43.

56. Kang, *The INS on the Line*, 45.

57. Act of February 27, 1925, Pub. L. No. 68-502, 43 Stat 1049-1050 (1925).

58. Act of March 4, 1929, Pub. L. No. 1018, 45 Stat 1551 (1929). See Nevins, *Operation Gatekeeper and Beyond*, 68; Cárdenas, "Immigration Policy toward Mexico," 73.

59. Library of Congress, "Immigration: Depression and the Struggle for Survival," http://www.loc.gov/teachers/classroommaterials/presentationsandactivities/presentations/immigration/mexican6.html.

60. Mae M. Ngai, *Impossible Subjects: Illegal Aliens and the Making of Modern America* (Princeton, NJ: Princeton University Press, 2014), 72–73. This estimate includes the number of Mexicans repatriated from the southwest and midwest of the United States.

61. See Olivier Razac, *Histoire politique du barbelé* (Paris: Flammarion, 2009); The Indian General Allotment Act, or Dawes Act, divided Indian reservations into individual plots of land that the US government could then distribute to individuals registered on a tribal roll. The stated aim of the act was to integrate Native tribes into the American community by favoring a sedentary way of life through farming. In effect, the act ruptured individual tribal members' connections with traditional tribal authorities and eroded Native culture: Michael R. McLaughlin, "The Dawes Act, or Indian General Allotment Act of 1887: The Continuing Burden of Allotment. A Selective Annotated Bibliography," *American Indian Culture and Research Journal* 20 (1996): 65. The Dawes Act also stated that any land remaining after allotment to Native Americans be made available for public sale. This provision, in conjunction with a 1981 amendment providing for the leasing of allotments to non-Natives, contributed to the appropriation of Native lands by white settlers: Paul Stuart, "United States Indian Policy: From the Dawes Act to the American Indian Policy Review Commission," *Social Service Review (Chicago)* 51, no. 3 (1977): 452–53; Indian General Allotment Act, 1887, 24 Pub. L. No. 49–105 388, (1887).

62. Razac, *Histoire politique du barbelé*, 36–37; According to McLaughlin, Native people held 55,000,000 acres of land in 1934, down from 147,000,000 acres in 1887: McLaughlin, "The Dawes Act," 65.

63. Martínez, "Tortilla Curtain."; On the construction of fences between the two cities of Nogales see Randall H. McGuire, "Steel Walls and Picket Fences: Rematerializing the U.S.–Mexican Border in Ambos Nogales," *American Anthropologist* 115, no. 3 (2013). The fence built in Nogales during the Mexican Revolution was erected with the assent of the Mexican government: St. John, *Line in the Sand*, 120.

64. Martínez, "Tortilla Curtain," 266–67.

65. Kang, *The INS on the Line*, 32.

66. R. M. Cousar, Inspector in Charge, Nogales, to District Director, Immigration Service, El Paso, November 22, 1928, file 55606/894, RG 85, National Archives.

67. Cousar to District Director, November 22, 1928.

68. G. C. Wilmoth, District Director, Immigration Service, El Paso, to Commissioner General of Immigration, Washington DC, May 2, 1930, file 55606/519, RG 85, National Archives.

69. Nick D. Collaer, Assistant Superintendent and H. C. Horsley, Chief Patrol Inspector, El Paso, to District Inspector, Immigration and Naturalization Service, El Paso, February 23, 1934, file 55606/894, RG 85, National Archives. See also Kang, *The INS on the Line*, 164, footnote 68.

70. R. G. Folk to Congressman R. E. Thomason, U.S. House of Representatives, December 7, 1933, file 55606/894, RG 85, National Archives; Morris Sheppard, Chairman of the Committee on Military Affairs, U.S. Senate, to Daniel MacCormack, Commissioner General of Immigration, January 8, 1934, file 55606/894, RG 85, National Archives.

71. See a reference to the letter by Justice Irby Dunklin in Morris Sheppard, Chairman of the Committee on Military Affairs, U.S. Senate, to Daniel MacCormack, Commissioner General of Immigration, January 8, 1934, file 55606/894, RG 85, National Archives.

72. D. W. MacCormack, General Commissioner of Immigration, to Morris Sheppard, Chairman of the Committee on Military Affairs, U.S. Senate, January 18, 1934, file 55606/894, RG 85, National Archives.

73. Collaer and Horsley to District Inspector, February 23, 1934.

74. Collaer and Horsley to District Inspector, February 23, 1934, 2.

75. Collaer and Horsley to District Inspector, February 23, 1934, 3.

76. Collaer and Horsley to District Inspector, February 23, 1934, 3.

77. Collaer and Horsley to District Inspector, February 23, 1934, 3.

78. Collaer and Horsley to District Inspector, February 23, 1934, 3.

79. Collaer and Horsley to District Inspector, February 23, 1934, 1.

80. Collaer and Horsley to District Inspector, February 23, 1934, 2.

81. Elizabeth Theiss-Morse, *Who Counts as an American?: The Boundaries of National Identity* (Cambridge: Cambridge University Press, 2009).

82. Theiss-Morse, *Who Counts as an American?*, 3–4.

83. Theiss-Morse, *Who Counts as an American?*, 13.

84. Theiss-Morse, *Who Counts as an American?*, 27.

85. Collaer and Horsley to District Inspector, February 23, 1934, 3.

86. Collaer and Horsley to District Inspector, February 23, 1934, 3.

87. Collaer and Horsley to District Inspector, February 23, 1934, 3.

88. Collaer and Horsley to District Inspector, February 23, 1934, 3.

89. Collaer and Horsley to District Inspector, February 23, 1934, 3.

90. Collaer and Horsley to District Inspector, February 23, 1934, 7.

91. Collaer and Horsley to District Inspector, February 23, 1934, 7.

92. Frances Perkins, Secretary of Labor, to Administrator of Public Work, Washington DC, March 7, 1934, file 55606/894, RG 85, National Archives. The request appears to have been unsuccessful since the department made a second request for the same purpose and amount the following year, in March 1935; see Turner W. Battle, Assistant to Frances Perkins, U.S. Secretary of Labor, to Harold L. Ickes, Administrator of Public Works, Washington, DC, March 7, 1935, file 55606/894, RG 85, National Archives.

93. 79 (3) Cong. Rec. 3066 (1935, House of Representatives).

94. The erection of fences was only one type of construction contemplated by this statute, the main purpose of which was to promote the conclusion of a treaty with Mexico on the equitable use of the waters of the Rio Grande, Colorado, and Tijuana rivers. Indeed, the act had two main purposes: to amend an Act of 1924 providing for a study regarding the equitable use of the waters of the Rio Grande in collaboration with Mexico, and the conclusion with Mexico of treaties on the division of water from the Rio Grande, the Colorado, and the Tijuana rivers and flood control; and to serve as a general enabling act so that the IBC, United States and Mexico, could conduct the various tasks required by its mandate, mostly regarding flood control and water conservation and the stabilization of the boundary between the two countries. The IBC was an international body comprising Mexican and American sections. It was renamed the International Boundary and Water Commission (IBWC) in 1944. The International Boundary Commission, United States and Canada, fulfills similar functions along the border the United States shares with Canada.

95. Act of August 19, 1935, 49 Stat. 660 (1935) § 2.

96. House of Representatives, Committee on Foreign Affairs, 74th Cong., 1st Session, H.R. 6453 (March 13, 1935), 1–2. The bill was passed unanimously in the House on April 1, 1935, and was referred to the Senate on April 3, 1935; see 79 (5) Cong. Rec. 4802–4803, 4900 (1935, House of Representatives).

97. House of Representatives, Subcommittee of the Committee on Foreign Affairs, 74th Cong., 1st Session, H.R. 6453 (March 7, 1935) 9, 16.

98. 79 (12) Cong. Rec. 13194 (1935, House of Representatives).

99. Frances Perkins, Secretary of Labor, to Cordell Hull, Secretary of State, August 7, 1935, file 55606/894, RG 85, National Archives.

100. Frances Perkins, Secretary of Labor, to Harry L. Hopkins, Works Progress Administration, August 26, 1935, file 56364/44.14, RG 85, National Archives; Richardson Saunders, Assistant Secretary of Labor to Frank C. Walker, Executive Director, Division of Applications and Information, National Emergency Council, September 7, 1935, file 55606/894, RG 85, National Archives. The amount requested for the construction of fences to the WPA represents approximately $75,500,000 in 2023 dollars.

101. After reviewing works funded by the WPA, it appears that the agency did not allot funds for the construction of fences at the border with Mexico. Concerning funding for the construction of observation towers, see G. C. Wilmoth, District Director, Immigration and Naturalization Service, El Paso, to W. H. Wagner, Immigration and Naturalization Service, September 9, 1936, file 55606/894, RG 85, National Archives; H. C. Horsley, Chief Patrol Inspector, El Paso, to G.C. Wilmoth, District Director, Immigration and Naturalization Service, El Paso, April 21, 1937, file 55 606/519, RG 85, National Archives.

102. Congressional records show that Congress gave the State Department $25,000 in 1938 and 1939 for the construction of border fences, but refused to allocate funding in 1940: Senate, Subcommittee of the Committee on Appropriations,

77th Cong., 1st Session, H.R. 4276: A Bill Making Appropriations for the Department of State, the Department of Commerce, the Department of Justice, and the Federal Judiciary, for the Fiscal Year Ending June 30, 1942, and for Other Purposes (April 30, 1941), 39.

103. Senate, Subcommittee of the Committee on Appropriations, 77th Cong., 1st Session, H.R. 4276, 52.

104. An Act Making Appropriations for the Department of State, the Department of Commerce, the Department of Justice, and the Federal Judiciary, for the Fiscal Year Ending June 30, 1942, and for Other Purposes, Pub. L. No. 135, 55 Stat. 265, 274 (1941).

105. Subcommittee of the Senate Committee on Appropriations (April 30, 1941) 40, 51.

106. An Act Making Appropriations for the Departments of State and Justice and for the Judiciary, and for the Departments of Commerce and Labor, for the Fiscal Year Ending June 30, 1939, and for Other Purposes, 75 Pub. L. No. 495, 52 Stat. 248, 256 (1938); An Act Making Appropriations for the Departments of State and Justice and for the Judiciary, and for the Department of Commerce, for the Fiscal Year Ending June 30, 1940, and for Other Purposes, 76 Pub. L. No. 156, 53 Stat. 885, 894 (1939); House of Representatives, Subcommittee of the Committee on Appropriations, 77th Cong., 1st Session, Department of State Appropriation Bill for 1942 (March 7, 1941), 463.

107. Subcommittee of the House of Representatives Committee on Appropriations (March 7, 1941), 462; An Act Making Appropriations for the Department of State, the Department of Commerce, the Department of Justice, and the Federal Judiciary, for the Fiscal Year Ending June 30, 1942, and for Other Purposes, Pub. L. No. 135, 55 Stat. 265, 274 (1941); An Act Making Appropriations for the Department of State, the Department of Justice, the Department of Commerce, and the Federal Judiciary, for the Fiscal Year Ending June 30, 1943, and for Other Purposes, 77 Pub. L .No. 644, 56 Stat. 468, 477 (1942).

108. Subcommittee of the Senate Committee on Appropriations (April 30, 1941), 49–51; Subcommittee of the House of Representatives Committee on Appropriations (March 7, 1941).

109. Subcommittee of the Senate Committee on Appropriations (April 30, 1941), 40.

110. The length for each section of the fence under the western land boundary fence project was as follows: Arizona, 289 miles; New Mexico, 179 miles; California, 108 miles. House of Representatives, Subcommittee of the Committee on Appropriations, 79th Congress, 1st Session, First Deficiency Appropriation Bill for 1946 (November 3, 1945), 678. Deficiency bills are usually adopted for emergencies and are distinct from the regular appropriation process. See also Senate, Subcommittee of the Committee on Foreign Relations, 80th Cong., 1st Session, S. J. Res. 46: Maintenance of the Western Land Boundary Fence Project and the Rio Grande Border Fence Project (March 13, 1947), 14.

111. Subcommittee of the House of Representatives Committee on Appropriations (November 3, 1945).

112. House of Representatives, Subcommittee of the Committee on Appropriations, 79th Cong., 1st Session, First Deficiency Appropriation Bill for 1946 (November 7, 1945), 877.

113. House of Representatives, Subcommittee of the Committee on Appropriations, 79th Cong., 1st Session, 877.

114. 93 (1) Cong. Rec. 646 (1947, Senate).

115. S. J. Res. 46, 80th Cong. (1947) §§ 1, 2.

116. S. J. Res. 46, 80th Cong. (1947) § 3. This is a power that is granted today to the secretary of homeland security in Section 102 of the Illegal Immigration Reform and Immigrant Responsibility Act of 1996, Pub. L. No. 104-208, Div C, 110 Stat 3009 (1996).

117. S. J. Res. 46, § 7.

118. S. J. Res. 46, § 5. The exception concerning the citizenship of workers employed on the project raises the question whether the drafters of S. J. Res. 46 had in mind the hiring of Mexican labor for the realization of the project, given the abundance of Mexican workers in the border region. The paradoxical situation where Mexican nationals work to build a wall aimed at stopping their fellow citizens from entering the United States has occurred with regard to border walls erected under the authority of the Secure Fence Act of 2006. In a 2017 report, the BBC interviewed Luis, a Mexican national living in Ciudad Juárez and working for an American concrete company that was reinforcing the border wall in El Paso. He told the BBC reporter that his relatives in Mexico joke with him and tell him "to leave a little opening for them to cross": "Life on the Border: The Mexican Building the Wall," *BBC News*, February 13, 2017 https://www.youtube.com/watch?v=mucl873ukjU.

119. In 1940, the INS was transferred from the Department of Labor to the Department of Justice as a national security measure to strengthen control over aliens. Sharon D. Masanz, *History of the Immigration and Naturalization Service,* Congressional Research Service (1980).

120. Subcommittee of the Senate Committee on Foreign Relations (March 13, 1947) 8, 11; See also, Senate, Committee on Foreign Relations, 80th Cong., Executive Session, S. J. Res. 46 (February 25, 1947).

121. It is unclear from his letter whether his suggestion aimed to prevent the entry of communist agents or stop "the constant traffic back and forth of 'peons'" that he witnessed during his visit to the border. John McDowell, U.S. House of Representatives, to Tom C. Clark, U.S. Attorney General, June 3, 1947, file 56364/042.40, RG 85, National Archives; "San Ysidro, Calexico Held Prime Immigration 'Leaks,'" *Alhambra Post Advocate,* June 18, 1947.

122. Based on a review of the Congressional debates for the year 1947 and early 1948, the Committee never presented S. J. Res. 46 to the whole House of Representatives.

123. See, for instance, the comments by Republican Representatives Chester H. Gross from Pennsylvania and Francis H. Case from South Dakota: 93 (1) Cong. Rec. 940-941, 1311 (1947, House of Representatives). On the creation of the Mexican-American Commission for the Eradication of Foot-and-Mouth Disease see William Dusenberry, "Foot and Mouth Disease in Mexico, 1946–1951," *Agricultural History* 29, no. 2 (1955).

124. David Snow, Patrol Inspector in Charge, Brownsville, Texas, report to Fletcher L. Rawls, Chief Patrol Inspector, McAllen, Texas, March 20, 1953, file 56363/44.14, RG 85, National Archives. 1.

125. Snow to Rawls, March 20, 1953, 2. Snow noted that burglary and robbery rates in 1952 in Brownsville were 2000 percent higher than in other comparable American cities.

126. Snow to Rawls, March 20, 1953, 2.

127. Snow to Rawls, March 20, 1953, 2.

128. Snow to Rawls, March 20, 1953, 4.

129. Leslie M. Gross, Lt Colonel, CE, Executive Officer, U.S. Army Engineers, to Division Engineer, Southwestern Division, September 10, 1953, file 56364/44.14, RG 85, National Archives; W. F. Kelly and D. R. Kelley, Ground Survey for Proposed Fence in McAllen Sector, September 15, 1953, file 56364/44.14, RG 85, National Archives. In their field notes the two officials remarked that local farmers were extremely hostile toward the Border Patrol and expected a violent opposition to right of way acquisitions.

130. D. R. Kelley to W. F. Kelly, memorandum of telephone conversation, September 11, 1953, file 56364/44.14, RG 85, National Archives; Kelly and Kelley, Ground Survey, 129.

131. District Director, Los Angeles, California, to Assistant Commissioner, Border Patrol, Detention and Deportation Division, September 18, 1953, file 56364/44.14, RG 85, National Archives, 8. The report on this section of the border noted that the fence would create new problems such as an increase in organized smuggling by air and sea and the perfection of methods to cross the border illegally. It also contended that illegal entries at ports of entry by fraud and misrepresentation would increase. To efficiently control the border, the report suggested other measures such as the fingerprinting of arrested aliens, rigorous prosecution of violations of the Immigration and Nationality Act, and the implementation of a more functional program for recruiting Mexican and other foreign agricultural laborers.

132. H. R. Landon, District Director, Los Angeles, to Commissioner, Central Office, August 13, 1954, file 56364/44.14, RG 85, National Archives.

133. Herbert Brownell Jr., U.S. Attorney General, to John Foster Dulles, Secretary of State, January 19, 1956, file 56364/44.14, RG 85, National Archives.

134. John P. Swanson, Chief Regional Enforcement Officer (Acting), Southwest Region, to Frank H. Partridge, Special Assistant to Commissioner, April 6, 1955, file 56364/44.14, RG 85, National Archives.

135. According to an unsigned memorandum, fences were erected in the following cities: Calexico (9 km), Nogales (3.2 km), Naco (1.6 km), Douglas (3.2 km), Columbus (1.6 km), San Ysidro (5.8 km), and San Luis (5.6 km). Memorandum, October 28, 1955, file 56364/44.14, RG 85, National Archives.

136. Kang, *The INS on the Line*, 6.

137. Senate Committee on Foreign Relations (February 25, 1947), 16.

138. H. R. Landon, District Director, Los Angeles, to Commissioner, Central Office, August 13, 1954, file 56364/44.14, RG 85, National Archives, 1. In his memo, the INS district director in Los Angeles explained that "so long as there continues to be a desire by large numbers of Mexican nationals to enter the United States illegally, the problem can be met only by the utilization of sufficient manpower for line, road block and mop-up operations, an adequate labor program, removal of apprehended wetbacks to central and southern Mexico and a vigorous prosecution and deportation program."

139. Subcommittee of the Senate Committee on Foreign Relations (March 13, 1947), 9.

140. See also Michael J. Garcia, *Barriers Along the U.S. Borders: Key Authorities and Requirements* (Congressional Research Service, 2015), footnote 18.

141. Democrat Senator Carl T. Hayden of Arizona appeared regularly before Congress to ask for funds for a border fence; see Subcommittee of the Senate Committee on Appropriations (April 30, 1941) 39. A comment by Republican Senator Henry Cabot Lodge Jr. of Massachusetts in 1947 suggests that Senator Hayden was influential in obtaining funding for the construction of small portions of the fence each year. See Senate Committee on Foreign Relations (February 25, 1947), 17.

142. The South-Western Cattle Raisers Association of Fort Worth, Texas, also appeared before Congress on more than one occasion to demand the construction of a fence. Subcommittee of the Senate Committee on Foreign Relations (March 13, 1947), 19.

143. See, for instance, James Boyd White, "Law as Rhetoric, Rhetoric as Law: The Arts of Cultural and Communal Life," *University of Chicago Law Review* 52, no. 3 (1985): 686; Eve Darian-Smith, *Laws and Societies in Global Contexts: Contemporary Approaches* (New York: Cambridge University Press, 2013); Margaret Davies, *Law Unlimited: Materialism, Pluralism, and Legal Theory* (Abingdon, UK: Routledge, 2017).

144. Robert M. Cover, "The Supreme Court, 1982 Term; Foreword: Nomos and Narrative," *Harvard Law Review* 97, no. 1 (1983): 9.

145. See, for instance, Edward W. Said, *Orientalism* (New York: Vintage Books, 1979); Ian Haney-López, *White by Law: The Legal Construction of Race*, rev. and updated 10th anniversary ed. (New York: New York University Press, 2006); Simone de Beauvoir, *Le deuxième sexe* (Paris: Gallimard, 1949); Iris Marion Young, "Throwing like a Girl: A Phenomenology of Feminine Body Comportment Motility and Spatiality," *Human Studies* 3, no. 2 (1980); Margaret Davies, "Exclusion and the Identity of

Law," *Macquarie Law Journal* 5 (2005); Teemu Ruskola, *Legal Orientalism: China, the United States, and Modern Law* (Cambridge, MA: Harvard University Press, 2013).

146. Ferdinand de Saussure, *Course in General Linguistics*, trans. Roy Harris (London: Bloomsbury, 2013), 137.

147. Davies, "Exclusion and the Identity of Law," 8.

148. Said, *Orientalism*; Iris Marion Young, "The Ideal of Community and the Politics of Difference," *Social Theory and Practice* 12, no. 1 (1986); Davies, "Exclusion and the Identity of Law."; Douzinas Costas, "The Paradoxes of Human Rights: The Paradox of Human Rights: Costas Douzinas," *Constellations* 20 (2013).

149. Anderson, *Imagined Communities*; Young, "Ideal of Community."

150. Theiss-Morse, *Who Counts as an American?*.

151. Davies, "Exclusion and the Identity of Law," 10.

152. Said, *Orientalism*, 296.

153. Edward W. Said, Moustafa Bayoumi, and Andrew Rubin, *The Edward Said Reader* (New York: Vintage Books, 2000), 53.

154. Said, *Orientalism*, 203.

155. Said, *Orientalism*, 207; See also Teemu Ruskola, "Legal Orientalism," *Michigan Law Review* 101, no. 1 (2002): 209. Ruskola notes that "structurally, Orientalism as a discourse entails the projection onto the Oriental Other of various sorts of things that "we" are not."

156. Said, *Orientalism*, 205.

157. Said, Bayoumi, and Rubin, *The Edward Said Reader*, 56.

158. Homi K. Bhabha, *The Location of Culture*, 2nd ed. (London: Routledge, 2004), 95.

159. Said, Bayoumi, and Rubin, *The Edward Said Reader*, 53.

160. Said, Bayoumi, and Rubin, *The Edward Said Reader*, 53.

161. James Boyd White, "Rhetoric and Law: The Arts of Cultural and Communal Life," in *The Rhetoric of the Human Sciences: Language and Argument in Scholarship and Public Affairs*, ed. John S. Nelson, Allan Megill, and Donald N. McCloskey (Madison: University of Wisconsin Press, 1987), 298–318.

162. White, "Rhetoric and Law," 302.

163. White, "Rhetoric and Law," 303.

164. White, "Rhetoric and Law," 304.

165. White, "Rhetoric and Law," 304.

166. White, "Rhetoric and Law," 304.

167. The National Prohibition Act, 1919, Pub. L. No. 66-66, 41 Stat 305-323 (1919) ch. 385.

168. Kang, *The INS on the Line*, 40.

169. Kang, *The INS on the Line*, 38.

170. Kang, *The INS on the Line*, 38; Dear, *Why Walls Won't Work*, 45.

171. Kang, *The INS on the Line*, 38.

172. Kang, *The INS on the Line*, 38.

173. Ngai, *Impossible Subjects*, 49.

174. Ngai, *Impossible Subjects*, 149.

175. Ngai, *Impossible Subjects*, 149.

176. Collaer and Horsley to District Inspector, Immigration and Naturalization Service, February 23, 1934, 3.

177. Said, *Orientalism*, 38.

178. Bhabha, *The Location of Culture*, 119.

179. Bhabha, *The Location of Culture*, 110–12.

180. Bhabha, *The Location of Culture*, 113.

181. Gerald B. Breitigam, "Welcomed Mexican Invasion," *New York Times*, June 20, 1920.

182. Jorge A. Bustamante, "The 'Wetback' as Deviant: An Application of Labeling Theory," *American Journal of Sociology* 77, no. 4 (1972): 706. The term *wetback* was originally used in reference to migrants who get their clothes wet crossing the Rio Grande River to avoid detection: Ngai, *Impossible Subjects*, 149.

183. Bustamante, "'Wetback' as Deviant," 714.

184. Gladwin Hill, "'Wetback' Invasion Is Broadening Despite All U. S. Counter-Moves," *New York Times*, February 11, 1952, https://www.nytimes.com/1952/02/11/archives/-wetback-invasion-is-broadening-despite-all-u-s-countermoves.html; Eleanor M. Hadley, "A Critical Analysis of the Wetback Problem," *Law and Contemporary Problems* 21, no. 2 (1956).

185. Report by Willard F. Kelly, *The Wetback Issue*, 2 (December 15, 1953) file 56321/448D, quoted in Ngai, *Impossible Subjects*, 149.

186. In mid-March 1953, three chiefs of police sent letters to the Border Patrol chief inspector to request the construction of a border fence between Brownsville, Texas, and Matamoros, Tamaulipas. The three letters expressed a similar view arguing that crimes in their city were mostly perpetrated by Mexicans entering the United States illegally in the Brownsville area. The letters were followed by a report by David Snow, patrol inspector in charge, Brownsville, which sustained the claims made in the letters: Boynton H. Fleming, Sheriff, Cameron County, to Fletcher L. Rawls, Chief Border, McAllen, March 17, 1953, file 56364/44.15, RG 85, National Archives; John L. Guseman, Chief of Police, Harlington, to Fletcher L. Rawls, Chief Border Patrol Inspector, McAllen, March 9, 1953, file 56364/44.15, RG 85, National Archives; Gus O. Krausse, Chief of Police, Brownsville, to Fletcher L. Rawls, Chief Border Patrol Inspector, McAllen, March 19, 1947, file 56364/44.15, RG 85, National Archives; David Snow, Patrol Inspector in Charge, Brownsville, Texas, report to Fletcher L. Rawls, Chief Patrol Inspector, McAllen, Texas, March 20, 1953, file 56363/44.14, RG 85, National Archives.

187. Snow to Rawls, March 20, 1953; Kelly and Kelley, September 15, 1953. However, the INS forwent the plan for fencing the border because of its cost. Instead, it responded to the "wetback situation" through the Bracero Program, which supplied legal labor to southwestern growers, and Operation Wetback, an immigration law enforcement campaign under which the INS deported more than one million undocumented migrants between June 1954 and June 1955; see Kitti Calavita, *Inside the*

State: The Bracero Program, Immigration and the I.N.S. (New York: Routledge, 1992); Kang, *The INS on the Line*, 161.

188. See, for instance, Wilmoth to Commissioner General of Immigration, May 2, 1930; Roy Jackson, District Attorney, El Paso, to Grover C. Wilmoth, District Director, INS, El Paso, February 26, 1934, file 55606/894, RG 85, National Archives; Perkins to Hull, August 7, 1935; Krausse to Rawls, March 19, 1947; Snow to Rawls, March 20, 1953; J. M. Swing, Commissioner General, to Senator Paul H. Douglas, March 29, 1956, file 56364/44.15, RG 85, National Archives.

189. See, for instance, Folk to Thomason, December 7, 1933, 10; Collaer and Horsley to District Inspector, Immigration and Naturalization Service, February 23, 1934; Subcommittee of the Senate Committee on Appropriations (April 30, 1941), 6, 54; Subcommittee of the Senate Committee on Foreign Relations (March 13, 1947).

190. Subcommittee of the Senate Committee on Foreign Relations (March 13, 1947), 22.

191. For a discussion in the context of child sexual offenses, see Anne-Marie McAlinden, "Re-Emotionalising Regulatory Responses to Child Sex Offenders," in *The Emotional Dynamics of Law and Legal Discourse*, ed. Heather Conway and John Stannard (Oxford: Hart, 2016); See also Sara Ahmed, "Collective Feelings: Or, the Impressions Left by Others," *Theory, Culture & Society* 21, no. 2 (2004): 26–27.

192. US Department of Agriculture Animal and Plant Health Inspection Service, "Foot-and-Mouth Disease," https://www.aphis.usda.gov/aphis/ourfocus/animalhealth/animal-disease-information/fmd/index#:~:text=Foot%2Dand%2Dmouth%20disease%20(,health%20or%20food%20safety%20threat.

193. US Department of Agriculture Animal and Plant Health Inspection Service, "Foot-and-Mouth Disease."

194. David Nesheim, "Machine Guns, Cows, and Quarantines: Foot and Mouth Disease in the United States, Mexico and Argentina" (Paper presented at the James A. Rawley Graduate Conference in the Humanities, University of Nebraska, Lincoln 2006).

195. Nesheim, "Machine Guns, Cows, and Quarantines."

196. Subcommittee of the Senate Committee on Foreign Relations (March 13, 1947), 4.

197. Subcommittee of the Senate Committee on Foreign Relations (March 13, 1947), 19.

198. Subcommittee of the Senate Committee on Foreign Relations (March 13, 1947), 4–5. There were also concerns that the sheep scab and cattle scab might be transmitted by stray animals from Mexico.

199. Quoted in Bess Furman, "Hoof Disease Stirs U.S.-Mexico Action: Cattle Ailment Below Border Expected to Be Subject of Truman Talks on Trip," *New York Times*, February 20, 1947.

200. *New York Times*, "Act to End Disease of Mexican Cattle," February 1, 1947; See also Waldemar Kaempffert, "Science in Review: A Fence 1,905 Miles Long

Is Proposed to Check the Spread of Foot-and-Mouth Disease," *New York Times*, February 23, 1947.

201. *New York Times*, "Act to End Disease"; *New York Times* "Ask Fence Along the Border," May 29, 1947.

202. Senate Committee on Foreign Relations (February 25, 1947), 14.

203. Senate, Committee on Foreign Relations, 80th Cong., Executive Session, *Whaling Convention and Protocols, Executives K, L and P; French Tax Convention; Trusteeship Agreement; World Health Organization, S. J. Res. 98; Western Land Boundary Fence, S. J. Res. 46; Appointments in the Diplomatic Service; Anglo-American Petroleum Agreement* (July 1, 1947), 17.

204. On February 28, 1947, President Harry Truman signed An Act to Authorize the Secretary of Agriculture to Cooperate with the Government of Mexico in the Control and Eradication of Foot-and-Mouth Disease and Rinderpest, 1947, Pub. L. No. 8, 61 Stat 7 (1947), to aid Mexico in suppressing the outbreak of foot-and-mouth disease, which led to the creation of the Mexican-American Commission for the Eradication of Foot-and-Mouth Disease. The binational commission oversaw the eradication quarantine, slaughter, burial, and disinfection of animals to suppress the disease: Dusenberry, "Foot and Mouth Disease in Mexico, 1946–1951," 84.

205. See Eve Darian-Smith, "Rabies Rides the Fast Train: Transnational Interactions in Post-colonial Times," in *The Legal Geographies Reader: Law, Power, and Space*, ed. Nicholas K. Blomley, David Delaney, and Richard T. Ford (Oxford: Wiley-Blackwell, 2001), 187–99.

206. Senate Committee on Foreign Relations (February 25, 1947), 17.

207. Senate Committee on Foreign Relations (February 25, 1947), 17.

208. Senate Committee on Foreign Relations (February 25, 1947), 15.

209. Senate Committee on Foreign Relations (February 25, 1947), 14; Subcommittee of the Senate Committee on Foreign Relations (March 13, 1947). A point was made that the plan's objective was "from a health standpoint in keeping all untested or uninspected animals out of this country from Mexico or Canada or any other area" and that it was "a sound livestock insurance procedure to have the fence there even though the foot-and-mouth disease were [*sic*] not in Mexico." This quote suggests that even in the absence of an outbreak, fences were required as a preventive measure to ensure that all animals entering the United States, from any land border or ports, would be free of contagious disease. In keeping with that objective, it would have been judicious to plan for the building of fences at the northern American border, but that was not considered. Perhaps, one reason for this was the absence of demands for this measure from constituents in the northern American states.

210. 93 (8) Cong. Rec. 9800 (1947, Senate).

211. See Darian-Smith, "Rabies Rides the Fast Train," 205.

212. Desmond Manderson, *Songs without Music: Aesthetic Dimensions of Law and Justice* (Berkeley: University of California Press, 2000), 135.

213. Manderson, *Songs without Music*, 135.

214. Manderson, *Songs without Music*, 135. See also Mary Douglas, *Purity and Danger: An Analysis of Concepts of Pollution and Taboo* (London: Routledge, 2002).

215. In 1917, in El Paso alone, 127,173 Mexicans nationals were bathed and physically screened for lice or other parasites before entering the United States: Nevins, *Operation Gatekeeper and Beyond*, 66.

216. Michael R. Kenwick and Beth A. Simmons, "Pandemic Response as Border Politics," *International Organization* 74, no. S1 (2020).

217. Kenwick and Simmons, "Pandemic Response as Border Politics,"11.

218. Darian-Smith, "Rabies Rides the Fast Train."

219. Darian-Smith, "Rabies Rides the Fast Train," 189.

220. Darian-Smith, "Rabies Rides the Fast Train," 189.

221. Darian-Smith, "Rabies Rides the Fast Train," 189.

222. Darian-Smith, "Rabies Rides the Fast Train," 190.

223. Convention Safeguarding Livestock Interests through the Prevention of Infectious and Contagious Diseases, signed March 16, 1928, TS 808 (entered into force January 18, 1930); 93 (1) Cong. Rec. 961 (1947, House); 93 (1) Cong. Rec. 959 (1947, House); 93 (1) Cong. Rec. 1071 (1947, Senate). The accusation was echoed in the media: *New York Times*, "Hoof Disease Stirs U.S.-Mexico Action." See also Dusenberry, "Foot and Mouth Disease in Mexico, 1946–1951," 123.

224. Subcommittee of the Senate Committee on Foreign Relations (March 13, 1947), 20.

225. US Department of Agriculture Animal and Plant Health Inspection Service, "Foot-and-Mouth Disease"; 93 (1) Cong. Rec. 959 (1947, House of Representatives).

226. 93 (1) Cong. Rec. 1315 (1947, House of Representatives).

227. See, for instance, Cousar to District Director, Immigration Service, November 22, 1928, 1; Turner W. Battle to Harold L. Ickes, Administrator of Public Works, March 7, 1935, file55606/894, RG 85, National Archives; Brownell Jr. to Dulles, January 19, 1956, 133.

228. This said, Democrat Senator Carl Hatch from New Mexico mentioned having received letters from his constituents as well. He does not say if those were for or against the project: Senate Committee on Foreign Relations (February 25, 1947) 120, 14.

229. Texas was excluded from the program at the demand of Mexico due to the history of discrimination and abuse of Mexican workers by employers in that state. Calavita, *Inside the State*, 20; Otey M. Scruggs, "Texas and the Bracero Program, 1942–1947," *Pacific Historical Review* 32, no. 3 (1963).

230. For a discussion on the influence of the farm industry on US border control policies during that period, see Calavita, *Inside the State*, 34–37. See also Kang, *The INS on the Line*, 106–7. A 1946 *Newsweek* article made the argument that the INS "know[s] that the wetback is the very backbone of the prosperity of the . . . lower Rio Grande Valley. . . . Without him, bank vaults in the Valley towns might not be bulging—as they are now—with farmers' cash." *Newsweek*, March 11, 1947, 71, quoted in Calavita, *Inside the State*, 34.

231. Kang, *The INS on the Line*, 98.

232. Kang, *The INS on the Line*, 104–5.

233. Kang, *The INS on the Line*, 105. Kitty Calavita writes that in the decade from 1942 to 1952, 818,545 bracero contracts were concluded while more than two million undocumented workers were apprehended by the INS: Calavita, *Inside the State*, 31–32.

234. C. A. Norton, President, Weslaco Chamber of Commerce, to Tom Connally, U.S. Senator, February 13, 1947, file 2750605, RG 59, National Archives.

235. Walter Hurst, President, Pharr Chamber of Commerce, to Arthur Vandenberg, U.S. Senator, March 11, 1947, file 2750605, RG 59, National Archives.

236. McAllen Chamber of Commerce (Directors), to Tom Connally, U.S. Senator, February 13, 1947, file 2750605, RG 59, National Archives.

237. J. D. Campbell, W. A. Bishops, W. S. Livingston to E. H. Moore, U.S. Senator, February 3, 1947, file 2750605, RG 59, National Archives.

238. J. K. Stirton to Tom Connally, U.S. Senator, February 6, 1947, file 2750605, RG 59, National Archives.

239. E. C. Breedlove, President, First National Bank, Harlingen, to Tom Connally, U.S. Senator, February 11, 1947, file 2750605, RG 59, National Archives.

240. Paul Heller, Ellis Seed Company, Weslaco, to Tom Connally, U.S. Senator, March 24, 1947, file 2750605, RG 59, National Archives. The author did not specify which policy he referred to, but it is most likely the Good Neighbor Policy of President Franklin Delano Roosevelt. Under that policy, military, economic, and cultural cooperation between Mexico and the United States was developed through binational program and border crossing was somewhat eased for local residents of both states, see Kang, *The INS on the Line*, 89–92. Similar views were expressed in 1955 when fences were considered again in Brownsville. The Kiwanis Club of Brownsville was a strong voice against the project at the time. In a resolution it forwarded to Democrat Senator Lyndon B. Johnson of Texas, the club protested against the construction of a fence and explained that "the unguarded frontier along both the Mexican and Canadian borders has become a matter of great national pride and a symbol of international peace, and the construction of such a fence is contrary to the Good Neighbor Policy of the United States Government, and such a fence might well be construed as an insult by our good Mexican neighbors and is almost certain to impair our long-standing friendly relations and provide material for Communistic propaganda." J. E. O' Brien, President, Kiwanis Club of Brownsville, to Lyndon B. Johnson, U.S. Senator, April 27, 1955, file 56364/44.15, RG 85, National Archives.

241. White, "Rhetoric and Law," 305.

242. These letters likely referred to President Roosevelt's Good Neighbor Policy.

243. Ngai, *Impossible Subjects*, 58.

244. Evelyne Ritaine, "La barrière et le checkpoint: mise en politique de l'asymétrie," *Cultures & Conflits* 73 (Spring 2009): 20.

245. See Bhabha, *The Location of Culture*, 119.

246. White, "Law as Rhetoric," 698.

247. Wolfe, *Traces of History*, 5.

248. Wolfe, *Traces of History*, 10.

Chapter 3

1. Gloria Anzaldúa, *Borderlands/La Frontera: The New Mestiza*, 5th ed. (San Francisco: Aunt Lute Books, 2022), 29.

2. Rita Dhamoon, "A Feminist Approach to Decolonizing Anti-Racism: Rethinking Transnationalism, Intersectionality, and Settler Colonialism," *Feral Feminisms* 4 (Summer 2015): 32.

3. Dhamoon, "A Feminist Approach to Decolonizing Anti-Racism," 32.

4. Kevin Bruyneel, *Settler Memory: The Disavowal of Indigeneity and the Politics of Race in the United States* (Chapel Hill: University of North Carolina Press, 2021), 8.

5. Stuart Hall and Charlotte Brunsdon, *Writings on Media: History of the Present. Stuart Hall: Selected Writings* (Durham, NC: Duke University Press, 2021), 186.

6. Saidiya V. Hartman, *Lose Your Mother: A Journey Along the Atlantic Slave Route* (New York: Farrar, Straus & Giroux, 2008), 133.

7. Bruyneel, *Settler Memory*, 5–6.

8. Hall and Brunsdon, *Writings on Media*, 185.

9. Hall and Brunsdon, *Writings on Media*, 186.

10. S. Deborah Kang, *The INS on the Line: Making Immigration Law on the US-Mexico Border, 1917–1954* (New York: Oxford University Press, 2017), 161–62. Kang notes that the decline in apprehension was not only a consequence of Operation Wetback but also resulted from the reduction in Border Patrol enforcement activities. Notably, the US Border Patrol uses apprehension data to measure its performance even though these data can be misleading because they do not account for the number of successful undocumented entries.

11. US Customs and Border Protection, "Southwest Border Sectors: Total Illegal Alien Apprehensions by Fiscal Year," https://www.cbp.gov/newsroom/media-resources/stats.

12. Joseph Nevins, *Operation Gatekeeper and Beyond: The War on Illegals and the Remaking of the U.S.-Mexico Boundary*, 2nd ed. (New York: Routledge, 2010), 141.

13. Hall and Brunsdon, *Writings on Media*, 180–81.

14. Hall and Brunsdon, *Writings on Media*, 184.

15. Nevins, *Operation Gatekeeper and Beyond*, 141. Between 1973 and 1980, the number of articles published annually by the *New York Times* on undocumented immigration increased by 650 percent.

16. Leo R. Chavez, *The Latino Threat: Constructing Immigrants, Citizens, and the Nation*, 2nd ed. (Stanford, CA: Stanford University Press, 2013); Emily M. Farris and Heather Silber Mohamed, "Picturing Immigration: How the Media Criminalizes Immigrants," *Politics, Groups & Identities* 6, no. 4 (2018): 814.

17. Nevins, *Operation Gatekeeper and Beyond*, 141–42.

18. Nevins, *Operation Gatekeeper and Beyond*, 142.

19. Nevins, *Operation Gatekeeper and Beyond*, 142.

20. Douglas S. Massey, Jorge Durand, and Karen A. Pren, "Why Border Enforcement Backfired," *American Journal of Sociology* 121, no. 5 (2016): 1561.

21. Quoted in Nevins, *Operation Gatekeeper and Beyond*, 142.

22. Regarding the negative coverage of the border and immigration, see Oscar J. Martínez, "Border Conflict, Border Fences, and the 'Tortilla Curtain' Incident of 1978–1979," *Journal of the Southwest* 50, no. 3 (2008): 270; Farris and Silber Mohamed, "Picturing Immigration," 814. A Gallup poll conducted in 1976 for the INS showed that half the participants had recently heard or read about the "problem of illegal aliens." In border states, this figure rose to two-thirds: Nevins, *Operation Gatekeeper and Beyond*, 142.

23. Martínez, "Tortilla Curtain," 270. However, controversy emerged when news broke that the fences would be topped with sharp razor wire that "would 'sever the toes of anyone trying to scale [them].'" Hence, protests against the fence arose from several circles, including the Mexican government and Mexican-American organizations in the United States. In El Paso, a 'Coalition Against the Fence' formed, resulting in manifestations and riots erupting that forced the government to renounce the controversial razor wire when it built the fences in 1979. Nevins explains that there was strong support for the proposed fence among the border population in the United States, but this group was unorganized and unprepared to counter critics of the fence. Nevins, *Operation Gatekeeper and Beyond*, 89.

24. "Tortilla curtain" is the name that was given to the events that occurred during that period, see Martínez, "Tortilla Curtain." *The Tortilla Curtain* is also the name of a novel by American author T. C. Boyle that addresses issues of immigration, nativism, and race in California. The novel was published in 1995 following the adoption of Proposition 187. This 1994 ballot initiative would have denied illegal immigrants social services, health care, and public education in the State of California. A total of 59 percent of Californians voted in favor of the measure. Only days after the ballot, the implementation of Proposition 187 was blocked by federal court injunction for being unconstitutional since immigration comes under the purview of the federal government. Five years later, a court-approved mediation confirmed the unconstitutionality of the Proposition. Justifications for Proposition 187 relied heavily on the narrative of the criminality of the undocumented immigrant: American Civil Liberties Union, "CA's Anti-immigrant Proposition 187 Is Voided, Ending State's Five-Year Battle With ACLU, Rights Groups," https://www.aclu.org/press-releases/cas-anti-immigrant-proposition-187-voided-ending-states-five-year-battle-aclu-rights. Barbara Coe, the drafter of the measure, and anti-immigrant activists wrote an opinion piece for *USA Today* stating that "violent crime is rampant. Illegal-alien gangs roam our streets, dealing drugs and searching for innocent victims to rob, rape and, in many cases, murder those who dare violate their 'turf'. . . . Nearly 90% of all illicit drugs are brought here by illegals." Barbara Coe, "Keep Illegals Out of State," *USA Today*, October 12, 1994. According to Kevin Johnson, Proposition 187 was directed specifically at Mexican immigrants. He explained that although

there were significant numbers of non-Mexican undocumented immigrants in the United States, the drafters' comments about the measure made it clear that the "illegal aliens" they were referring to were Mexican nationals: Kevin R. Johnson, "An Essay on Immigration Politics, Popular Democracy, and California's Proposition 187: The Political Relevance and Legal Irrelevance of Race," *Washington Law Review* 70, no. 3 (1995): 660.

25. US Customs and Border Protection, "Southwest Border Sectors: Total Illegal Alien Apprehensions by Fiscal Year," https://www.cbp.gov/newsroom/media-resources/stats.

26. Nevins, *Operation Gatekeeper and Beyond*, 96–97; Peter Andreas, *Border Games: Policing the U.S.-Mexico Divide*, 2nd ed. (Ithaca, NY: Cornell University Press, 2009), 52.

27. Nevins, *Operation Gatekeeper and Beyond*, 105–7.

28. Nevins, *Operation Gatekeeper and Beyond*, 111.

29. Peter Andreas, "The Escalation of U.S. Immigration Control in the Post-NAFTA Era," *Political Science Quarterly* 113, no. 4 (1998): 596.

30. Andreas, "The Escalation of U.S. Immigration Control," 593.

31. David Newman, "On Borders and Power: A Theoretical Framework," *Journal of Borderlands Studies* 18, no. 1 (2003): 21.

32. Patricia Fernández-Kelly and Douglas S. Massey, "Borders for Whom? The Role of NAFTA in Mexico-U.S. Migration," *Annals of the American Academy of Political and Social Science* 610, no. 1 (2007): 99, 105, 109.

33. Fernández-Kelly and Massey, "Borders for Whom?," 99.

34. Nevins, *Operation Gatekeeper and Beyond*, 100.

35. Nevins, *Operation Gatekeeper and Beyond*, 99; Chad C Haddal, Yule Kim, and Michael J. Garcia, *Border Security: Barriers Along the U.S. International Border*, Congressional Research Service (2009), 1.

36. Gustavo De La Viňa quoted in Nevins, *Operation Gatekeeper and Beyond*, 100.

37. Nevins, *Operation Gatekeeper and Beyond*, 101. See also US Government Accountability Office, *Border Control: Revised Strategy Is Showing Some Positive Results* (March 10, 1995).

38. Nevins, *Operation Gatekeeper and Beyond*, 100.

39. Haddal, Kim, and Garcia, *Border Security*. See also Jason De Léon, *The Land of Open Graves: Living and Dying on the Migrant Trail* (Oakland: University of California Press, 2015).

40. Brown, *Walled States, Waning Sovereignty*, 47. For an ethnographic study of the experiences of Mexican migrants' crossings being aided by coyotes at the Texas-Mexico border, see David Spener, *Clandestine Crossings: Migrants and Coyotes on the Texas-Mexico Border* (Ithaca, NY: Cornell University Press, 2010).

41. Eventually more fences were built in the following areas: Campo, California; Yuma, Nogales, Naco, and Douglas, Arizona; and El Paso, Texas. These represent a total of approximately sixty-two miles. Jones, *Border Walls*, 31.

42. Sandia National Laboratories, *Systematic Analysis of the Southwest Border* (January 1993), 2.

43. Sandia National Laboratories, *Systematic Analysis of the Southwest Border*, 3–4.

44. Sandia National Laboratories, *Systematic Analysis of the Southwest Border*, 4.

45. Sandia National Laboratories, *Systematic Analysis of the Southwest Border*, 5.

46. Sandia National Laboratories, *Systematic Analysis of the Southwest Border*, ES-10.

47. Sandia National Laboratories, *Systematic Analysis of the Southwest Border*, ES-4, 9. Sandia National Laboratories proposed the construction of an initial 10-foot-high opaque fence (such as the one erected at the time in El Paso), a second 15-foot-high fence anticlimb fence, and a third 10-foot-high chain-link fence. Sandia National Laboratories, *Systematic Analysis of the Southwest Border*, 6.

48. Illegal Immigration Reform and Immigrant Responsibility Act of 1996, Pub. L. No. 104-208, Div C, 110 Stat 3009 (1996).

49. Jennifer M. Chacon, "Unsecured Borders: Immigration Restrictions, Crime Control and National Security," *Connecticut Law Review* 39, no. 5 (2007): 1842.

50. Mae M. Ngai, *Impossible Subjects: Illegal Aliens and the Making of Modern America* (Princeton, NJ: Princeton University Press, 2014), 268. Some of the harshest measures initially proposed in H.R. 2202, which became the IIRIRA, did not pass Congress or were vetoed by President Bill Clinton. One of the most contentious provisions would have allowed states to deny the children of undocumented immigrants access to public schooling. It was removed from the bill following threats of a bipartisan Senate filibuster and presidential veto. See also Eric Schmitt, "New Demands by White House Are Made on Immigration Bill," *New York Times*, September 27, 1996; Eric Schmitt, "Milestones and Missteps on Immigration," *New York Times*, October 26, 1996.

51. California's Proposition 187 is one example of such a policy.

52. Nevins, *Operation Gatekeeper and Beyond*, 109.

53. Richard Rayner, "What Immigration Crisis?: An Alien's Tour Through the Back Rooms of What Is Becoming America's Most Exaggerated Threat," *New York Times*, January 7, 1996.

54. 142 (4) Cong. Rec. 5304 (1996, House of Representatives).

55. 142 (4) Cong. Rec. 5304 (1996, House of Representatives).

56. Anthony Lewis, "Why the Cruelty?," *New York Times*, September 23, 1996.

57. Robert Pear, "U.S. Strengthening Patrols Along the Mexican Border," *New York Times*, January 13, 1996.

58. 142 (4) Cong. Rec. 5318 (1996, House of Representatives).

59. *Chicago Tribune*, "'Steel Curtain' Falls on Mexico's Border—and its Feelings," November 12, 1991.

60. 142 (4) Cong. Rec. 5315 (1996, House of Representatives).

61. See, for instance, 142 (7) Cong. Rec. 9514 (1996, Senate).

62. See 142 (17) Cong. Rec. 24779 (1996, House of Representatives).

63. 142 (17) Cong. Rec. 24779 (1996, House of Representatives), 24783. See also 142 (17) Cong. Rec. 24779 (1996, House of Representatives), 24794.

64. REAL ID Act of 2005, Pub L No 109–13, 119 Stat 302 (2005). The REAL ID Act of 2005 (hereinafter REAL ID Act) amended the IIRIRA. Among other things, the REAL ID Act authorizes the director of Homeland Security, at his/her sole discretion, to waive all legal requirements he/she "determines necessary to ensure expeditious construction of the barriers and roads." The act was a response to the difficulties that arose when attempting to complete parts of the San Diego fence due to challenges stemming from environmental regulations.

65. Michael J. Garcia, *Barriers Along the U.S. Borders: Key Authorities and Requirement*, Congressional Research Service (2017), 22–25.

66. Kenneth D. Madsen, "Institutionalising the Exception: Homeland Security Section 102(c) Waivers and the Construction of Border Barriers," *Geopolitics* 28, no. 5 (2023). Environmental advocacy groups, including Defenders of Wildlife, Sierra Club, and the Center for Biological Diversity, contested the constitutionality of these waivers in courts; however, their claims were rejected by the courts in all cases. See Defenders of Wildlife v. Chertoff, 527 F. Supp. 2d 119 (D.D.C. 2007); Defenders of Wildlife, 527 F. Supp. 2d 119 (D.D.C. 2007), cert. denied, 128 S. Ct. 2962 (2008); Sierra Club v. Ashcroft, No. 04-CV-272, 2005 U.S. Dist. LEXIS 44244 (S.D. Cal. Dec. 13, 2005); Heritage Organization v. Gonzalez, 533 F. Supp. 2d 58 (D.D.C. 2008); County of El Paso v. Chertoff, No. EP-08-CA-196, 2008 WL 4372693 (W.D. Tex. Aug. 29, 2008); County of El Paso, No. EP-08-CA-196, 2008 WL 4372693 (W.D. Tex. Aug. 29, 2008), cert denied, 129 S. Ct. 2789 (2009). In 2017, the Center for Biological Diversity challenged the waivers for the replacement of dilapidated fences, arguing that the waiver authority only applied to new fences. This argument was also dismissed by the courts. In re: Border Infrastructure Environmental Litigation 284 F. Supp. 3d 1092 (S.D Cal. 2018) and 915 F. 3d 1213 (9th Cir. 2019).

67. Secure Fence Act of 2006, Pub. L. No. 109–367, 120 Stat 2638 (2006). See also Michael J. Garcia, *Barriers Along the U.S. Borders: Key Authorities and Requirements* (Congressional Research Service, 2015). The Secure Fence Act was amended by the Consolidated Appropriations Act of 2008.

68. Doris Meissner, "Keynote Address," *Temple Political & Civil Rights Law Review* 16, no. 2 (2007): 310. Meissner noted that the issue of "immigration reform is going straight to the electorate in November in the form of something called the 'Secure Fence Act.'"

69. Meissner, "Keynote Address," 311.

70. Meissner, "Keynote Address," 310.

71. Meissner, "Keynote Address," 311. Senate Bill S. 2611 was the result of a compromise between lawmakers on a previous Senate bill introduced on May 12, 2005, by Senators Kennedy and McCain (S. 1033).

72. As explained in the previous chapter, it is not a crime to be unlawfully present in American territory. What is criminalized is illegal entry into the United States territory.

73. Meissner, "Keynote Address," 313. Meissner contends that votes on the Secure Fence Act demonstrate that lawmakers and constituencies most favorable to a border

wall were those that had the least contact with immigrants. Of the thirteen states in which their members of Congress in both the House and the Senate voted unanimously in favor of the bill, eleven were located in the US heartland: Iowa, Kansas, Kentucky, Montana, Nebraska, North Dakota, Oklahoma, South Dakota, Tennessee, Utah, West Virginia, and Wyoming. See Pratheepan Gulasekaram, "Why a Wall?," *UC Irvine Law Review* 2, no. 1 (2012): 160–61.

74. 152 (13) Cong. Rec. 18292 (2006, House of Representatives).

75. 151 (21) Cong. Rec. 28690 (2005, House of Representatives).

76. Jeffrey S. Passel, *Size and Characteristics of the Unauthorized Migrant Population in the US*, Pew Research Centre (March 7, 2006), https://www.pewresearch.org/hispanic/2006/03/07/size-and-characteristics-of-the-unauthorized-migrant-population-in-the-us/.

77. Passel, *Size and Characteristics.*

78. 152 (16) Cong. Rec. 21395 (2006, Senate). Arizona governor Janet Napolitano shared the view that fences alone were not a solution to undocumented immigration: "You show me a 50-foot wall and I'll show you a 51-foot ladder at the border." The formula became popular among those opposed to the erection of a border wall.

79. Meissner, "Keynote Address," 313–14.

80. Meissner, "Keynote Address," 314.

81. 152 (6) Cong. Rec. 8157 (2006, Senate).

82. Hall and Brunsdon, *Writings on Media*, 180.

83. Hall and Brunsdon, *Writings on Media*, 180.

84. Gary Gerstle, *American Crucible: Race and Nation in the Twentieth Century* (Princeton, NJ: Princeton University Press, 2017), 380.

85. Gerstle, *American Crucible*, 380.

86. Gerstle, *American Crucible*, 380. According to Gary Gerstle, President Bush was not so much concerned about religious affiliations, whether Protestant, Jewish, or Muslim. Regarding Islam, the author notes that although his administration subjected Muslim and Arab communities to intense surveillance following September 11, 2001, Bush insisted on distinguishing between radical Islamists and Islam. Still, his policies created significant obstacles to immigrants from Muslim and Arab countries. Several of his responses to the attack also tarnished his credentials as a multilateralist, notably the Iraq War of 2003, the establishment of a prison at Guantánamo Bay, the violation of international humanitarian law, as did his response to Hurricane Katrina.

87. *New York Times*, "Bush's Speech on Immigration," May 15, 2006, https://www.nytimes.com/2006/05/15/washington/15text-bush.html.

88. *New York Times*, "Bush's Speech on Immigration."

89. *New York Times*, "Bush's Speech on Immigration."

90. 152 (6) Cong. Rec. 8335 (2006, Senate). The fence, Session explained, would show other countries that the American border is closed, a comment that highlighted the highly symbolic quality of the fence.

91. Paul Engler and Mark Engler, "The Massive Immigrant-Rights Protests of 2006 Are Still Changing Politics," *Los Angeles Times*, March 4, 2016, https://www.latimes.com/opinion/op-ed/la-oe-0306-engler-immigration-protests-2006-20160306-story.html.

92. Carl Hulse, "A Build-a-Protest Approach to Immigration: Advocates of Border Security Are Trying to Inundate Congress," *New York Times*, May 31, 2006.

93. Hulse, "A Build-a-Protest Approach to Immigration."

94. A 2006 Gallup poll demonstrated that 56 percent of respondents were opposed to building a wall along the border with Mexico. Jim Norman, "Solid Majority Still Opposes New Construction on Border Wall," *Gallup*, February 4, 2019, https://news.gallup.com/poll/246455/solid-majority-opposes-new-construction-border-wall.aspx.

95. Carl Hulse, "G.O.P in Senate Narrows Immigration Focus to 700-Mile Fence," *New York Times*, September 21, 2006.

96. 152 (13) Cong. Rec. 18279 (2006, House of Representatives).

97. *New York Times*, "G.O.P in Senate."

98. On the use of symbolic actions in a political context, see, for instance, Murray J. Edelman, *The Symbolic Uses of Politics* (Urbana: University of Illinois Press, 1964).

99. Julia Gelatt, "President Signs DHS Appropriations and Secure Fence Act, New Detainee Bill Has Repercussions for Noncitizens, Migration Policy Institute," *Policy Beat*, November 1, 2006, https://www.migrationpolicy.org/article/president-signs-dhs-appropriations-and-secure-fence-act-new-detainee-bill-has-repercussions.

100. Gelatt, "President Signs DHS Appropriations and Secure Fence Act."

101. Despite the flexibility afforded to the administration for the design and location of border fences in the appropriation bill, the border wall remained high on the political agenda of Congress members, stirred by voters' concerns over undocumented migration amid the 2007 economic crisis and the continued fear of terrorism. This helps to explain why the DHS remained committed to the construction of a physical border wall: Robert Lee Maril, *The Fence: National Security, Public Safety, and Illegal Immigration along the U.S.-Mexico Border* (Lubbock: Texas Tech University Press, 2011), 140–42.

102. Gulasekaram, "Why a Wall?," 161.

103. Jennifer M. Chacón, "Immigration and the Bully Pulpit," *Harvard Law Review* 130, no. 7 (2017): 249.

104. Chacón, "Immigration and the Bully Pulpit," 249.

105. Chacón, "Immigration and the Bully Pulpit," 249.

106. Two significant exceptions include Republicans Pete Wilson and Patrick Buchanan. Pete Wilson, a former US senator (1983–1991) and governor of California (1991–1999), was one of the first US national politicians to rely on fears about Mexican immigration to promote his political agenda. In his 2006 book *State of Emergency: The Third World Invasion and Conquest of America*, Patrick Buchanan, a retired right-wing conservative American journalist, politician, and commentator, compared Mexican immigration to the United States to an invasion. He described that invasion as a "Aztlan plot" to recapture lands lost following the Mexican-American

War, "not militarily, but ethnically, linguistically, and culturally, through the transfer of millions of Mexicans into the United States." Patrick J. Buchanan, *State of Emergency: The Third World Invasion and Conquest of America* (New York: Thomas Dunne Books/St. Martin's, 2006), 135. See Gerstle, *American Crucible*, 397.

107. Gerstle, *American Crucible*, 394–95.

108. Hall and Brunsdon, *Writings on Media*, 189.

109. E. Tendayi Achiume, "Racial Borders," *Georgetown Law Journal* 110, no. 3 (2022): 447.

110. Debra Thompson, "Through, Against and Beyond the Racial State: The Transnational Stratum of Race," *Cambridge Review of International Affairs* 26, no. 1 (2013): 135.

111. Thompson, "Through, Against and Beyond the Racial State," 135.

112. Thompson, "Through, Against and Beyond the Racial State," 134.

113. Thompson, "Through, Against and Beyond the Racial State," 135.

114. See, for instance, Homi K. Bhabha, *The Location of Culture*, 2nd ed. (London: Routledge, 2004).

115. See Mary Neal, "Discovering Dignity: Unpacking the Emotional Content of 'Killing Narratives,'" in *The Emotional Dynamics of Law and Legal Discourse*, ed. Heather Conway and John Stannard (Oxford: Hart, 2016), 83–104.

116. Martha C. Nussbaum, *Political Emotions: Why Love Matters for Justice* (Cambridge, MA: Harvard University Press, 2013), ch. 10.

117. Sara Ahmed, *The Cultural Politics of Emotion*, 2nd ed. (Edinburgh: Edinburgh University Press, 2014), 68.

118. Martha Nussbaum also discusses the role of love in justice at the state level. In her book, she argues that cultivating love at the national level is necessary to overcome fear, envy, and other emotions that prevent us from achieving justice and equality.

119. Vincent F. Sacco and William Glackman, "Vulnerability, Locus of Control and Worry about Crime," in *The Fear of Crime*, ed. Jason Ditton and Stephen Farrall (Aldershot, UK: Ashgate, 2000), 415–27.

120. Ahmed, *The Cultural Politics of Emotion*, 68–69. Italics are mine.

121. Ahmed, *The Cultural Politics of Emotion*, 69.

122. Ahmed, *The Cultural Politics of Emotion*, 69–70.

123. Ahmed, *The Cultural Politics of Emotion*, 72.

124. Brown, *Walled States, Waning Sovereignty*, 127.

125. Brown, *Walled States, Waning Sovereignty*, 127.

126. Brown, *Walled States, Waning Sovereignty*, 128–29.

127. See Brown, *Walled States, Waning Sovereignty*, ch. 4.

128. Michel Foucher, *L'obsession des frontières* (Paris: Perrin, 2012), 76.

129. For a discussion on the role of borders in the production of territory, see David Newman and Anssi Paasi, "Fences and Neighbours in the Postmodern World: Boundary Narratives in Political Geography," *Progress in Human Geography* 22, no. 2 (1998): 187.

130. Desmond Manderson, *Songs without Music: Aesthetic Dimensions of Law and Justice* (Berkeley: University of California Press, 2000), 133–35.

131. Notably, it is now well recognized that territorial jurisdiction and border control do not necessarily coincide with the border. Some have discussed the multiplication of borders to explain the disjunction between territorial boundaries and economic, cultural, and jurisdictional borders. See Ayelet Shachar, *The Shifting Border: Legal Cartographies of Migration and Mobility* (Manchester, UK: Manchester University Press, 2020).

132. Andreas, *Border Games*, 142–44.

133. Emilie Cloatre and Dave Cowan explain how the concept of the rule of law has become the proud symbol of Western democratic thought despite its evident shortcomings: Emilie Cloatre and Dave Cowan, "Legalities and materialities," in *Routledge Handbook of Law and Theory*, ed. Andreas Philippopoulos-Mihalopoulos (London: Routledge, 2019), 433–52.

134. Jones, *Border Walls*, 39.

135. House of Representatives, Committee on the Judiciary, 109th Cong., 2nd Session, *Should Mexico Hold Veto Power over U.S. Border Security Decision?* (August 17, 2006), 28.

136. James McKinley Jr., "With Beheadings and Attacks, Drug Gangs Terrorize Mexico," *New York Times*, October 26, 2006. See also Jones, *Border Walls*, 40.

137. 152 (13) Cong. Rec. 18236 (2006, House of Representatives).

138. See Brown, *Walled States, Waning Sovereignty*, ch. 4.

139. Juliet P. Stumpf, "The Crimmigration Crisis: Immigrants, Crime, and Sovereign Power," in *Governing Immigration Through Crime: A Reader*, ed. Julie A. Dowling and Jonathan Xavier Inda (Stanford, CA: Stanford University Press, 2020), 59–76.

140. Stumpf, "The Crimmigration Crisis," 61.

141. 152 (16) Cong. Rec. 21489 (2006, Senate).

142. House of Representatives, Subcommittee on Investigations, 109th Cong., 2nd Session, *Armed and Dangerous: Confronting the Problem of Border Incursions* (February 7, 2006).

143. House of Representatives, Subcommittee on Immigration, Border Security, and Claims and the Subcommittee on Crime, Terrorism, and Homeland Security of the Committee on the Judiciary, 109th Cong., 2nd Session, *Outgunned and Outmanned: Local Law Enforcement Confronts Violence Along the Southern Border* (March 2, 2006); House of Representatives, Committee on Armed Services, 109th Cong., 2nd Session, *U.S. Southern Border Security—National Security Implications and Issues for the Armed Services* (August 2, 2006); House of Representatives, Subcommittee on Investigations, 109th Cong., 2nd Session, *Criminal Activity and Violence Along the Southern Border* (August 16, 2006).

144. Subcommittee on Investigations (August 16, 2006), 1.

145. For a comparative study of pro-immigrant and immigration-restrictonist activists in the United States, see Emine Fidan Elcioglu, *Divided by the Wall: Progressive*

and Conservative Immigration Politics at the U.S.-Mexico Border (Oakland: University of California Press, 2020).

146. Kristin Haltinner, "Minutewomen, Victims, and Parasites: The Discursive and Performative Construction of Women by the Minuteman Civil Defense Corps," *Sociological Inquiry* 86, no. 4 (2016): 611; Jennifer L. Johnson, *Border Politics* (New York: New York University Press, 2020), 35–59.

147. "The Botany of Illegal Immigration," *Free Republic*, 2005, http://www.freerepublic.com/focus/f-news/1471676/posts. This quote also reveals that the tension between America's north and south, present at the time the Treaty of Guadalupe Hidalgo was negotiated and during the American Civil War, endures in certain segments of the population.

148. Haltinner, "Minutewomen, Victims, and Parasites," 611.

149. Miriam Ticktin, "Sexual Violence as the Language of Border Control: Where French Feminist and Anti-immigrant Rhetoric Meet," *Signs: Journal of Women in Culture and Society* 33, no. 4 (2008): 865.

150. Ticktin, "Sexual Violence," 864–65.

151. Ticktin, "Sexual Violence," 883.

152. Chacón, "Unsecured Borders," 1850.

153. Jones, *Border Walls*, 32.

154. Jones, *Border Walls*, 32.

155. George W. Bush, 'Address to a Joint Session of Congress and the American People' (Washington, DC, September 20, 2001), https://georgewbush-whitehouse.archives.gov/news/releases/2001/09/20010920-8.html.

156. Jones, *Border Walls*, 35.

157. See Jones, *Border Walls*, ch. 2.

158. Gulasekaram, "Why a Wall?," 164.

159. Lou Dobbs, "Dobbs: Bush Speech Satisfies Nobody," *CNN*, May 17, 2006, http://edition.cnn.com/2006/US/05/17/dobbs.bushspeech/.

160. Pipa Noris, Montague Kern, and Marion Just, "The Lessons of Framing Terrorism," in *Framing Terrorism: The News Media, the Government and the Public*, ed. Pipa Noris, Montague Kern, and Marion Just (New York: Routledge, 2003), 294.

161. Subcommittee on Investigations of the House of Representatives (February 7, 2006), 7.

162. House of Representatives, Subcommittee on International Terrorism and Nonproliferation of the Committee on International Relations, 109th Cong., 2nd Session, *Checking Terrorism at the Border* (April 6, 2006); House of Representatives, Subcommittee on International Terrorism and Nonproliferation of the Committee on International Relations, 109th Cong., 2nd Session, *Border Vulnerabilities and International Terrorism* (July 5–7, 2006). See also Committee on Armed Services (August 2, 2006).

163. Subcommittee on International Terrorism and Nonproliferation (July 5–7, 2006), 2.

164. Subcommittee on International Terrorism and Nonproliferation (July 5–7, 2006), 3.

165. 152 (13) Cong. Rec. 18281 (2006, House of Representatives).

166. The CATO Institute reports that seven individuals who initially entered the United States illegally have been convicted of planning a terrorist attack on US soil. These individuals either entered illegally from Canada or through an American maritime port. David Bier and Alex Nowrasteh, *45,000 "Special Interest Aliens" Caught Since 2007, But No U.S. Terrorist Attacks from Illegal Border Crossers*, CATO Institute (2018).

167. See Achiume, "Racial Borders"; Hannah Gordon, "Cowboys and Indians: Settler Colonialism and the Dog Whistle in U.S. Immigration Policy," *University of Miami Law Review* 74, no. 2 (2020): 520.

168. Secure Fence Act § 2(b).

169. This alignment was also made in the past. The language of the Secure Fence Act strikingly resembles the discourse held by the INS and other US officials in the early 1900s to justify fencing the southern land border. It is also reminiscent of the definition of "adversaries" in the 1993 report of Sandia National Laboratories, conflating commuter aliens and illegal aliens along with drug smugglers and alien smugglers.

170. Sara Ahmed, "Collective Feelings: Or, the Impressions Left by Others," *Theory, Culture & Society* 21, no. 2 (2004): 26.

171. Ahmed, "Collective Feelings," 26. Ahmed briefly discusses the joining of the figure of the terrorist and asylum seekers by liberal democracies after September 11, 2001, 79–80.

172. Ahmed, *The Cultural Politics of Emotion*, 72.

173. Anna Trosborg, *Rhetorical Strategies in Legal Language: Discourse Analysis of Statutes and Contracts* (Tübingen, Germany: Narr, 1997), 14, 23.

174. Eve Darian-Smith, "Precedents of Injustice: Thinking About History in Law and Society Scholarship," in *Studies in Law, Politics and Society*, vol. 41, ed. Austin Sarat (Bingley, UK: Emerald Group, 2007), 61–81.

175. Darian-Smith, "Precedents of Injustice," 61–81.

176. Gulasekaram, "Why a Wall?," 169–70.

177. Gulasekaram, "Why a Wall?," 170.

178. Darian-Smith, "Precedents of Injustice," 66.

179. Gulasekaram, "Why a Wall?," 183. Gulasekaram argues that the effect of the wall in promoting defensive strategies is only temporary. Nonetheless, the author recognizes that once legislated and erected, the wall becomes a "sticky public policy," 161. The border wall appears to remain a popular measure among anti-immigrant politicians and continues to appeal to a section of the American public. A survey conducted by the Pew Research Center in 2018 shows that 40 percent of Americans supported substantially extending the wall, while 58 percent were against it. The percentage of people in support of expanding the wall was much higher among Republicans and Republican-leaning independents, with 82 percent in favor. By contrast,

92 percent of Democrats opposed its expansion, see John Gramlich, "How Americans See Illegal Immigration, the Border Wall and Political Compromise," Pew Research Center, January 16, 2019, https://www.pewresearch.org/fact-tank/2019/01/16/how-americans-see-illegal-immigration-the-border-wall-and-political-compromise/. Since then, support for the wall has increased: Jamie Ballard, "As Congress Considers a Shutdown, Here's What Americans Think of U.S. Immigration Policies," *YouGov*, January 13, 2024, https://today.yougov.com/politics/articles/48352-congress-considers-shutdown-what-americans-think-us-immigration-policies-poll.

180. Brown, *Walled States, Waning Sovereignty*, 52. See also Gulasekaram, "Why a Wall?"

181. For instance, Rescinding DHS' Waiver Authority for the Border Wall Act (2021) and Prioritizing Pandemic Prevention Act (2020).

182. A December 2023 YouGov poll shows that a small majority of Americans are in favor of building a wall. While 53 percent are in favor, 31 percent oppose it. Overall, 85 and 32 percent of Republicans and Democrats, respectively, support the policy: Jamie Ballard, "As Congress Considers a Shutdown, Here's What Americans Think of U.S. Immigration Policies," *YouGov*, January 13, 2024, https://today.yougov.com/politics/articles/48352-congress-considers-shutdown-what-americans-think-us-immigration-policies-poll.

183. Proclamation No. 10142, Fed. Reg. 86 Fed. Reg. 7225 (2021); Eileen Sullivan and Colbi Edmonds, "Biden, the Border, and Why a New Wall Is Going Up," *New York Times*, October 6, 2023, https://www.nytimes.com/2023/10/06/us/border-wall-biden.html#:~:text=Alejandro%20N.,to%20do%20so%20in%202019.

184. United States v. Arizona, No. 2:10-cv-01413-SRB, Order No. CV 10-1413-PHX-SRB dismissing Az.'s Countercls. (D. Az., Oct. 21, 2011).

185. We Build the Wall, "About Us," https://webuildthewall.us/about-us/.

186. Exec. Order No. 2022-04, Securing Arizona's Southern Border (August 12, 2022); Jack Healy, "One Governor's Border Wall Is Another Governor's Headache," *New York Times*, December 19, 2022.

187. United States of America v. Douglas A. Ducey et al. Case 2:22-cv-02107-SMB.

188. Manderson, *Songs without Music*, 58.

Chapter 4

1. I understand orality as the quality of being oral or orally communicated.

2. Kevin Bruyneel, *Settler Memory: The Disavowal of Indigeneity and the Politics of Race in the United States* (Chapel Hill: University of North Carolina Press, 2021), 13.

3. Bruyneel, *Settler Memory*, 14.

4. Stuart Hall, "Race—The Sliding Signifier," in *The Fateful Triangle* (Cambridge, MA: Harvard University Press, 2017), 31–79. 48.

5. Bruyneel, *Settler Memory*, 14.

6. Gloria Anzaldúa, *Borderlands/La Frontera: The New Mestiza*, 5th ed. (San Francisco: Aunt Lute Books, 2022), 16.

7. Margaret Davies, *Law Unlimited: Materialism, Pluralism, and Legal Theory* (Abingdon, UK: Routledge, 2017), 136.

8. Peter Goodrich, "Specula Laws: Image, Aesthetic and Common Law," *Law and Critique* 2, no. 2 (1991): 238.

9. Serghei Golunov, "Border Fences in the Globalizing World: Beyond Traditional Geopolitics and Post-positivist Approaches," in *Borders, Fences and Walls: State of Insecurity?*, ed. Élisabeth Vallet (Farnham, UK: Ashgate, 2014), 117–29. 121.

10. Davies, *Law Unlimited*, 69–70.

11. Desmond Manderson, "Interstices: New Work on Legal Spaces," *Law, Text, Culture* 9 (2005).

12. Manderson, "Interstices," 5.

13. See Eve Darian-Smith, *Bridging Divides: The Channel Tunnel and English Legal Identity in the New Europe* (Berkeley: University of California Press, 1999), 21.

14. Sarah Keenan, *Subversive Property: Law and the Production of Spaces of Belonging* (Abingdon, UK: Routledge, 2014), 42.

15. See Donald W. Meinig, "The Beholding Eye: Ten Versions of the Same Scene," in *The Interpretation of Ordinary Landscapes: Geographical Essays*, ed. Donald W. Meinig and John B. Jackson (New York: Oxford University Press, 1979); W. J. T. Mitchell, *Landscape and Power*, 2nd ed. (Chicago: University of Chicago Press, 2002); Darian-Smith, *Bridging Divides*.

16. Mitchell, *Landscape and Power*, 1. Mitchell opens his book by explaining that his aim is to "change 'landscape' from a noun to a verb."

17. Darian-Smith, *Bridging Divides*.

18. Darian-Smith, *Bridging Divides*, 21–24. For instance, Darian-Smith explains that the reification of the rural landscapes of Scotland, Wales, and England works as an instrument of British territorialization that reinforces British sovereignty and territorial cohesion.

19. Darian-Smith, *Bridging Divides*, 22.

20. See Darian-Smith, *Bridging Divides*, 21.

21. Keenan, *Subversive Property: Law and the Production of Spaces of Belonging*, 29.

22. This said, Philippopoulos-Mihalopoulos distinguishes between the *lawscape* and the *landscape*. For him, the landscape is merely an oculocentric manipulation of space; it is not a space shaped by a plurality of individuals. By contrast, Darian-Smith's landscape is a process in which everyone can intervene to configure space; therefore, it is closer to Philippopoulos-Mihalopoulos's notion of the lawscape. See Andreas Philippopoulos-Mihalopoulos, *Spatial Justice: Body, Lawscape, Atmosphere* (Abingdon, UK: Routledge, 2015), 39–74.

23. Philippopoulos-Mihalopoulos, *Spatial Justice*, 39.

24. David Delaney, *The Spatial, the Legal and the Pragmatics of World-Making: Nomospheric Investigations* (New York: Routledge, 2010), ii. Like Philippopoulos-Mihalopoulos, Delaney distinguishes between the landscape and his neologism, the *nomoscape*, pointing out that the former conveys a static image of space while the latter refers to a space that is lived through. In this sense, the concept

of landscape used here, as well as by Darian-Smith, is closer to Delaney's nomoscape, at least to the extent that it is understood as a space that is performed and where individuals have a degree of agency (Delaney, *The Spatial*, 104).

25. Richard T. Ford, "Law's Territory (A History of Jurisdiction)," *Michigan Law Review* 97, no. 4 (1999): 855. Delaney, *The Spatial*, 26.

26. Ford, "Law's Territory," 855.

27. Ford, "Law's Territory," 898.

28. Ford, "Law's Territory," 855.

29. Ford, "Law's Territory," 856.

30. See Andrea Mubi Brighenti, "Lines, Barred Lines. Movement, Territory and the Law," *International Journal of Law in Context* 6, no. 3 (2010): 24. Brighenti argues that the act of drawing of boundaries turns ideas into material force.

31. Desmond Manderson, *Songs without Music: Aesthetic Dimensions of Law and Justice* (Berkeley: University of California Press, 2000); Yi-Fu Tuan, *Space and Place: The Perspective of Experience* (Minneapolis: University of Minnesota Press, 1977).

32. Tuan, *The Perspective of Experience*, 9.

33. Layli Long Soldier, "Layli Long Soldier on Wounded Knee and the Murder of George Floyd," *Literary Hub*, June 3, 2020, https://lithub.com/layli-long-soldier-on-wounded-knee-and-the-murder-of-george-floyd/.

34. Golunov, "Border Fences in the Globalizing World," 122.

35. Christine Leuenberger, "Technologies, Practices and the Reproduction of Conflict: The Impact of the West Bank Barrier on Peace Building," in *Borders, Fences and Walls: State of Insecurity?*, ed. Élisabeth Vallet (Farnham, UK: Routledge, 2014), 213.

36. Leuenberger, "Technologies, Practices and the Reproduction of Conflict," 213.

37. Sara Ahmed, *Living a Feminist Life* (Durham, NC: Duke University Press, 2017), 136.

38. Ahmed, *Living a Feminist Life*, 138.

39. Claude Quétel, *Histoire des murs* (Paris: Perrin, 2012), 7.

40. Iris Marion Young, "House and Home: Feminist Variations on a Theme," in *On Female Body Experience: "Throwing like a Girl" and Other Essays* (Oxford: Oxford University Press, 2005), 139.

41. Young, "House and Home," 139.

42. Mary Douglas, "The Idea of a Home: A Kind of Space," *Social Research* 58, no. 1 (1991): 288.

43. Douglas, "The Idea of a Home," 299.

44. Douglas, "The Idea of a Home," 289.

45. Young, "House and Home," 147.

46. Margaret Davies, "Home and State: Reflections on Metaphor and Practice," *Griffith Law Review* 23, no. 2 (2014).

47. Davies, "Home and State," 155.

48. Davies, "Home and State," 156.

49. Pratheepan Gulasekaram, "Why a Wall?," *UC Irvine Law Review* 2, no. 1 (2012): 173–76.

50. See also Reece Jones, *Border Walls: Security and the War on Terror in the United States, India and Israel* (London: Zed Books, 2012). Jones argues that in the context of terrorism, the symbol of the wall deploys a narrative of territorial control that makes the intangible concept of territory tangible. The wall solidifies the divide between two countries and their populations; it dehumanizes those outside and conveys the impression that they stand outside the pale of civilization and governable politics.

51. Wendy Brown, *Walled States, Waning Sovereignty*, 2nd ed. (New York: Zone Books, 2017), 38.

52. Brown, *Walled States*, 37.

53. Brown, *Walled States*, 38.

54. Brown, *Walled States*, 131.

55. Evelyne Ritaine, "La barrière et le checkpoint: mise en politique de l'asymétrie," *Cultures & Conflits* 73 (Spring 2009): 28. For a study of the esthetic of border walls, see Elisa Ganivet, *Esthétique du mur géopolitique* (Québec: Presses de l'Université du Québec, 2015).

56. Reece Jones, *Border Walls*, 176.

57. Interview with staff at a Washington-based immigration research institute, Washington, DC, June 21, 2016.

58. See Quétel, *Histoire des murs*; Arthur Waldron, *The Great Wall of China: From History to Myth* (Cambridge: Cambridge University Press, 1989). Most of these walls had more than just a defensive function. For instance, the Roman *limes* marked the territorial limits of the Roman Empire, which, in addition to their defensive function, operated as an economic frontier and assisted in controlling people's movement.

59. For an illustration of artistic work inspired by or representing walls, see Ganivet, *Esthétique du mur géopolitique*. One artistic performance using the Great Wall of China as a stage is Marina Abramović and Ulay's video performance *The Lovers—The Great Wall Walk*.

60. Gregory Ashworth and David M. Bruce, "Town Walls, Walled Towns and Tourism: Paradoxes and Paradigms," *Journal of Heritage Tourism* 4, no. 4 (2009): 301.

61. M. J. Kuipers and Gregory Ashworth, "Managing the Heritage of Fortress Towns: The Cases of Naarden and Bourtange," in *The Construction of Built Heritage: A North European Perspective on Policies, Practices and Outcomes*, ed. Gregory Ashworth, Angela Phelps, and Bengt O. H. Johannsson (Aldershot, UK: Ashgate, 2002), 142.

62. See Reviel Netz, *Barbed Wire: An Ecology of Modernity* (Middletown, CT: Wesleyan University Press, 2009).

63. On the symbolism of the barbed wire, see Olivier Razac, *Histoire politique du barbelé* (Paris: Éditions Flammarion, 2009), 60.

64. Alain Brossat, "Préface," in *Histoire politique du barbelé* (Paris: Flammarion, 2009), 7–21. My translation.

65. Razac, *Histoire politique du barbelé*, 77. My translation.

66. Brossat, "Préface," 9. My translation.

67. The association between the wall and violence is intensified and kept alive today through vestiges, memorials, museums, and commemoration ceremonies. Memorial sites such as the *Tränenpalast* (Palace of Tears), a check-in hall for West German families crossing to visit their relatives to the East, reminds us of the pain inflicted by the division of a community, families, and friends. Similarly, artistic representations of the wall and its fall have served, and continue to serve, an essential role in the transformation of the wall into a symbolic object of international resonance, see Nicole Colin et al., eds., *Le Mur de Berlin: histoire, mémoires, représentations* (Bruxelles: PIE Peter Lang, 2016).

68. Quoted in Mark Tran, "Mexico Fury as Bush Gives Go-ahead to Border Fence," *The Guardian*, October 27, 2006, https://www.theguardian.com/world/2006/oct/27/usa.mexico. There were other instances when the US-Mexico border wall was compared to the Berlin Wall. In 2005, John P. Clark, a former deputy assistant secretary for immigration and customs enforcement, reportedly stated during congressional testimony that an extension of the existing border fencing "harkens back to the Chinese wall and the Berlin Wall, not the message we want to send to the Mexican government, the Canadian government, and the rest of the world," quoted in Chad C. Haddal, Yule Kim, and Michael J. Garcia, *Border Security: Barriers Along the U.S. International Border,* Congressional Research Service (2009), 31. More recently, in 2017, a resident of Naco, Arizona, compared the new wall built by the Trump administration to replace an old fence to the Berlin Wall, stating "We got the Berlin Wall torn down. Why build another one?," quoted in Erik Kolsrud, "A Wall Being Built in Naco's Backyard Stirs Up Emotions," *Arizona Sonora News*, February 10, 2017, https://arizonasonoranewsservice.com/a-wall-being-built-in-nacos-backyard-stirs-up-emotions/.

69. Razac, *Histoire politique du barbelé*, 73. See also Netz, *Barbed Wire: An Ecology of Modernity.*

70. Razac, *Histoire politique du barbelé.*

71. Corine Defrance, "'Cette histoire de la brutalité du mur': du 'viol de Berlin' au symbole de la liberté," in *Le mur de Berlin: histoire, mémoires, représentations*, ed. Nicole Colin et al. (Bruxelles: PIE Peter Lang, 2016), 61–78.

72. Leuenberger, "Technologies, Practices and the Reproduction of Conflict," 225.

73. Dallen J. Timothy and Cevat Tosun, "Tourists' Perceptions of the Canada–USA Border as a Barrier to Tourism at the International Peace Garden," *Tourism Management* 24, no. 4 (2003): 415.

74. Dallen J. Timothy, "Cross-Border Partnership in Tourism Resource Management: International Parks along the US-Canada Border," *Journal of Sustainable Tourism* 7, no. 3–4 (1999).

75. Timothy and Tosun, "Tourists' Perceptions," 418.

76. International Peace Garden, "Maps of Our Park," https://peacegarden.com/wp-content/uploads/2019/06/IPG-Map-with-Key.pdf.

77. International Peace Garden, "Preparing for Your Visit," https://peacegarden.com/discover#preparevisit.

78. Timothy, "Cross-Border Partnership," 192.

79. Timothy, "Cross-Border Partnership," 188; Timothy and Tosun, "Tourists' Perceptions," 418.

80. Timothy, "Cross-Border Partnership," 191.

81. Timothy and Tosun, "Tourists' Perceptions," 415.

82. Timothy and Tosun, "Tourists' Perceptions," 417.

83. Timothy and Tosun, "Tourists' Perceptions," 418.

84. Still, a minority of visitors at the park found the border formalities intimidating and confusing. Timothy and Tosun, "Tourists' Perceptions," 417.

85. Timothy and Tosun, "Tourists' Perceptions," 417.

86. Communities in Bloom, "International Peace Garden: Dedicated to the Celebration of Peace," https://www.collectivitesenfleurs.ca/international-peace-garden-dedicated-to-the-celebration-of-peace/.

87. Charles Thomsen, "A Border Vision: The International Peace Garden," *Manitoba History* 31 (1996), http://www.mhs.mb.ca/docs/mb_history/31/peacegarden.shtml.

88. Thomsen, "A Border Vision."

89. International Peace Garden, "Home," https://peacegarden.com/.

90. Thomsen, "A Border Vision: The International Peace Garden."

91. Jackson J. Faber, "Becoming Friendship Park: The History of Border Field State Park" (master's thesis, San Diego State University, 2015), 13.

92. Faber, "Becoming Friendship Park," 13.

93. Faber, "Becoming Friendship Park," 10. Cornell hoped the park would create "a new mood in the border area."

94. Joseph Nevins, *Operation Gatekeeper and Beyond: The War on Illegals and the Remaking of the U.S.-Mexico Boundary*, 2nd ed. (New York: Routledge, 2010), 190.

95. Faber, "Becoming Friendship Park," 16.

96. Faber, "Becoming Friendship Park," 17–18.

97. Faber, "Becoming Friendship Park," 20.

98. Faber, "Becoming Friendship Park," 30, 41.

99. Faber, "Becoming Friendship Park," 50–51.

100. Kathryn Balint, "It's Iffy, but Border Park Might Be Open," *San Diego Union Tribune*, October 26, 1995.

101. Faber, "Becoming Friendship Park," 61. Even though a large section of the border within the park was divided by a chain-link fence, the weathered metal pillars closer to the beach had gaps large enough for people to touch and embrace each other. As noted by Faber, these were less than ideal conditions since encounters among families and friends unavoidably occurred under the gaze of federal agents.

102. Faber, "Becoming Friendship Park," 66.

103. California Department of Parks and Recreation, "Border Field State Park," https://www.parks.ca.gov/?page_id=664.

104. Kate Morrissey, "Border Patrol Changes Rules at Friendship Park, Upsetting Frequent Visitors," *San Diego Union-Tribune*, February 14, 2018, https://www.sandiegouniontribune.com/news/immigration/sd-me-friendship-park-20180214-story.html.

105. See Friends of Friendship Park, "Status of Binational Friendship Garden of Native Plants," May 5, 2022, https://www.friendshippark.org/post/status-of-binational-friendship-garden-of-native-plants. The binational garden was an initiative initiated by Dan Watman, who, through the Border Encuentro project, first brought students from Tijuana and San Diego together in 2007 to plant the garden, which consisted of two garden plots, one on each side of the border. In 2009, the US Border Patrol removed the garden, claiming that the plants could hinder border enforcement activities. Eventually, a US Border Patrol officer offered to replant the garden even though it was not possible to restore public access to the site. Again, in 2011, the US Border Patrol requested the removal of the garden to allow for work on the replacement of the fence. All the plants were removed and stored in a nursery by a team of landscape architects, native plant experts, gardeners, and volunteers until the end of the work. Once finished, the team designed a new layout for the garden made of three circles that are crossed by the fence. The idea behind this design was to suggest a truly binational garden as opposed to two separate ones on each side of the border. The US Border Patrol bulldozed the latest iteration of the garden in 2020 and partially replanted it afterward. However, it has not been maintained since the closure of Friendship Park that same year.

106. At the Edge, "Friendship Park," http://www.attheedges.com/border-stories/friendship-park/.

107. Morrissey, "Border Patrol Changes Rules at Friendship Park, Upsetting Frequent Visitors."

108. See Jean Guerrero, "A Trump-like Border Wall Is About to be Built—Unless Biden Stops It," *Los Angeles Times*, February 27, 2023. Customs and Border Protection announced its intention to reopen Friendship Park after the construction of the new border wall. US Customs and Border Protection, "CBP Announces New Path Forward for the Replacement of Deteriorated Border Barrier Near Friendship Park," news release, January 17, 2023, https://www.cbp.gov/newsroom/local-media-release/cbp-announces-new-path-forward-replacement-deteriorated-border-barrier.

109. Edward S. Casey and Mary M. Watkins, *Up Against the Wall: Re-imagining the U.S.-Mexico Border* (Austin: University of Texas Press, 2014), 28.

110. Allison Fish, "A Border Seeping in All Directions: Technologies of Separation Along the U.S.-Mexico Border in Ambos Nogales," in *Information, Technology and Control in a Changing World: Understanding Power Structures in the 21st Century*, ed. Blayne Haggart, Kathryn Henne, and Natasha Tusikov (Cham, Switzerland: Springer International Publishing, 2019): 253.

111. Casey and Watkins, *Up Against the Wall*, 29.

112. Fish, "A Border Seeping in All Directions," 256.

113. Fish, "A Border Seeping in All Directions," 257.

114. R. M. Cousar, Inspector in Charge, Nogales, to District Director, Immigration Service, El Paso, November 22, 1928, file 55 606/894, RG 85, National Archives. Still, in his letter, Cousar requested the erection of a "well-constructed, substantial, durable, non-climbable fence to discourage illegal entries."

115. Randall H. McGuire, "Steel Walls and Picket Fences: Rematerializing the U.S.–Mexican Border in Ambos Nogales," *American Anthropologist* 115, no. 3 (2013): 469.

116. McGuire, "Steel Walls and Picket Fences," 470.

117. Irasema Coronado, "Towards the Wall between Nogales, Arizona and Nogales, Sonora," in *Borders, Fences and Walls: State of Insecurity?*, ed. Élisabeth Vallet (Farnham, UK: Ashgate, 2014), 247.

118. Casey and Watkins, *Up Against the Wall*, 31.

119. Paul Theroux, "The Country Just Over the Fence," *New York Times*, February 23, 2012, https://www.nytimes.com/2012/02/26/travel/nogales-mexico-a-few-steps-and-a-whole-world-away.html; McGuire, "Steel Walls and Picket Fences."

120. McGuire, "Steel Walls and Picket Fences," 472.

121. McGuire, "Steel Walls and Picket Fences," 472–73. The author explains that they have been able to collaborate in some cases. For instance, when a fire broke out in an abandoned hotel in Nogales, Sonora, the fire department in Nogales, Arizona, hosed the fire from across the wall and provided hoses for their Mexican counterparts.

122. McGuire, "Steel Walls and Picket Fences," 474.

123. Casey and Watkins, *Up Against the Wall*, 31.

124. Casey and Watkins, *Up Against the Wall*, 31.

125. McGuire, "Steel Walls and Picket Fences," 475. The annual number of crossings has remained relatively stable since 2011, except during the COVID-19 pandemic in 2020 and 2021. See US Department of Transportation, "Border Crossing Entry Data," https://explore.dot.gov/views/BorderCrossingData/PercentChange?%3Aembed=y&%3AisGuestRedirectFromVizporal=y.

126. McGuire, "Steel Walls and Picket Fences," 467.

127. Gloria Anzaldúa, *Borderlands/La Frontera: The New Mestiza*, 5th ed. (San Francisco: Aunt Lute Books, 2022), 17.

128. Theroux, "The Country Just over the Fence."

129. Theroux, "The Country Just over the Fence."

130. Casey and Watkins, *Up Against the Wall*, 48.

131. Casey and Watkins, *Up Against the Wall*, 48.

132. Casey and Watkins, *Up Against the Wall*, 50.

133. Casey and Watkins, *Up Against the Wall*, 50.

134. Statistics Canada, "Census Profile, 2016," https://www12.statcan.gc.ca/census-recensement/index-eng.cfm; US Census Bureau, "American Fact Finder," https://factfinder.census.gov/faces/nav/jsf/pages/community_facts.xhtml.

135. At that time, the town of Stanstead was composed of three villages: Stanstead Plain, Rock Island, and Beebe Plain. The three villages were merged into one town, Stanstead, in 1995.

136. Jan Lounder, "This Town's a Tale of Two Countries," *Sunday Sun*, August 31, 1980.

137. Phil Blampied, "Partly in Vermont: A Borderline Case," *Time*, August 13, 1979.

138. Todd Hataley and Scott J. Mason, "Collective Efficacy Across Borders: The Case of Stanstead, Quebec and Derby Line, Vermont," *Journal of Borderlands Studies* 33, no. 3 (2018): 435.

139. Hataley and Mason, "Collective Efficacy Across Borders," 435; *The Gazette*, "Phoning U.S. Without Fee Privilege of Rock Islanders," May 24, 1954.

140. Steve Blake, "Boundary Rotary Club Viable Despite Declining Membership," *Sherbrooke Record*, February 9, 2017.

141. Hataley and Mason, "Collective Efficacy Across Borders," 435.

142. Hataley and Mason, "Collective Efficacy Across Borders," 436.

143. John Donnelly, "They're Bilingual on Both Sides of Street," *Burlington Free Press*, February 11, 1980.

144. *Los Angeles Times*, "U.S.-Canada Border Cuts 20-Foot Swath," April 17, 1972; Stephanie Lim, "This Border-Straddling U.S. Home Has a Door that Leads Right to Canada," *Global News*, June 29, 2017, https://globalnews.ca/news/3567283/this-border-straddling-u-s-home-has-a-door-that-leads-right-to-canada/.

145. *Stanstead Journal*, "Haskell Free Library," May 26, 1904; Sally Johnson, "Life on the Line: Vermont and Canada," *New York Times*, February 7, 1988.

146. Haskell Free Library & Opera House, "History," https://haskellopera.com/history/.

147. Haskell Free Library & Opera House, "History."

148. *Boston Sunday Herald*, "Unique Border Library Was Opened in '04," July 11, 1976.

149. In 1984, during the trial of Canadian Clement Daigneault, who was accused of smuggling twelve people from Haiti, El Salvador, and the Dominican Republic through Quebec and into the United States, the court held the court rogatory at the library. Canadian witnesses were needed for the prosecutor to make his case, but Canadians cannot be forced to appear as witness in the United States. At the same time, American defendants have a right to be present at deposition hearings. In the Daigneault case, that would have required bringing the accused into Canada; however, this was not possible because American law enforcement does not have the jurisdiction to detain Canadians in Canada. To circumvent these jurisdictional hurdles, the trial temporarily moved to the Haskell Library. David Johnston, "Judge Draws Fine Line at Cross-Border Hearing," *Montreal Gazette*, February 1983. The experience was repeated in 1988 for the trial of three Canadians charged with smuggling a homemade bomb through US-Canada border: Judith Shulevitz, "Bomb Trial to Feature Border-Line Testimony," *Burlington Free Press*, June 23, 1988.

150. Colin Nickerson, "Haskell Library Straddles the Border," *The Chronicle*, April 20, 1978; Colin Nickerson, "International Border Slices Library in Half, Producing Unique Diplomatic Interactions," *Sunday Rutland Herald and Sunday Times Argus*,

April 30, 1978; Christopher Bain, "Separation Crosses the Borderline," *Ottawa Journal*, December 22, 1979.

151. Exec. Order No. 13780, 82 F.R. 13209 (2017).

152. Yeganeh Torbati, "Separated by Travel Ban, Iranian Families Reunite at Border Library," *Reuters*, November 28, 2018, https://www.reuters.com/article/us-usa-immigration-ban-insight/separated-by-travel-ban-iranian-families-reunite-at-border-library-idUSKCN1NX1P2.

153. Jillian Kestler-D'Amours, "Inside the Library Where You Can Read in Two Countries at Once," *Al Jazeera*, December 26, 2022, https://www.aljazeera.com/news/2022/12/26/inside-the-library-where-you-can-read-in-two-countries-at-once.

154. Hataley and Mason, "Collective Efficacy Across Borders: The Case of Stanstead, Quebec and Derby Line, Vermont," 437.

155. Vincent Boucher, Cloutier-Roy Christophe, and Élisabeth Vallet, "Frontiérités québécoises: Représentations de la zone transfrontalière québéco-américaine au Congrès des États-Unis, 2001–2016," *Canadian Geographer* 63, no. 1 (2019): 34.

156. Victor A. Konrad and Heather N. Nicol, *Beyond Walls: Re-inventing the Canada-United States Borderlands* (London: Routledge, 2016), 4.

157. See Victor Konrad and Emmanuel Brunet-Jailly, "Approaching Borders, Creating Borderland Spaces, and Exploring the Evolving borders Between Canada and the United States," *Canadian Geographer* 63, no. 1 (2019).

158. The decision to mark the border with flowers was made by a committee led by community leaders from Stanstead and Derby Line and negotiated with the US Border Patrol, US Customs and Border Protection, and the Royal Canadian Mounted Police to "suit the community values and needs." Other concessions included permission to visit the Haskell Library without a passport or identity card and an easing of the policy of automatic detention for residents crossing between ports of entry. Hataley and Mason, "Collective Efficacy Across Borders: The Case of Stanstead, Quebec and Derby Line, Vermont," 437.

159. See, for instance, Martha C. Nussbaum, *Political Emotions: Why Love Matters for Justice* (Cambridge, MA: Harvard University Press, 2013).

160. See Davina Cooper, "Against the Current: Social Pathways and the Pursuit of Enduring Change," *Feminist Legal Studies* 9, no. 2 (2001): ch. 9; Davies, *Law Unlimited*.

161. Cooper, "Against the Current," 129.

162. See Brighenti, "Lines, Barred Lines," 221.

163. Davina Cooper, "Reading the State as a Multi-Identity Formation: The Touch and Feel of Equality Governance," *Feminist Legal Studies* 19, no. 1 (2011): 7. For Cooper, touch constitutes a "linguistic register."

164. Delaney, *The Spatial*, 22.

165. Sociologists Miguel Díaz-Barriga and Margaret E. Dorsey similarly discuss how the wall has disrupted the daily patterns of everyday life in the border town of Hidalgo, Texas. Miguel Díaz-Barriga and Margaret E. Dorsey, *Fencing in Democracy:*

Border Walls, Necrocitizenship, and the Security State (Durham, NC: Duke University Press, 2020), 39.

166. Paul Hirst argues that buildings do not mean nor narrate, and that the material they are made of—steel, wood or concrete—have no signifying value. Yet, the discussion about the symbolic meanings of barbed wire indicates otherwise. Paul Q. Hirst, *Space and Power: Politics, War and Architecture* (Cambridge: Polity, 2005).

167. Lindsay Nash, "Mending Wall: Playing the Game of Neighborhood Ordering," *Yale Journal of Law & the Humanities* 21, no. 1 (2009): 187.

168. Anzaldúa, *Borderlands/La Frontera*, 77.

169. Nash, "Mending Wall," 188.

170. Nash, "Mending Wall," 188–89.

171. Nash, "Mending Wall," 189.

172. Nash, "Mending Wall," 189.

173. Nash, "Mending Wall," 190–91.

174. Nash, "Mending Wall," 191.

175. Evelyne Ritaine, "La barrière et le checkpoint," 32. My translation.

176. Nussbaum, *Political Emotions*, 331.

177. Nussbaum, *Political Emotions*, 331.

178. Nussbaum, *Political Emotions*, 360.

179. Nussbaum, *Political Emotions*, 361.

180. Nussbaum, *Political Emotions*, 361–62.

181. Nussbaum, *Political Emotions*, 361.

182. Ahmed, *Living a Feminist Life*, 136, 146.

183. Anzaldúa, *Borderlands/La Frontera*, 85.

184. Sara Ahmed, "A Phenomenology of Whiteness," *Feminist Theory* 8, no. 2 (2007): 153.

185. Ahmed, "A Phenomenology of Whiteness," 153, 156.

186. In this regard, there is a link between what Ahmed says and the crystallization of de jure pathways in Cooper's work.

187. Ahmed, "A Phenomenology of Whiteness," 159.

188. Ahmed, "A Phenomenology of Whiteness," 157–58.

189. Ahmed, "A Phenomenology of Whiteness," 158.

190. Ahmed, "A Phenomenology of Whiteness," 158.

191. Ahmed, "A Phenomenology of Whiteness," 158.

192. Ahmed, "A Phenomenology of Whiteness," 161.

193. I use the term *Chicano* to generally refer to Americans of Mexican descent.

194. Anzaldúa, *Borderlands/La Frontera*, 17. My translation.

195. The distinction that Mary Neal makes between the terms *abjectification* and *dehumanization* is helpful here. Whereas dehumanization can be understood as a denial of humanity, abjectification is the process of making a person or group "negatively Other." In this process, a group is constructed as the site of revulsion and distanced from the moral community. I believe the word *abjectification* better captures the ongoing process of differentiation and division at the US-Mexico border. Mary

Neal, "Discovering Dignity: Unpacking the Emotional Content of 'Killing Narratives,'" in *The Emotional Dynamics of Law and Legal Discourse*, ed. Heather Conway and John Stannard (Oxford: Hart, 2016), 83–104.

196. Anne-Laure Amilhat Szary, "Walls and Border Art: The Politics of Art Display," *Journal of Borderlands Studies* 27, no. 2 (2012): 214.

197. Szary, "Walls and Border Art: The Politics of Art Display," 222.

198. At the Edge, "Friendship Park"; Border Angels, "Events," Facebook, last updated May 25, 2022, https://www.facebook.com/pg/BorderAngels/events/?ref=page_internal.

199. Valeria Bigurra, "Wallyball: Playing Volleyball on the Border," *Mexico News Network*, August 22, 2015, http://www.mexiconewsnetwork.com/en/noticias-en/wallyball-border/. Wallyball is a fast-paced game that resembles volleyball but is usually played on a racquetball court.

200. See Davies, *Law Unlimited*, 116.

201. See, for instance, Davies, *Law Unlimited*, 116; Desmond Manderson, "Beyond the Provincial: Space, Aesthetics, and Modernist Legal Theory," *Melbourne University Law Review* 20, no. 4 (1997); Martha-Marie Kleinhans and Roderick A. Macdonald, "What Is a Critical Legal Pluralism?," *Canadian Journal of Law and Society* 12, no. 2 (1997).

202. Desmond, "Beyond the Provincial," 1064.

Conclusion

1. Gloria Anzaldúa, *Borderlands/La Frontera: The New Mestiza*, 5th ed. (San Francisco: Aunt Lute Books, 2022), 16. Again, while I emphasize the effects of the new border on people of Mexican descent, I am conscious of the fact that indigenous tribes are not deeply affected by the border and the contemporary border wall. Kevin Bruyneel notes that the Treaty of Guadalupe Hidalgo and the 1854 Gadsden Purchase (an agreement in which the United States agreed to pay Mexico US$10 million for a 29,670-square-mile section of Mexico's territory that became part of Arizona and New Mexico) split the traditional homelands of thirty-six recognized tribes. Kevin Bruyneel, *Settler Memory: The Disavowal of Indigeneity and the Politics of Race in the United States* (Chapel Hill: University of North Carolina Press, 2021), 158–59.

2. Eve Darian-Smith, *Bridging Divides: The Channel Tunnel and English Legal Identity in the New Europe* (Berkeley: University of California Press, 1999), 190.

3. See Homi K. Bhabha, *The Location of Culture*, 2nd ed. (London: Routledge, 2004), 101.

4. Marianne Constable, *Our Word Is Our Bond: How Legal Speech Acts* (Stanford, CA: Stanford University Press, 2014), 132.

5. Patrick Wolfe, *Traces of History: Elementary Structures of Race* (London: Verso, 2016), 8.

6. Bruyneel, *Settler Memory*, 142.

7. Bruyneel, *Settler Memory*, 137.

8. See Eve Darian-Smith, "Precedents of Injustice: Thinking About History in Law and Society Scholarship," in *Studies in Law, Politics and Society*, vol. 41, ed. Austin Sarat (Bingley: Emerald Group, 2007), 61–81.

9. Darian-Smith, "Precedents of Injustice," 63.

10. Darian-Smith, "Precedents of Injustice," 63.

11. Nicholas Pedriana and Robin Stryker, "Political Culture Wars 1960s Style: Equal Employment Opportunity–Affirmative Action Law and the Philadelphia Plan," *American Journal of Sociology* 103, no. 3 (1997): 642. As the authors explain, law incorporates values through the language of political and legal debates over law enactment, as well as through statutory and court language.

12. Constable, *Our Word Is Our Bond: How Legal Speech Acts*, 132.

13. Darian-Smith, "Precedents of Injustice," 65.

14. Bruyneel, *Settler Memory*, 13.

15. Debra Thompson, "Through, Against and Beyond the Racial State: The Transnational Stratum of Race," *Cambridge Review of International Affairs* 26, no. 1 (2013).

16. Darian-Smith, "Precedents of Injustice," 66.

17. James Boyd White, *Heracles' Bow: Essays on the Rhetoric and Poetics of the Law* (Madison: University of Wisconsin Press, 1985), xi.

18. Exec. Order No. 13767, 82 C.F.R. 8793 (2017).

19. Proclamation No. 9844, 84 Fed. Reg. 4949 (2019).

20. *The Guardian*, "'Immoral': Nancy Pelosi on Trump's Border Wall—Video (online)," January 4, 2019, https://www.theguardian.com/us-news/video/2019/jan/04/immoral-nancy-pelosi-on-trumps-border-wall-video.

21. Audrey Signer and William L. Painter, *DHS Border Barrier Funding*, Congressional Research Service (January 29, 2020).

22. Eileen Sullivan and Colbi Edmonds, "Biden, the Border, and Why a New Wall Is Going Up," *New York Times*, October 6, 2023, https://www.nytimes.com/2023/10/06/us/border-wall-biden.html#:~:text=Alejandro%20N.,to%20do%20so%20in%202019.

23. See, for instance, Wendy Brown, *Walled States, Waning Sovereignty*, 2nd ed. (New York: Zone Books, 2017); Reece Jones, *Border Walls: Security and the War on Terror in the United States, India and Israel* (London: Zed Books, 2012); Evelyne Ritaine, "La barrière et le checkpoint: mise en politique de l'asymétrie," *Cultures & Conflits* 73 (2009); Jean-Marc Sorel, ed., *Les murs et le droit international* (Paris: Pedone, 2010).

24. See Desmond Manderson, *Songs without Music: Aesthetic Dimensions of Law and Justice* (Berkeley: University of California Press, 2000); Brian E. Butler, "Aesthetics and American Law," 27, no. 1 (2003).

25. Peter Goodrich, "Specula Laws: Image, Aesthetic and Common Law," *Law and Critique* 2, no. 2 (1991): 235.

26. Yet, as noted in chapter 2, its monumentality simultaneously reassures, much like the walls of a home make us feel sheltered from outside threats.

27. Goodrich, "Specula Laws," 235.

28. E. Tendayi Achiume, "Racial Borders," *Georgetown Law Journal* 110, no. 3 (2022).

29. Achiume, "Racial Borders," 448.

30. Wolfe, *Traces of History*, 17.

31. Ritaine, "La barrière et le checkpoint."

32. It is specifically these "counterhegemonic" pathways—practices that confront dominant discourses—that interest Davina Cooper: "Against the Current: Social Pathways and the Pursuit of Enduring Change," *Feminist Legal Studies* 9, no. 2 (2001).

33. Margaret Davies, "Exclusion and the Identity of Law" *Macquarie Law Journal* 5 (2005): 6.

Appendix

1. *USA Today*, "The Wall," 2017, https://www.usatoday.com/border-wall/; Nash Jenkins, "Donald Trump's Border Wall Is Already a Reality in This Texas Town," *Time*, May 1, 2018, https://time.com/5260569/brownsville-border-wall-texas-mexico/. For this review of the walled border, I relied primarily on my partial tour of the border in July and August 2016 and a *USA Today* 2017 report, which provides the most complete picture of the border wall structure. Some of the sections described may have been replaced by more robust fences since the report was produced. I relied on news reports and an interactive map by Customs and Border Protection to identify sections of the border where bollard-style walls have replaced older fences: US Customs and Border Protection, "Border Wall System," July 24, 2023, https://www.cbp.gov/border-security/along-us-borders/border-wall-system. Estimates suggest that 452 miles of wall were constructed during Donald Trump's presidency. Of this, only 40 miles were built where there was previously no fence, whereas over 400 miles replaced older structures. These news walls mainly consist of 18- to 30-foot steel bollards with a concrete foundation.

2. USA Today, "The Wall."

3. USA Today, "The Wall."

4. Santa Elena Canyon features the tallest cliffs in the area.

5. US Customs and Border Protection, "Large Groups of Aliens Encountered in Big Bend Sector," news release, March 7, 2019, https://www.cbp.gov/newsroom/local-media-release/large-groups-aliens-encountered-big-bend-sector.

6. Patrick Timmons, "El Paso Border Wall Rises at Place Once Marked by Unity," *United Press International*, October 2 2018, https://www.upi.com/Top_News/US/2018/10/02/El-Paso-border-wall-rises-at-place-once-marked-by-unity/3151538421151/.

7. USA Today, "The Wall."; Karklis et al., "Borderline: Navigating the Invisible Boundary and Physical Barriers that Define the U.S.-Mexico Border," *Washington Post*, October 17 2018, https://www.washingtonpost.com/graphics/2018/national/us-mexico-border-flyover/.

8. Ronald Rael and Teddy Cruz, *Borderwall as Architecture: A Manifesto for the U.S.-Mexico Boundary* (Oakland: University of California Press, 2017), 12.

Bibliography

Articles and Books

Achiume, E. Tendayi. "Racial Borders." *Georgetown Law Journal* 110, no. 3 (2022): 445–508.

Adelman, Robert, Lesley Williams Reid, Gail Markle, Saskia Weiss, and Charles Jaret. "Urban Crime Rates and the Changing Face of Immigration: Evidence across Four Decades." *Journal of Ethnicity in Criminal Justice* 15, no. 1 (2017): 52–77.

Agnew, John. "The Territorial Trap: The Geographical Assumptions of International Relations Theory." *Review of International Political Economy: RIPE* 1, no. 1 (1994): 53–80.

Ahmed, Sara. "Collective Feelings: Or, the Impressions Left by Others." *Theory, Culture & Society* 21, no. 2 (2004): 25–42.

Ahmed, Sara. *The Cultural Politics of Emotion*. 2nd ed. Edinburgh: Edinburgh University Press, 2014.

Ahmed, Sara. *Living a Feminist Life*. Durham, NC: Duke University Press, 2017

Ahmed, Sara. "A Phenomenology of Whiteness." *Feminist Theory* 8, no. 2 (2007): 149–68.

Anderson, Benedict. *Imagined Communities: Reflections on the Origin and Spread of Nationalism*. Rev. ed. London: Verso, 2016.

Andreas, Peter. *Border Games: Policing the U.S.-Mexico Divide*. 2nd ed. Ithaca, NY: Cornell University Press, 2009.

Andreas, Peter. "The Escalation of U.S. Immigration Control in the Post-NAFTA Era." *Political Science Quarterly* 113, no. 4 (1998): 591–615.

Anzaldúa, Gloria. *Borderlands/La Frontera: The New Mestiza*. 5th ed. San Francisco: Aunt Lute Books, 2022.

Ashworth, Gregory, and David M. Bruce. "Town Walls, Walled Towns and Tourism: Paradoxes and Paradigms." *Journal of Heritage Tourism* 4, no. 4 (2009): 299–313.

Ashworth, Gregory, and M. J. Kuipers. "Managing the Heritage of Fortress Towns: The Cases of Naarden and Bourtange." In *The Construction of Built Heritage: A North European Perspective on Policies, Practices and Outcomes*, edited by Gregory Ashworth, Angela Phelps, and Bengt O.H. Johannsson 131–43. Aldershot, UK: Ashgate, 2002.

Balderrama, Francisco E., and Raymond Rodriguez. *Decade of Betrayal: Mexican Repatriation in the 1930s*. Albuquerque: University of New Mexico Press, 1995.

Barad, Karen. "Posthumanist Performativity: Toward an Understanding of How Matter Comes to Matter." *Signs: Journal of Women in Culture and Society* 28, no. 3 (2003): 801–31.

Beaulieu-Brossard, Philippe, and Charles-Philippe David. "Le blindage des frontières selon les théories des Relations Internationales: contribution et dialogue." *L'Espace Politique* 20 (2013), http://journals.openedition.org/espacepolitique/2637.

Beauvoir, Simone de. *Le Deuxième Sexe*. Paris: Gallimard, 1949.

Bhabha, Homi K. *The Location of Culture*. 2nd ed. London: Routledge, 2004.

Bissonnette, Andréanne, and Élisabeth Vallet, eds. *Borders and Border Walls: In-Security, Symbolism, Vulnerabilities*. Abingdon, UK: Routledge, 2021.

Blomley, Nicholas K. "From 'What?' to 'So What?': Law and Geography in Retrospect." In *Law and Geography*, edited by Jane Holder and Carolyn Harrison, 17–33. Oxford: Oxford University Press, 2003.

Blomley, Nicholas K. *Law, Space, and the Geographies of Power*. New York: Guilford, 1994.

Boucher, Vincent, Christophe Cloutier-Roy, and Élisabeth Vallet. "Frontiérités Québécoises: Représentations de la zone transfrontalière québéco-américaine au Congrès des États-Unis, 2001–2016." *Canadian Geographer* 63, no. 1 (2019): 27–42.

Boyce, Geoffrey Alan, Samuel N. Chambers, and Sarah Launius. "Bodily Inertia and the Weaponization of the Sonoran Desert in US Boundary Enforcement: A GIS Modeling of Migration Routes through Arizona's Altar Valley." *Journal on Migration and Human Security* 7, no. 1 (2019): 23–35.

Braverman, Irus. *Planted Flags: Trees, Land, and Law in Israel/Palestine*. New York: Cambridge University Press, 2009.

Brighenti, Andrea Mubi. "Lines, Barred Lines. Movement, Territory and the Law." *International Journal of Law in Context* 6, no. 3 (2010): 217–27.

Brooks, Peter. "The Law as Narrative and Rhetoric." In *Law's Stories: Narrative and Rhetoric in the Law*, edited by Peter Brooks and Paul Gewirtz. New Haven, CT: Yale University Press, 1996.

Brooks, Peter, and Paul Gewirtz, eds. *Law's Stories: Narrative and Rhetoric in the Law*. New Haven, CT: Yale University Press, 1996.

Brossat, Alain. "Préface." In *Histoire Politique Du Barbelé*, 7–21. Paris: Flammarion, 2009.

Brown, Wendy. *Walled States, Waning Sovereignty*. 2nd ed. New York: Zone Books, 2017.

Brunet-Jailly, Emmanuel, "Special Section: Borders, Borderlands and Theory: An Introduction." *Geopolitics* 16 (2011): 1–6.

Bruyneel, Kevin. *Settler Memory: The Disavowal of Indigeneity and the Politics of Race in the United States.* Chapel Hill: University of North Carolina Press, 2021.

Buchanan, Patrick J. *State of Emergency: The Third World Invasion and Conquest of America.* New York: Thomas Dunne Books/St. Martin's, 2006.

Burgis, Michelle L. *Boundaries of Discourse in the International Court of Justice: Mapping Arguments in Arab Territorial Disputes.* Leiden: Martinus Nijhoff, 2009.

Bustamante, Jorge A. "The 'Wetback' as Deviant: An Application of Labeling Theory." *American Journal of Sociology* 77, no. 4 (1972): 706–18.

Butler, Brian E. "Aesthetics and American Law." *Legal Studies Forum* 27, no. 1 (2003): 203–20.

Calavita, Kitty. *Inside the State: The Bracero Program, Immigration, and the I.N.S.* New York: Routledge, 1992.

Calavita, Kitty. *Invitation to Law and Society: An Introduction to the Study of Real Law.* Chicago: University of Chicago Press, 2010.

Cárdenas, Gilberto. "United States Immigration Policy toward Mexico: An Historical Perspective." *Chicano-Latino Law Review* 2 (1975).

Casey, Edward S., and Mary M. Watkins. *Up against the Wall: Re-Imagining the U.S.-Mexico Border.* Austin: University of Texas Press, 2014.

Chacón, Jennifer M. "Essay: Immigration and the Bully Pulpit." *Harvard Law Review* 130, no. 7 (2017).

Chacón, Jennifer M. "Unsecured Borders: Immigration Restrictions, Crime Control and National Security." *Connecticut Law Review* 39, no. 5 (2007): 1827–92.

Chaichian, Mohammad A. *Empires and Walls: Globalization, Migration, and Colonial Domination.* Chicago: Haymarket Books, 2014.

Chavez, Leo R. *The Latino Threat: Constructing Immigrants, Citizens, and the Nation.* 2nd ed. Stanford, CA: Stanford University Press, 2013.

Chemillier-Gendreau, Monique. "Les murs, quelles conséquences en matière de droit humanitaire et de droits de l'Homme?." In *Les murs en droit international,* edited by Jean-Marc Sorel, 161–70. Paris: Pedone, 2010.

Chryssostalis, Julia H. "Reading Arendt 'Reading' Schmitt: Reading Nomos Otherwise?" In *Feminist Encounters with Legal Philosophy,* edited by Maria Drakopoulou, 158–84. Abingdon, UK: Routledge, 2013.

Cloatre, Emilie, and Dave Cowan. "Legalities and Materialities." In *Routledge Handbook of Law and Theory,* edited by Andreas Philippopoulos-Mihalopoulos, 433–52. London: Routledge, 2019.

Colin, Nicole, Corine Defrance, Ulrich Pfeil, and Joachim Umlauf, eds. *Le mur de Berlin: histoire, mémoires, représentations.* Bruxelles: Peter Lang, 2016.

Constable, Marianne. "Law as Language." *Critical Analysis of Law: An International & Interdisciplinary Law Review* 1, no. 1 (2014): 63–74.

Constable, Marianne. *Our Word Is Our Bond: How Legal Speech Acts.* Stanford, CA: Stanford University Press, 2014.

Conway, Heather, and John Stannard, eds. *The Emotional Dynamics of Law and Legal Discourse*. Oxford: Hart, 2016.

Cooper, Davina. "Against the Current: Social Pathways and the Pursuit of Enduring Change." *Feminist Legal Studies* 9, no. 2 (2001): 119–48.

Cooper, Davina. "Reading the State as a Multi-Identity Formation: The Touch and Feel of Equality Governance." *Feminist Legal Studies* 19, no. 1 (2011): 3–25.

Cooper, Davina. "Talmudic Territory? Space, Law, and Modernist Discourse." *Journal of Law and Society* 23, no. 4 (1996): 529–48.

Coronado, Irasema. "Towards the Wall between Nogales, Arizona and Nogales, Sonora." In *Borders, Fences and Walls: State of Insecurity?*, edited by Élisabeth Vallet, 247–66. Farnham, UK: Routledge, 2014.

Costas, Douzinas. "The Paradoxes of Human Rights: The Paradox of Human Rights: Costas Douzinas." *Constellations* 20 (2013): 51–67.

Coutin, Susan Bibler. *Legalizing Moves: Salvadoran Immigrants' Struggle for U.S. Residency*. Ann Arbor: University of Michigan Press, 2000.

Cover, Robert M. "The Supreme Court, 1982 Term; Foreword: Nomos and Narrative." *Harvard Law Review* 97, no. 1 (1983): 4–68.

Creighton, Oliver. "Contested Townscapes: The Walled City as World Heritage." *World Archaeology* 39, no. 3 (2007): 339–54.

Dalh, Adam *Empire of the People: Settler Colonialism and the Foundations of Modern Democratic Thought*. Lawrence: University Press of Kansas, 2018.

Darian-Smith, Eve. *Bridging Divides: The Channel Tunnel and English Legal Identity in the New Europe*. Berkeley: University of California Press, 1999.

Darian-Smith, Eve. *Laws and Societies in Global Contexts: Contemporary Approaches*. New York: Cambridge University Press, 2013.

Darian-Smith, Eve. "Precedents of Injustice: Thinking About History in Law and Society Scholarship." In *Studies in Law, Politics and Society; Special Issue Law and Society Reconsidered*, vol. 41, edited by Austin Sarat, 61–81. Bingley, UK: Emerald Group, 2007.

Darian-Smith, Eve. "Rabies Rides the Fast Train: Transnational Interactions in Post-colonial Times." In *The Legal Geographies Reader: Law, Power, and Space*, edited by Nicholas K. Blomley, David Delaney and Richard T. Ford, 187–99. Oxford: Wiley-Blackwell, 2001.

Darian-Smith, Eve. *Religion, Race, Rights: Landmarks in the History of Modern Anglo-American Law*. Oxford: Hart, 2010.

Davies, Margaret. *Asking the Law Question*. 3rd ed. Pyrmont, Australia: Thomson Legal & Regulatory, 2008.

Davies, Margaret. "Exclusion and the Identity of Law." *Macquarie Law Journal* 5 (2005): 5–30.

Davies, Margaret. "Home and State: Reflections on Metaphor and Practice." *Griffith Law Review* 23, no. 2 (2014): 153–75.

Davies, Margaret. *Law Unlimited: Materialism, Pluralism, and Legal Theory*. Abingdon, UK: Routledge, 2017.

Dear, Michael J. *Why Walls Won't Work: Repairing the US-Mexico Divide.* New York: Oxford University Press, 2013.

Defrance, Corine, "'Cette histoire de la brutalité du mur': du 'viol de Berlin' au symbole de la Liberté." In *Le mur de Berlin: histoire, mémoires, représentations*, edited by Nicole Colin, Corine Defrance, Ulrich Pfeil, and Joachim Umlauf, 61–78. Bruxelles: Peter Lang, 2016.

Delaney, David. *The Spatial, the Legal and the Pragmatics of World-Making: Nomospheric Investigations.* New York: Routledge, 2010.

Delaney, David. *Territory: A Short Introduction.* Malden, MA: Blackwell, 2005.

De Léon, Jason, *The Land of Open Graves: Living and Dying on the Migrant Trail.* Oakland: University of California Press, 2015.

Demata, Massimiliano. *Discourses of Borders and the Nation in the USA: A Discourse-Historical Analysis.* London: Routledge, 2023.

De Saint Victor, Jacques. "Le retour des murs: une mondialisation fermée?." *Cités* 31 (2007): 15–20.

Dhamoon, Rita. "A Feminist Approach to Decolonizing Anti-Racism: Rethinking Transnationalism, Intersectionality, and Settler Colonialism." *Feral Feminisms* 4 (Summer 2015) 20–37.

Díaz-Barriga, Miguel and Margaret E. Dorsey. *Fencing in Democracy: Border Walls, Necrocitizenship, and the Security State.* Durham, NC: Duke University Press, 2020.

Douglas, Mary. "The Idea of a Home: A Kind of Space." *Social Research* 58, no. 1 (1991): 287–307.

Douglas, Mary. *Purity and Danger: An Analysis of Concepts of Pollution and Taboo.* London: Routledge, 2002.

Dusenberry, William. "Foot and Mouth Disease in Mexico, 1946–1951." *Agricultural History* 29, no. 2 (1955): 82–90.

Edelman, Murray J. *The Symbolic Uses of Politics.* Urbana: University of Illinois Press, 1964.

Elcioglu, Emine Fidan. *Divided by the Wall: Progressive and Conservative Immigration Politics at the U.S.-Mexico Border.* Oakland: University of California Press, 2020.

Fabri, Hélène R."Murs, accessibilité et libre circulation." In *Les murs en droit international*, ed. Jean-Marc Sorel, 153–59. Paris: Pedone, 2010.

Farris, Emily M., and Heather Silber Mohamed. "Picturing Immigration: How the Media Criminalizes Immigrants." *Politics, Groups & Identities* 6, no. 4 (2018): 814–24.

Feinstein, Barry A., and Justus Reid Weiner. "Israel's Security Barrier: An International Comparative Analysis." *George Washington International Law Review* 37, no. 309 (2005): 309–467.

Feldman, David. "Beginning at the Beginning: The Relationships between Politics and Law." In *Law in Politics, Politics in Law*, edited by David Feldman, 3–14. Oxford: Hart, 2013.

Fernández-Kelly, Patricia, and Douglas S. Massey. "Borders for Whom? The Role of NAFTA in Mexico-U.S. Migration." *Annals of the American Academy of Political and Social Science* 610, no. 1 (2007): 98–118.

Fish, Allison. "A Border Seeping in All Directions: Technologies of Separation Along the U.S.-Mexico Border in Ambos Nogales." In *Information, Technology and Control in a Changing World*, edited by Blayne Haggart, Kathryn Henne and Natasha Tusikov, 247–72. Cham, Switzerland: Springer, 2019.

Fisher, David. "The U.S.-Mexico Border Wall and the Case for 'Environmental Rights.'" *Texas International Law Journal* 50, no. 1 (2015): 145–68.

Foley, Neil. *Mexicans in the Making of America*. Cambridge, MA: Harvard University Press, 2014.

Foucher, Michel. *L'obsession des frontières*. Paris: Perrin, 2012.

Ford, Richard T. "Law's Territory (A History of Jurisdiction)." *Michigan Law Review* 97, no. 4 (1999): 843–930.

Fowler, Norma, Tim Keitt, Olivia Schmidt, Martin Terry, and Keeper Trout. "Border Wall: Bad for Biodiversity." *Frontiers in Ecology and the Environment* 16, no. 3 (2018): 137–38.

Ganivet, Elisa. *Esthétique du mur géopolitique*. Québec: Presses de l'Université du Québec, 2015.

Gareau, Jean-François. "Shouting at the Wall: Self-Determination and the Legal Consequences of the Construction of a Wall in the Occupied Palestinian Territory." *Leiden Journal of International Law* 18, no. 3 (2005): 489–521.

Genova, Nicholas de. "The Legal Production of Mexican/Migrant 'Illegality.'" In *Governing Immigration Through Crime*, edited by Julie A. Dowling and Jonathan Xavier Inda, 41–58. Stanford, CA: Stanford University Press, 2020.

Gerstle, Gary. *American Crucible: Race and Nation in the Twentieth Century*. Princeton, NJ: Princeton University Press, 2017.

Geslin, Albane. "Sémantique, sémiotique et matérialité des murs." In *Les murs en droit international*, edited by Jean-Marc Sorel, 47–74. Paris: Pedone, 2010.

Gilman, Denise. "Seeking Breaches in the Wall: An International Human Rights Law Challenge to the Texas-Mexico Border Wall." *Texas International Law Journal* 46, no. 2 (2011): 257–94.

Glenn, Evelyn Nakano. "Settler Colonialism as Structure: A Framework for Comparative Studies of U.S. Race and Gender Formation." *Sociology of Race and Ethnicity* 1, no. 1 (2015): 52–72.

Golunov, Serghei. "Border Fences in the Globalizing World: Beyond Traditional Geopolitics and Post-positivist Approaches." In *Borders, Fences and Walls: State of Insecurity?*, edited by Élisabeth Vallet, 117–29. Farnham, UK: Routledge, 2014.

Goodall, Laura M. "The 'Otherized' Latino: Edward Said's Orientalism Theory and Reforming Suspect Class Analysis." *University of Pennsylvania Journal of Constitutional Law* 16, no. 3 (2014): 835–60.

Goodrich, Peter. "Specula Laws: Image, Aesthetic and Common Law." *Law and Critique* 2, no. 2 (1991): 233–54.

Gordon, Hannah. "Cowboys and Indians: Settler Colonialism and the Dog Whistle in U.S. Immigration Policy." *University of Miami Law Review* 74, no. 2 (2020): 520–62.

Gordon, Linda. *The Great Arizona Orphan Abduction*. Cambridge, MA: Harvard University Press, 1999.

Gross, Aeyal M. "The Construction of a Wall between The Hague and Jerusalem: The Enforcement and Limits of Humanitarian Law and the Structure of Occupation." *Leiden Journal of International Law* 19, no. 2 (2006): 393–440.

Guardino, Peter. *The Dead March: A History of the Mexican-American War*. Cambridge, MA: Harvard University Press, 2017.

Gulasekaram, Pratheepan. "Why a Wall." *UC Irvine Law Review* 2, no. 1 (2012): 147–92.

Gutiérrez, David. *Walls and Mirrors: Mexican Americans, Mexican Immigrants, and the Politics of Ethnicity*. Berkeley: University of California Press, 1995.

Hadley, Eleanor M. "A Critical Analysis of the Wetback Problem." *Law and Contemporary Problems* 21, no. 2 (1956): 334–57.

Hall, Stuart. "Race—The Sliding Signifier." In *The Fateful Triangle*, 31–79. Cambridge, MA: Harvard University Press, 2017.

Hall, Stuart, and Charlotte Brunsdon. *Writings on Media: History of the Present. Stuart Hall: Selected Writings*. Durham, NC: Duke University Press, 2021.

Haltinner, Kristin. "Minutewomen, Victims, and Parasites: The Discursive and Performative Construction of Women by the Minuteman Civil Defense Corps." *Sociological Inquiry* 86, no. 4 (2016): 593–617.

Haney-López, Ian. *White by Law: The Legal Construction of Race*. Rev. and updated 10th anniversary ed. New York: New York University Press, 2006.

Harrall, Simon. "The Federal Government's Power of Eminent Domain over State Lands Regarding the U.S.-Mexico Border Wall." *Houston Law Review* 56, no. 3 (2019): 635–66.

Hartman, Saidiya V. *Lose Your Mother: A Journey along the Atlantic Slave Route*. New York: Farrar, Straus and Giroux, 2008.

Hassner, Ron E., and Jason Wittenberg. "Barriers to Entry: Who Builds Fortified Boundaries and Why?" *International Security* 40, no. 1 (2015): 157–90.

Hataley, Todd, and Scott J. Mason. "Collective Efficacy Across Borders: The Case of Stanstead, Quebec and Derby Line, Vermont." *Journal of Borderlands Studies* 33, no. 3 (2018): 433–44.

Herzog, Benno. *Discourse Analysis as Social Critique: Discursive and Non-Discursive Realities in Critical Social Research*. London: Palgrave Macmillan, 2016.

Hirst, Paul Q. *Space and Power: Politics, War and Architecture*. Cambridge: Polity, 2005.

Jacobson, Matthew Frye. *Whiteness of a Different Color: European Immigrants and the Alchemy of Race*. Cambridge, MA: Harvard University Press, 1998.

Johnson, Jennifer L. *Border Politics*. New York: New York University Press, 2020.

Johnson, Kevin R. "An Essay on Immigration Politics, Popular Democracy, and California's Proposition 187: The Political Relevance and Legal Irrelevance of Race." *Washington Law Review* 70, no. 3 (1995): 629–74.

Jones, Reece. *Border Walls: Security and the War on Terror in the United States, India and Israel.* London: Zed Books, 2012.

Jutte, Daniel. "Entering a City: On a Lost Early Modern Practice." *Urban History* 41, no. 2 (2014): 204–27.

Kang, S. Deborah. *The INS on the Line: Making Immigration Law on the US-Mexico Border, 1917–1954.* New York: Oxford University Press, 2017.

Keenan, Sarah. *Subversive Property: Law and the Production of Spaces of Belonging.* Abingdon, UK: Routledge, 2014

Kenwick, Michael R., and Beth A. Simmons. "Pandemic Response as Border Politics." *International Organization* 74, no. S1 (2020): E36– E58.

Kesby, Alison. "The Shifting and Multiple Border and International Law." *Oxford Journal of Legal Studies* 27, no. 1 (2007): 101–19.

Kleinhans, Martha-Marie, and Roderick A. Macdonald. "What Is a Critical Legal Pluralism?" *Canadian Journal of Law and Society* 12, no. 2 (1997): 25–46.

Kohen, Marcelo G. "Murs, souveraineté et frontières," In *Les murs en droit international*, edited by Jean-Marc Sorel, 127–34. Paris: Pedone, 2010.

Konrad, Victor, and Emmanuel Brunet-Jailly. "Approaching Borders, Creating Borderland Spaces, and Exploring the Evolving Borders between Canada and the United States." *Canadian Geographer* 63, no. 1 (2019): 4–10.

Konrad, Victor A., and Heather N. Nicol. *Beyond Walls: Re-Inventing the Canada-United States Borderlands.* London: Routledge, 2016.

Koskenniemi, Martti. "Letter to the Editors of the Symposium." *American Journal of International Law* 93, no. 2 (1999): 351–61.

Laclau, Ernesto, and Chantal Mouffe. *Hegemony and Socialist Strategy: Towards a Radical Democratic Politics.* 2nd ed. London: Verso, 2014.

Lara-Valencia, Francisco, and Margaret Wilder. "Jump It, Climb It, Dig It for the Environment: Meddling with Trump's Border Wall." *Journal of Latin American Geography* 17, no. 3 (2018): 258–61.

Latour, Bruno. *The Making of Law: An Ethnography of the Conseil d'Etat.* Cambridge: Polity, 2010.

Lavorel, Sabine. "Walls and Access to Natural Resources." In *Borders, Fences and Walls: State of Insecurity?*, edited by Élisabeth Vallet, 159–74. Farnham, UK: Routledge, 2014.

Leuenberger, Christine. "Constructions of the Berlin Wall: How Material Culture Is Used in Psychological Theory." *Social Problems* 53, no. 1 (2006): 18–37.

Leuenberger, Christine. "Technologies, Practices and the Reproduction of Conflict: The Impact of the West Bank Barrier on Peace Building" In *Borders, Fences and Walls: State of Insecurity?*, edited by Élisabeth Vallet, 211–30. Farnham, UK: Routledge, 2014.

Longo, Matthew. *The Politics of Borders: Sovereignty, Security, and the Citizen after 9/11.* Cambridge: Cambridge University Press, 2017.

Macías-Rojas, Patrisia. "Immigration and the War on Crime: Law and Order Politics and the Illegal Immigration Reform and Immigrant Responsibility Act of 1996." *Journal on Migration and Human Security* 6, no. 1 (2018): 1–25.

Madsen, Kenneth D. "A Basis for Bordering: Land, Migration, and Inter-Tohono O'odham Distinction along the US-Mexico Line." In *Placing the Border in Everyday Life*, edited by Reece Jones and Corey Johnson, 93–116. Abingdon, UK: Routledge, 2016.

Madsen, Kenneth D. "Institutionalising the Exception: Homeland Security Section 102(c) Waivers and the Construction of Border Barriers." *Geopolitics* 28, no. 5 (2023): 1783–806.

Mafart, Bertrand, and Jean-Luc Perret. "Histoire du concept de la quarantaine." *Médecine Tropicale* 58 2S (1998): 14–20.

Malagamba-Ansótegui, Amelia, and Sarah J. Moore. "A Conversation on Border Art and Space." In *Border Spaces: Visualizing the US-Mexico Frontera*, edited by Katherine G. Morrissey and John-Michael H. Warner, 113–33. Tucson: University of Arizona Press, 2018.

Manderson, Desmond. "Beyond the Provincial: Space, Aesthetics, and Modernist Legal Theory." *Melbourne University Law Review* 20, no. 4 (1997): 1048–71.

Manderson, Desmond. "Interstices: New Work on Legal Spaces." *Law, Text, Culture* 9 (2005): 1–10.

Manderson, Desmond. "Introduction: Imaginal Law." In *Law and the Visual: Representations, Technologies, and Critique*, edited by Desmond Manderson, 3–20. Toronto: University of Toronto Press, 2018.

Manderson, Desmond. *Songs without Music: Aesthetic Dimensions of Law and Justice.* Berkeley: University of California Press, 2000.

Maril, Robert Lee. *The Fence: National Security, Public Safety, and Illegal Immigration along the U.S.-Mexico Border.* Lubbock: Texas Tech University Press, 2011.

Marshall, Tim. *The Age of Walls: How Barriers between Nations Are Changing Our World.* New York: Scribner, 2018.

Martínez, Oscar J. "Border Conflict, Border Fences, and the 'Tortilla Curtain' Incident of 1978–1979." *Journal of the Southwest* 50, no. 3 (2008): 263–78.

Massey, Douglas S., Jorge Durand, and Karen A. Pren. "Why Border Enforcement Backfired." *American Journal of Sociology* 121, no. 5 (2016): 1557–600.

McAlinden, Anne-Marie. "Re-Emotionalising Regulatory Responses to Child Sex Offenders." In *The Emotional Dynamics of Law and Legal Discourse*, edited by Heather Conway and John Stannard. Oxford: Hart, 2016.

McGuire, Randall H. "Steel Walls and Picket Fences: Rematerializing the U.S.–Mexican Border in Ambos Nogales." *American Anthropologist* 115, no. 3 (2013): 466–80.

McLaughlin, Michael R. "The Dawes Act, or Indian General Allotment Act of 1887: The Continuing Burden of Allotment. A Selective Annotated Bibliography." *American Indian Culture and Research Journal* 20 (1996): 59–105.

Meinig, Donald W. "The Beholding Eye: Ten Versions of the Same Scene." In *The Interpretation of Ordinary Landscapes: Geographical Essays*, edited by Donald W. Meinig and John B. Jackson. New York: Oxford University Press, 1979.

Meissner, Doris. "Keynote Address," *Temple Political & Civil Rights Law Review* 16, no. 2 (Spring 2007): 309–20.

Miller, Nicole. "How Property Rights Are Affected by the Texas-Mexico Border Fence: A Failure Due to Insufficient Procedure." *Texas International Law Journal* 45, no. 3 (2010): 631–54.

Mitchell, W. J. Thomas. *Landscape and Power*. 2nd ed. Chicago: University of Chicago Press, 2002.

Morales, Daniel Ibsen. "In Democracy's Shadow: Fences, Raids, and the Production of Migrant Illegality," *Stanford Journal of Civil Rights & Civil Liberties* 5, no. 1 (April 2009): 23–88.

Nail, Thomas. *Theory of the Border*. New York: Oxford University Press, 2016.

Nash, Lindsay. "Mending Wall: Playing the Game of Neighborhood Ordering." *Yale Journal of Law & the Humanities* 21, no. 1 (2009): 173–202.

Neal, Mary. "Discovering Dignity: Unpacking the Emotional Content of 'Killing Narratives.'" In *The Emotional Dynamics of Law and Legal Discourse*, edited by Heather Conway and John Stannard, 83–104. Oxford: Hart, 2016.

Nesheim, David. "Machine Guns, Cows, and Quarantines: Foot and Mouth Disease in the United States, Mexico and Argentina." Paper presented at the James A. Rawley Graduate Conference in the Humanities, University of Nebraska, Lincoln, 2006.

Netz, Reviel. *Barbed Wire: An Ecology of Modernity*. Middletown, CT: Wesleyan University Press, 2009.

Neustadt, Robert. "Intervention II: Borders: Strangers and Neighbors: The Tohono O'odham and the Myth of 'Us versus Them' on the US/Mexico Border." *Cross Currents* 67, no. 3 (2017): 577–89.

Nevins, Joseph. *Operation Gatekeeper and Beyond: The War on Illegals and the Remaking of the U.S.-Mexico* Boundary. 2nd ed. New York: Routledge, 2010.

Newman, David. "On Borders and Power: A Theoretical Framework." *Journal of Borderlands Studies* 18, no. 1 (2003): 13–25.

Newman, David, and Anssi Paasi. "Fences and Neighbours in the Postmodern World: Boundary Narratives in Political Geography." *Progress in Human Geography* 22, no. 2 (1998): 186–207.

Ngai, Mae M. *Impossible Subjects Illegal Aliens and the Making of Modern America*. Princeton, NJ: Princeton University Press, 2014.

Nieto-Gomez, Rodrigo. "Walls, Sensors and Drones: Technology and Surveillance on the US-Mexico Border." In *Borders, Fences and Walls: State of Insecurity?*, edited by Élisabeth Vallet, 191–210. Farnham, UK: Routledge, 2014.

Norris, Pippa, Montague Kern, and Marion Just. "Framing Terrorism: The News Media, the Government and the Public." In *Framing Terrorism: The News Media, the Government, and the Public*, edited by Pippa Norris, Montague Kern, Marion Just, 281–302. New York: Routledge, 2003.

Novosseloff, Alexandra. "La vision historique des murs." In *Les murs en droit international*, edited by Jean-Marc Sorel, 27–35. Paris: Pedone, 2010.

Nussbaum, Martha C. *Political Emotions: Why Love Matters for Justice*. Cambridge, MA: Harvard University Press, 2013.

Osete, Jesus A. "The Praetorians: An Analysis of U.S. Border Patrol Checkpoints Following Martinez-Fuerte." *Washington University Law Review* 93 (2016): 803–45.

Scruggs, Otey M. "Texas and the Bracero Program, 1942–1947." *Pacific Historical Review* 32, no. 3 (1963): 251–64.

Paasi, Anssi. "Boundaries as Social Processes: Territoriality in the World of Flows." *Geopolitics* 3, no. 1 (1998): 69–88.

Paz, Moria. "Between the Kingdom and the Desert Sun: Human Rights, Immigration, and Border Walls." *Berkeley Journal of International Law* 34, no. 1 (2016): 1–43.

Pécoud, Antoine, and Paul de Guchteneire. "International Migration, Border Controls and Human Rights: Assessing the Relevance of a Right to Mobility." *Journal of Borderlands Studies* 21, no. 1 (2006): 69–86.

Pedriana, Nicholas, and Robin Stryker. "Political Culture Wars 1960s Style: Equal Employment Opportunity–Affirmative Action Law and the Philadelphia Plan." *American Journal of Sociology* 103, no. 3 (1997): 633–91.

Philippopoulos-Mihalopoulos, Andreas. *Routledge Handbook of Law and Theory.* Abingdon, UK: Routledge, 2018.

Philippopoulos-Mihalopoulos, Andreas. *Spatial Justice: Body, Lawscape, Atmosphere.* Abingdon, UK: Routledge, 2015.

Pusterla, Elia, and Francesca Piccin. "The Loss of Sovereignty Control and the Illusion of Building Walls." *Journal of Borderlands Studies* 27, no. 2 (2012): 121–38.

Quétel, Claude. *Histoire des* murs. Paris: Perrin, 2012.

Rael, Ronald. "Borderwall as Architecture: The Divided States of North America." In *Borderwall as Architecture: A Manifesto for the US-Mexico Boundary*, edited by Ronald Rael, 10–21. Oakland: University of California Press, 2017.

Razac, Olivier. "La gestion de la perméabilité." *L'espace politique* 20 (2013).

Razac, Olivier. *Histoire politique du barbelé.* Paris: Flammarion, 2009.

Regan, Margaret. "How the Border Wall Became a Canvas: Political Art in the U.S.-Mexico Border Towns of Ambos Nogales." In *Border Spaces*, edited by Katherine G. Morrissey and John-Michael H. Warner, 151–74. Tucson: University of Arizona Press, 2018.

Reséndez, Andrés. *Changing National Identities at the Frontier: Texas and New Mexico, 1800–1850.* Cambridge: Cambridge University Press, 2004.

Reséndez, Andrés. "National Identity on a Shifting Border: Texas and New Mexico in the Age of Transition, 1821–1848." *Journal of American History* 86, no. 2 (1999): 668–88.

Ritaine, Evelyne. "La barrière et le checkpoint: mise en politique de l'asymétrie." *Cultures & Conflits* 73 (2009): 15–33.

Roche, Jean-Jacques. "Walls and Borders in a Globalized World: The Paradoxical Revenge of Territorialization." In *Borders, Fences and Walls: State of Insecurity?*, edited by Élisabeth Vallet, 105–14. Farnham, UK: Ashgate, 2014.

Rosière, Stéphane, and Reece Jones. "Teichopolitics: Re-Considering Globalisation Through the Role of Walls and Fences." *Geopolitics* 17, no. 1 (2012): 217–34.

Ruskola, Teemu. "Legal Orientalism." *Michigan Law Review* 101, no. 1 (2002): 179–234.

Ruskola, Teemu. *Legal Orientalism: China, the United States, and Modern Law*. Cambridge, MA: Harvard University Press, 2013.

Sacco, Vincent F., and William Glackman. "Vulnerability, Locus of Control, and Worry about Crime." In *The Fear of Crime*, edited by Jason Ditton and Stephen Farrall, 415–27. Aldershot, UK: Ashgate, 2000.

Saddiki, Said. "Border Fences as an Anti-Immigration Device: A Comparative View of American and Spanish Policies." In *Borders, Fences and Walls: State of Insecurity?*, edited by Élisabeth Vallet, 175–89. Farnham, UK: Routledge, 2014.

Saddiki, Said. *World of Walls: The Structure, Roles and Effectiveness of Separation Barriers*. Cambridge: Open Book, 2017.

Said, Edward W. *Orientalism*. New York: Vintage Books, 1979.

Said, Edward W., Moustafa Bayoumi, and Andrew Rubin. *The Edward Said Reader*. New York: Vintage Books, 2000.

Saint-Exupéry, Antoine de. *Wind, Sand and Stars*. [Terre des Hommes]. Translated by Lewis Galantière. New York: Reynal & Hitchcock, 1939.

Sanders, Carol. *Cours de linguistique générale de Saussure*. Paris: Hachette, 1979.

Sarat, Austin, Lawrence Douglas, and Martha Merrill Umphrey. "Negotiating (with) Strangers." In *Law and the Stranger*, edited by Austin Sarat, Lawrence Douglas, and Martha Merrill Umphrey, 1–20. Stanford, CA: Stanford University Press, 2020.

Saussure, Ferdinand de. *Course in General Linguistics*. Translated by Roy Harris. London: Bloomsbury, 2013.

Schlag, Pierre. "The Aesthetics of American Law." *Harvard Law Review* 115, no. 4 (2002): 1047–118.

Schlögel, Karl. *Le Berlin Russe*. Paris: Éditions de la Maison des Sciences de l'Homme, 2014.

Schneider, Dorothee. *Crossing Borders: Migration and Citizenship in the Twentieth-Century United States*. Cambridge, MA: Harvard University Press, 2011.

Scobbie, Iain. "Unchart(Er)Ed Waters?: Consequences of the Advisory Opinion on the Legal Consequences of the Construction of a Wall in the Occupied Palestinian Territory for the Responsibility of the UN for Palestine." *European Journal of International Law* 16, no. 5 (2005): 94–61.

Scruggs, Otey M. "Texas and the Bracero Program, 1942–1947." *Pacific Historical Review* 32, no. 3 (1963): 251–64.

Shachar, Ayelet. "The Shifting Border of Immigration Regulation." *Michigan Journal of International Law* 30, no. 3 (2009): 809–40.

Shachar, Ayelet. *The Shifting Border: Legal Cartographies of Migration and Mobility: Ayelet Shachar in Dialogue*. Manchester, UK: Manchester University Press, 2020.

Shamir, Ronen. "Without Borders? Notes on Globalization as a Mobility Regime." *Sociological Theory* 23, no. 2 (2005): 197–217.

Shields, Rob. "Spatial Stress and Resistance: Social Meanings of Spatialization." In *Space & Social Theory: Interpreting Modernity and Postmodernity*, edited by Georges Benko and Ulf Strohmayer, 186–202. Oxford: Wiley-Blackwell, 1997.

Slack, Jeremy, and Howard Campbell. "On Narco-Coyotaje: Illicit Regimes and Their Impacts on the U.S.-Mexico Border." In *The Shadow of the Wall: Violence and Migration on the US-Mexico Border*, edited by Jeremy Slack, Daniel E. Martínez and Scott Whiteford, 166–89. Tucson: University of Arizona Press, 2018.

Slotkin, Richard. *The Fatal Environment: The Myth of the Frontier in the Age of Industrialization, 1800–1890*. New York: Atheneum, 1985.

Sorel, Jean-Marc. "Is the Wall Soluble into International Law?" In *Borders, Fences and Walls: State of Insecurity?*, edited by Élisabeth Vallet, 133–41. Farnham, UK: Routledge, 2014.

Sorel, Jean-Marc, ed. *Les murs et le droit international*. Paris: Pedone, 2010.

Sorel, Jean-Marc. "Les murs murent." In *Les murs en droit international*, edited by Jean-Marc Sorel, 7– 23. Paris: Pedone, 2010.

Soto, Gabriella, and Daniel E. Martínez. "The Geography of Migrant Death: Implications for Policy and Forensic Science." In *Sociopolitics of Migrant Death and Repatriation*, edited by Krista E. Latham and Alyson J. O' Daniel, 67–82. Cham, Switzerland: Springer, 2017.

Spener, David. *Clandestine Crossings: Migrants and Coyotes on the Texas-Mexico Border*. Ithaca, NY: Cornell University Press, 2010.

Sterling, Brent L. *Do Good Fences Make Good Neighbors?: What History Teaches Us About Strategic Barriers and International Security*. Washington, DC: Georgetown University Press, 2009.

St. John, Rachel C. *Line in the Sand: A History of the Western U.S.-Mexico Border*. Princeton, NJ: Princeton University Press, 2011.

Stuart, Paul. "United States Indian Policy: From the Dawes Act to the American Indian Policy Review Commission." *Social Service Review (Chicago)* 51, no. 3 (1977): 451–63.

Stumpf, Juliet P. "The Crimmigration Crisis: Immigrants, Crime, and Sovereign Power." In *Governing Immigration Through Crime*, edited by Julie A. Dowling and Jonathan Xavier Inda, 59–76. Stanford, CA: Stanford University Press, 2020.

Szary, Anne-Laure Amilhat. "Walls and Border Art: The Politics of Art Display." *Journal of Borderlands Studies* 27, no. 2 (2012): 213–28.

Tasker, Keegan C. "Waived: The Detrimental Implications of U.S. Immigration and Border Security Measures on Southern Border Tribes; an Analysis of the Impact of President Trump's Border Wall on the Tohono O'odham Nation." *American Indian Law Journal* 8, no. 1 (2019): 303–29.

Theiss-Morse, Elizabeth. *Who Counts as an American?: The Boundaries of National Identity*. Cambridge: Cambridge University Press, 2009.

Thompson, Debra. "Through, Against and Beyond the Racial State: The Transnational Stratum of Race." *Cambridge Review of International Affairs* 26, no. 1 (2013): 133–51.

Thomsen, Charles. "A Border Vision: The International Peace Garden." *Manitoba History* 31 (spring 1996), http://www.mhs.mb.ca/docs/mb_history/31/peacegarden.shtml.

Ticktin, Miriam. "Sexual Violence as the Language of Border Control: Where French Feminist and Anti-immigrant Rhetoric Meet." *Signs: Journal of Women in Culture and Society* 33, no. 4 (2008): 863–89.

Timothy, Dallen J. "Cross-Border Partnership in Tourism Resource Management: International Parks along the US-Canada Border." *Journal of Sustainable Tourism* 7, no. 3–4 (1999): 182–205.

Timothy, Dallen J., and Cevat Tosun. "Tourists' Perceptions of the Canada–USA Border as a Barrier to Tourism at the International Peace Garden." *Tourism Management* (1982) 24, no. 4 (2003): 411–21.

Tomuschat, Christian. "Murs et responsibilité des états." In *Les murs en droit international*, edited by Jean-Marc Sorel, 172–81. Paris: Pedone, 2010.

Trosborg, Anna. *Rhetorical Strategies in Legal Language: Discourse Analysis of Statutes and Contracts*. Tübingen, Germany: Narr, 1997.

Tuan, Yi-Fu. "Space and Place: Humanistic Perspective." In *Philosophy in Geography*, edited by Stephen Gale and Gunnar Olsson, 387–427. Dordrecht, The Netherlands: D. Reidel, 1979.

Tuan, Yi-Fu. *Space and Place: The Perspective of Experience*. Minneapolis: University of Minnesota Press, 1977.

Vagnoux, Isabelle. "États-Unis et Mexique: le mur de la discorde." (2007) 31 *Cités* 41.

Vallet, Élisabeth, ed. *Borders, Fences and Walls: State of Insecurity?* Farnham, UK: Routledge, 2014).

Vallet, Élisabeth, and Charles-Philippe David. "Introduction: The (Re)Building of the Wall in International Relations." *Journal of Borderlands Studies* 27, no. 2 (2012): 111–19.

Vallet, Élisabeth, and Charles-Philippe David. "Walls of Money: Securitization of Border Discourse and Militarization of Markets." In *Borders, Fences and Walls: State of Insecurity?*, edited by Élisabeth Vallet, 155–68. Farnham, UK: Routledge, 2014.

Veracini, Lorenzo. "Introducing: Settler Colonial Studies." *Settler Colonial Studies* 1, no. 1 (2011): 1–12.

Waldron, Arthur. *The Great Wall of China: From History to Myth*. Cambridge: Cambridge University Press, 1990.

Weissman, Deborah. "The Politics of Narrative: Law and the Representation of Mexican Criminality." *Fordham International Law Journal* 38, no. 1 (2015): 141–204.

White, James Boyd. *Heracles' Bow: Essays on the Rhetoric and Poetics of the Law*. Madison: University of Wisconsin Press, 1985.

White, James Boyd. "Law as Rhetoric, Rhetoric as Law: The Arts of Cultural and Communal Life." *University of Chicago Law Review* 52, no. 3 (1985): 684–702.

White, James Boyd. "Rhetoric and Law: The Arts of Cultural and Communal Life." In *The Rhetoric of the Human Sciences: Language and Argument in Scholarship and*

Public Affairs, edited by John S. Nelson, Allan Megill, and Donald N. McCloskey, 298–318. Madison: University of Wisconsin Press, 1987.

Winant, Howard. *The New Politics of Race: Globalism, Difference, Justice*. Minneapolis: University of Minnesota Press, 2004.

Wolfe, Patrick. "Settler Colonialism and the Elimination of the Native." *Journal of Genocide Research* 8, no. 4 (2006): 387–409.

Wolfe, Patrick. *Settler Colonialism and the Transformation of Anthropology: The Politics and Poetics of an Ethnographic Event*. London: Cassell, 1999.

Wolfe, Patrick. *Traces of History: Elementary Structures of Race*. London: Verso, 2016.

Young, Iris Marion. "House and Home: Feminist Variations on a Theme." In *On Female Body Experience*: "Throwing like a Girl" and Other Essays, 123–54. New York: Oxford University Press, 2005.

Young, Iris Marion. "The Ideal of Community and the Politics of Difference." *Social Theory and Practice* 12, no. 1 (1986): 1–26.

Young, Iris Marion. "Throwing like a Girl: A Phenomenology of Feminine Body Comportment Motility and Spatiality." *Human Studies* 3, no. 2 (1980): 137–56.

Legislation

Statutes

Act of August 19, 1935, Pub. L. No. 286, 49 Stat. 660 (1935).

An Act to Authorize the Secretary of Agriculture to Cooperate with the Government of Mexico in the Control and Eradication of Foot-and-mouth Disease and Rinderpest, 1947, Pub. L. No. 8, 61 Stat 7 (1947).

Act of February 27, 1925, Pub. L. No. 68-502, 43 Stat. 1049-1050 (1925).

An Act Making Appropriations for the Department of State, the Department of Commerce, the Department of Justice, and the Federal Judiciary, for the Fiscal Year Ending June 30, 1942, and for Other Purposes, Pub. L. No. 135, 55 Stat. 265, 274 (1941).

An Act Making Appropriations for the Department of State, the Department of Justice, the Department of Commerce, and the Federal Judiciary, for the Fiscal Year Ending June 30, 1943, and for Other Purposes, Pub. L. No. 644, 56 Stat. 468, 477 (1942).

An Act Making Appropriations for the Departments of State and Justice and for the Judiciary, and for the Departments of Commerce and Labor, for the Fiscal Year Ending June 30, 1939, and for Other Purposes, Pub. L. No. 495, 52 Stat. 248, 256 (1938).

An Act Making Appropriations for the Departments of State and Justice and for the Judiciary, and for the Department of Commerce, for the Fiscal Year Ending June 30, 1940, and for Other Purposes, Pub. L. No. 156, 53 Stat. 885, 894 (1939).

Act of March 4, 1929, Pub. L. No. 70-1018, 45 Stat. 1551 (1929).

An Act to Prevent in Time of War Departure from or Entry into the United States Contrary to the Public Safety, Pub. L. No. 65-154, 40 Stat. 559 (1918).

Consolidated Appropriations Act, 2008, Pub. L. No. 110-161, div. E., 121 Stat. 1844 (2007).
Illegal Immigration Reform and Immigrant Responsibility Act of 1996, Pub. L. No. 104-208, Division C, 110 Stat. 3009 (1996).
Immigration Act of 1917, Pub. L. No. 64-301, 39 Stat. 874 (1917).
Immigration and Nationality Act of 1952, Pub. L. No. 82-414, 66 Stat. 163 (1952).
National Prohibition Act, 1919, Pub. L. No. 66-66, 41 Stat. 305-323 (1919).
REAL ID Act of 2005, Pub. L. No. 109-13, 119 Stat. 302 (2005).
Secure Fence Act of 2006, Pub. L. No. 109-367, 120 Stat. 2638 (2006).

Executive Orders and Proclamation

Exec. Order No. 13767, 82 C.F.R. 8793 (2017).
Exec. Order No. 13780, 82 C.F.R. 13209 (2017).
Exec. Order No. 2022-04 (Arizona), Securing Arizona's Southern Border (August 12, 2022).
Proclamation No 9844, 84 Fed. Reg. 4949 (2019).

Bills

Border Protection, Antiterrorism, and Illegal Immigration Control Act of 2005, H.R. 4437, 109th Cong. (2005–2006).
Comprehensive Immigration Reform Act of 2006, S 2611, 109th Cong. (2006).
S.J. Res. 46, 80th Cong. (1947).

Treaties

Convention Between the United States of America and the United Mexican States for the Solution of the Problem of The Chamizal, signed August 29, 1963, 505 U.N.T.S. 185 (entered into force January 14, 1964).
Convention Safeguarding Livestock Interests through the Prevention of Infectious and Contagious Diseases, signed March 16, 1928, T.S. 808 (entered into force January 18, 1930).
International Covenant on Civil and Political Rights, opened for signature December 19, 1966, 999 U.N.T.S. 171 (entered into force March 23, 1976).
Treaty of Peace, Friendship, Limits, and Settlement with the Republic of Mexico (Treaty of Guadalupe Hidalgo), signed February 2, 1848, T.S. 207 (entered into force May 30, 1948).

Cases

United States

Ashcroft v. Sierra Club No. 04-Cv-272, 2005 U.S. Dist. Lexis 44244 (S.D. Cal. Dec. 13, 2005).
County of El Paso, 2008 WL 4372693 (W.D. Tex. August 29, 2008), cert. denied, 129 S. Ct. 2789 (2009).

County of El Paso v. Chertoff, 2008 WL 4372693 (W.D. Tex. August 29, 2008).
Defenders of Wildlife, 527 F. Supp. 2d 119 (D.C., 2007), cert. denied, 128 S. Ct. 2962 (2008).
Defenders of Wildlife v. Chertoff, 527 F. Supp. 2d 119 (D.C. 2007).
Heritage Organization v. Gonzalez, 533 F. Supp. 2d 58 (D.C. 2008).
In Re Border Infrastructure Environmental Litigation, 284 F. Supp. 3d 1092 (S.D. Cal., February 27, 2018).
In Re Border Infrastructure Environmental Litigation, 915 F.3d 1213 (9th Cir., February 22, 2019).
United States v. Arizona, No. 2:10-cv-01413-SRB, Order No. CV 10-1413-PHX-SRB dismissing Az.'s Countercls. (D. Az., Oct. 21, 2011).
United States of America v. Douglas A. Ducey et als. Case 2:22-cv-02107-SMB.

International

Legal Consequences of the Construction of a Wall in the Occupied Palestinian Territory, Advisory Opinion, 2004, I.C.J. Rep. 136 (July 9).

U.S. Congressional Hearings

House of Representatives

Armed and Dangerous: Confronting the Problem of Border Incursions, Subcommittee on Investigations, 109th Congress, 2nd Session (February 7, 2006).
Border Vulnerabilities and International Terrorism, Subcommittee on International Terrorism and Nonproliferation of the Committee on International Relations, 109th Congress, 2nd Session, *Border Vulnerabilities and International Terrorism* (July 5, 7, 2006).
Checking Terrorism at the Border, Subcommittee on International Terrorism and Nonproliferation of the Committee on International Relations, 109th Congress, 2nd Session (April 6, 2006).
Criminal Activity and Violence Along the Southern Border, Subcommittee on Investigations, 109th Congress, 2nd Session (August 16, 2006).
Department of State Appropriation Bill for 1942, Subcommittee of the Committee on Appropriations, 77th Congress, 1st Session (March 7, 1941).
First Deficiency Appropriation Bill for 1946, Subcommittee of the Committee on Appropriations, 79th Congress, 1st Session (November 3, 1945).
First Deficiency Appropriation Bill for 1946, Subcommittee of the Committee on Appropriations, 79th Congress, 1st Session (November 7, 1945).
H.R. 6453, Committee on Foreign Affairs, 74th Congress, 1st Session (March 13, 1935).
H.R. 6453, Subcommittee of the Committee on Foreign Affairs, 74th Congress, 1st Session (March 7, 1935).
Outgunned and Outmanned: Local Law Enforcement Confronts Violence Along the Southern Border, Subcommittee on Immigration, Border Security, and Claims and the Subcommittee on Crime, Terrorism, and Homeland Security of the Committee on the Judiciary, 109th Congress, 2nd Session (March 2, 2006).

Should Mexico Hold Veto Power over U.S. Border Security Decision?, Committee on the Judiciary, 109th Congress, 2nd Session (August 17, 2006).
U.S. Southern Border Security—National Security Implications and Issues for the Armed Services, Committee on Armed Services, 109th Congress, 2nd Session (August 2, 2006)

Senate

H.R. 4276: A Bill Making Appropriations for the Department of State, the Department of Commerce, the Department of Justice, and the Federal Judiciary, for the Fiscal Year Ending June 30, 1942, and for Other Purposes, Subcommittee of the Committee on Appropriations, 77th Congress, 1st Session (April 30, 1941).
S. J. Res. 46, Committee on Foreign Relations, 80th Congress, Executive Session (February 25, 1947).
S. J. Res. 46: Maintenance of the Western Land Boundary Fence Project and the Rio Grande Border Fence Project, Subcommittee of the Committee on Foreign Relations, 80th Congress, 1st Session (March 13, 1947).
Whaling Convention and Protocols, Executives K, L and P; French Tax Convention; Trusteeship Agreement; World Health Organization, S. J. Res. 98; Western Land Boundary Fence, S. J. Res. 46; Appointments in the Diplomatic Service; Anglo-American Petroleum Agreement, Committee on Foreign Relations, 80th Congress, Executive Session (July 1, 1947).

Congressional Records

79 (3) *Cong. Rec.* (1935).
79 (5) *Cong. Rec.* (1935).
79 (12) *Cong. Rec.* (1935).
93 (1) *Cong. Record* (1947).
93 (1) *Congressional Rec.* (1947).
93 (8) *Cong. Rec.* (1947).
142 (4) Cong. Rec. 5304 (1996).
142 (7) Cong. Rec. 9514 (1996).
142 (17) Cong. Rec. 24779 (1996).
151 (21) Cong. Rec. 28690 (2005).
152 (6) Cong. Rec. 8157 (2006).
152 (13) Cong. Rec. 18279 (2006).
152 (16) Cong. Rec. 21395 (2006).

Archival Documents

Battle, Turner W., Assistant to the U.S. Secretary of Labor to Harold L. Ickes, Administrator of Public Work, Washington DC, March 7, 1935, file 55606/894, RG 85, National Archives.
Breedlove, E. C., President, First National Bank, Harlingen to Tom Connally, U.S. Senator, February 11, 1947, file 2750605, RG 59, National Archives.

Brownell, Herbert Jr., U.S. Attorney-General to John Foster Dulles, Secretary of State, January 19, 1956, file 56364/44.14, RG 85, National Archives.

Campbell, J. D., W. A. Bishops, and W. S. Livingston to E. H. Moore, U.S. Senator, February 3, 1947, file 2750605, RG 59, National Archives.

Collaer, Nick D. , and H. C. Horsley to District Inspector, Immigration and Naturalization Service, February 23, 1934, file 55606/894 RG 85, National Archives.

Cousar, R. M., Inspector in Charge, Nogales, to District Director, Immigration Service, El Paso, November 22, 1928, file 55 606/894, RG 85, National Archives.

Fleming, Boynton H., Sheriff, Cameron County to Fletcher L. Rawls, Chief Border, McAllen, March 17, 1953, file 56364/44.15, RG 85, National Archives.

Folk, R. G., to Congressman R. E. Thomason, U.S. House of Representatives, December 7, 1933, file 55606/894, RG 85, National Archives.

Gross, Leslie M., Lt Colonel, CE, Executive Officer, U.S. Army Engineers to Division Engineer, Southwestern Division, September 10, 1953, file 56364/44.14, RG 85, National Archives.

Guseman, John L., Chief of Police, Harlington, to Fletcher L. Rawls, Chief Border Patrol Inspector, McAllen, March 9, 1953, file 56364/44.15, RG 85, National Archives.

Heller, Paul, Ellis Seed Company, Weslaco, to Tom Connally, U.S. Senator, March 24, 1947, file 2750605, RG 59, National Archives.

Horsley, H. C., Chief Patrol Inspector, El Paso, to District Inspector, Immigration and Naturalization Service, El Paso, February 23, 1934, file 55606/894, RG 85, National Archives.

Horsley, H. C., Chief Patrol Inspector, El Paso, to G. C. Wilmoth, District Director, Immigration and Naturalization Service, El Paso, April 21, 1937, file 55 606/519, RG 85, National Archives.

Hurst, Walter, President, Pharr Chamber of Commerce, to Arthur Vandenberg, U.S. Senator, March 11, 1947, file 2750605, RG 59, National Archives.

Jackson, Roy, District Attorney, El Paso, to Grover C. Wilmoth, District Director, Immigration and Naturalization Service, El Paso, February 26, 1934, file 55606/894, RG 85, National Archives.

Kelley, D. R., to W. F. Kelly, memorandum of telephone conversation, September 11, 1953, file 56364/44.14, RG 85, National Archives.

Kelly, W. F., and D. R. Kelley, Ground Survey for Proposed Fence in McAllen Sector, September 15, 1953, file 56364/44.14, RG 85, National Archives.

Krausse, Gus O., Chief of Police, Brownsville, to Fletcher L. Rawls, Chief Border Patrol Inspector, McAllen, March 19, 1947, file 56364/44.15, RG 85, National Archives.

Landon, H. R., District Director, Los Angeles, to Commissioner, Central Office, August 14, 1954, file 56364/44.14, RG 85, National Archives.

MacCormack, D. W., General Commissioner of Immigration to Morris Sheppard, Chairman of the Committee on Military Affairs, U.S. Senate, January 18, 1934, file 55606/894, RG 85, National Archives.

McAllen Chamber of Commerce (Directors) to Tom Connally, U.S. Senator, February 13, 1947, file 2750605, RG 59, National Archives.

McDowell, John, U.S. House Representative, to Tom C. Clark, U.S. Attorney-General, June 3, 1947, file 56364/042.40, RG 85, National Archives.

Norton, C. A., President, Weslaco Chamber of Commerce, to Tom Connally, U.S. Senator, February 13, 1947, file 2750605, RG 59, National Archives.

O' Brien, J. E., President, Kiwanis Club of Brownsville, to Lyndon B. Johnson, U.S. Senator, April 21, 1955, file 56364/44.15, RG 85, National Archives.

Perkins, Frances, Secretary of Labor, to Administrator of Public Works, Washington DC, March 7, 1934, file 55606/894, RG 85, National Archives.

Perkins, Frances, Secretary of Labor, to Cordell Hull, Secretary of State, August 7, 1935, file 55606/894, RG 85, National Archives.

Perkins, Frances, Secretary of Labor, to Harry L. Hopkins, Works Progress Administration, August 26, 1935, file 56364/44.14, RG 85, National Archives.

Saunders, Richardson, Assistant Secretary of Labor, to Frank C. Walker, Executive Director, Division of Applications and Information, National Emergency Council, September 7, 1935, file 55606/894, RG 85, National Archives.

Sheppard, Morris, Chairman of the Committee on Military Affairs, U.S. Senate, to Daniel MacCormack, Commissioner General of Immigration, January 8, 1934, file 55606/894, RG 85, National Archives.

Snow, David, Patrol Inspector in Charge, Brownsville, Texas, report to Fletcher L. Rawls, Chief Patrol Inspector, McAllen, Texas, March 20, 1953, file 56363/44.14, RG 85, National Archives.

Stirton, J. K., to Tom Connally, U.S. Senator, February 6, 1947, file 2750605, RG 59, National Archives.

Swanson, John P., Chief Regional Enforcement Officer (Acting), Southwest Region, to Frank H. Partridge, Special Assistant to Commissioner, April 6, 1955, file 56364/44.14, RG 85, National Archives.

Swing, J. M., Commissioner General, Immigration and Naturalization Service, to Senator Paul H. Douglas, March 29, 1956, file 56364/44.15, RG 85, National Archives.

Wilmoth, G. C., District Director, Immigration Service, El Paso, to Commissioner General of Immigration, Washington, DC, May 2, 1930, file 55606/519, RG 85, National Archives.

Wilmoth, G. C., District Director, Immigration and Naturalization Service, El Paso, to W. H. Wagner, Immigration and Naturalization Service, September 9, 1936, file 55606/894, RG 85, National Archives.

Others

Alhambra Post Advocate. "San Ysidro, Calexico Held Prime Immigration 'Leaks.'" June 18, 1947.

American Civil Liberties Union. "CA's Anti-immigrant Proposition 187 Is Voided, Ending State's Five-Year Battle with ACLU, Rights Groups." July 29, 1999, https://www.aclu.org/press-releases/cas-anti-immigrant-proposition-187-voided-ending-states-five-year-battle-aclu-rights>.

Amnesty International USA. *In Hostile Terrain: Human Rights Violations in Immigration Enforcement in the US Southwest.* New York: Amnesty International USA, 2012.

Argueta, Carla N. *Border Security: Immigration Enforcement Between Ports of Entry.* Congressional Research Service, 2016.

At the Edge. "Friendship Park." 2023, http://www.attheedges.com/border-stories/friendship-park/.

Bain, Christopher. "Separation Crosses the Borderline." *Ottawa Journal*, December 22, 1979.

Balint, Kathryn. "It's Iffy, but Border Park Might Be Open." *San Diego Union Tribune*, October 26, 1995.

Ballard, Jamie. "As Congress Considers a Shutdown, Here's What Americans Think of U.S. Immigration Policies." *YouGov*, January 13, 2024, https://today.yougov.com/politics/articles/48352-congress-considers-shutdown-what-americans-think-us-immigration-policies-poll.

BBC News. "Life on the Border: The Mexican Building the Wall." February 13, 2017, https://www.youtube.com/watch?v=mucl873ukjU.

Bier, David, and Alex Nowrasteh. *45,000 "Special Interest Aliens" Caught since 2007, but No U.S. Terrorist Attacks from Illegal Border Crossers.* CATO Institute, 2018.

Bigurra, Valeria. "Wallyball: Playing Volleyball on the Border." *Mexico News Network*. August 22, 2015, http://www.mexiconewsnetwork.com/en/noticias-en/wallyball-border/.

Blake, Steve. "Boundary Rotary Club Viable Despite Declining Membership." *Sherbrooke Record*, February 9, 2017.

Blampied, Phil. "Partly in Vermont: A Borderline Case." *Time*, August 13, 1979.

Border Angeles. Events, Facebook, https://www.facebook.com/pg/BorderAngels/events/?ref=page_internal.

Boston Sunday Herald. "Unique Border Library Was Opened in '04." July 11, 1976.

Breitigam, Gerald B. "Welcomed Mexican Invasion." *New York Times*, June 20, 1920.

Bush, George W. "Address to a Joint Session of Congress and the American People." Washington, DC, September 20, 2001, https://georgewbush-whitehouse.archives.gov/news/releases/2001/09/20010920-8.html.

California Department of Parks and Recreation. "Border Field State Park." https://www.parks.ca.gov/?page_id=664.

Carter, Nicole T. *Army Corps of Engineers and U.S. Southern Border Barriers.* Congressional Research Service, 2019.

Haddal, Chad C., Yule Kim, and Michael J. Garcia. *Border Security: Barriers Along the U.S. International Border.* Congressional Research Service, 2009.

Chicago Tribune. "'Steel Curtain' Falls on Mexico's Border—and Its Feelings." November 12, 1991.

Clark, Gerald. "International Opera: Entrance in Canada and U.S." The Standard, September 28, 1940.

Coe, Barbara. "Keep Illegals Out of State." *USA Today*, October 12, 1994.

Communities in Bloom. "International Peace Garden: Dedicated to the Celebration of Peace." https://www.collectivitesenfleurs.ca/international-peace-garden-dedicated-to-the-celebration-of-peace/.

Directory of Federal Heritage Designations. "Haskell Free Library and Opera House National Historic Site of Canada." https://www.pc.gc.ca/apps/dfhd/page_nhs_eng.aspx?id=704.

Dobbs, Lou. "Dobbs: Bush Speech Satisfies Nobody." *CNN.com*, May 17, 2006, http://edition.cnn.com/2006/US/05/17/dobbs.bushspeech/.

Donnelly, John. "They're Bilingual on Both Sides of Street." *Burlington Free Press*, February 11, 1980.

Drury, Colin. "Trump Has Not Built Single Mile of New Border Wall since Taking Office" *Independent*, July 22, 2019, https://www.independent.co.uk/news/world/americas/us-politics/donald-trump-border-wall-not-built-2020-campaign-a9015181.html.

Engler, Mark, and Paul Engler. "The Massive Immigrant-Rights Protests of 2006 Are Still Changing Politics." *Los Angeles Times*, March 4, 2016, https://www.latimes.com/opinion/op-ed/la-oe-0306-engler-immigration-protests-2006-20160306-story.html.

Faber, Jackson James. "Becoming Friendship Park: The History of Border Field State Park." Master's thesis, San Diego State University, 2015.

Furman, Bess. "Hoof Disease Stirs U.S.-Mexico Action: Cattle Ailment Below Border Expected to Be Subject of Truman Talks on Trip." *New York Times*, February 20, 1947.

Garcia, Michael J. *Barriers Along the U.S. Borders: Key Authorities and Requirements*. Congressional Research Service, 2015.

Garcia, Michael J. *Barriers Along the U.S. Borders: Key Authorities and Requirement*. Congressional Research Service, 2017.

The Gazette. "Phoning U.S. Without Fee Privilege of Rock Islanders." May 24, 1954.

Gelatt, Julia. "President Signs DHS Appropriations and Secure Fence Act, New Detainee Bill Has Repercussions for Noncitizens, Migration Policy Institute." *Policy Beat*, November 1, 2006, https://www.migrationpolicy.org/article/president-signs-dhs-appropriations-and-secure-fence-act-new-detainee-bill-has-repercussions.

Giles, Christopher. "Trump's Wall: How Much Has Been Built During His Term?" *BBC News*, January 12, 2021, https://www.bbc.com/news/world-us-canada-46748492.

Gramlich, John. "How Americans See Illegal Immigration, the Border Wall and Political Compromise." Pew Research Center, January 16, 2019, https://www.pewresearch.org/fact-tank/2019/01/16/how-americans-see-illegal-immigration-the-border-wall-and-political-compromise/.

Granados, Samuel, Zoeann Murphy, Kevin Schaul, and Anthony Faiola. "Raising Barriers: A New Age of Walls." *Washington Post*, October 12, 2016, https://www.washingtonpost.com/graphics/world/border-barriers/global-illegal-immigration-prevention/?hpid=hp_no-name_graphic-story-b%3Ahomepage%2Fstory.

The Guardian, "'Immoral': Nancy Pelosi on Trump's Border Wall—Video (Online)." January 4, 2019, https://www.theguardian.com/us-news/video/2019/jan/04/immoral-nancy-pelosi-on-trumps-border-wall-video.

Guerrero, Jean. "A Trump-Like Border Wall Is About to Be Built—Unless Biden Stops It." *Los Angeles Times*, February 27, 2023.

Haskell Free Library & Opera House. "History." https://haskellopera.com/history/.

Healy, Jack. "One Governor's Border Wall Is Another Governor's Headache." *New York Times*, December 2022.

Hill, Gladwin. "'Wetback' Invasion Is Broadening Despite All U. S. Counter-Moves." *New York Times*, February 11,1952, https://www.nytimes.com/1952/02/11/archives/-wetback-invasion-is-broadening-despite-all-u-s-countermoves.html.

Hulse, Carl. "A Build-a-Protest Approach to Immigration: Advocates of Border Security Are Trying to Inundate Congress." *New York Times*, May 31, 2006.

Hulse, Carl. "G.O.P in Senate Narrows Immigration Focus to 700-Mile Fence." *New York Times*, September 21, 2006.

Inewsource KPBS. "America's Wall," November 13, 2017, https://www.kpbs.org/news/2017/nov/13/americas-wall/#explore.

International Peace Garden. "Home." https://peacegarden.com/.

International Peace Garden. "Maps of Our Park." https://peacegarden.com/wp-content/uploads/2019/06/IPG-Map-with-Key.pdf.

International Peace Garden. "Preparing for Your Visit." https://peacegarden.com/discover#preparevisit.

Jenkins, Nash. "Donald Trump's Border Wall Is Already a Reality in This Texas Town." *Time*, May 1, 2018, https://time.com/5260569/brownsville-border-wall-texas-mexico/.

Johnson, Sally. "Life on the Line: Vermont and Canada" *New York Times*, February 7, 1988.

Johnston, David. "Judge Draws Fine Line at Cross-Border Hearing." *Montreal Gazette*, February 1983.

Kaempffert, Waldemar. "Science in Review: A Fence 1,905 Miles Long Is Proposed to Check the Spread of Foot-and-Mouth Disease." *New York Times*, February 23, 1947.

Karklis, Laris, Ann Gerhart, Joe Fox, Armand Emamdjomeh, and Kevin Schaul. "Borderline: Navigating the Invisible Boundary and Physical Barriers that Define the U.S.-Mexico Border." *Washington Post*, October 17, 2018, https://www.washingtonpost.com/graphics/2018/national/us-mexico-border-flyover/.

Kestler-D'Amours, Jillian. "Inside the Library Where You Can Read in Two Countries at Once." *Al Jazeera*, December 26, 2022. https://www.aljazeera.com/news/2022/12/26/inside-the-library-where-you-can-read-in-two-countries-at-once.

Kolsrud, Erik. " A Wall Being Built in Naco's Backyard Stirs up Emotions." *Arizona Sonora News*, February 10, 2017, https://arizonasonoranewsservice.com/a-wall-being-built-in-nacos-backyard-stirs-up-emotions/.

Kulish, Nicholas. "What It Costs to Be Smuggled across the U.S. Border." *New York Times*, June 30, 2018, https://www.nytimes.com/interactive/2018/06/30/world/smuggling-illegal-immigration-costs.html.

Lewis, Anthony. "Why the Cruelty?" *New York Times*, September 23, 1996.

Library of Congress. "Immigration: Depression and the Struggle for Survival." http://www.loc.gov/teachers/classroommaterials/presentationsandactivities/presentations/immigration/mexican6.html.

Lim, Stephanie. "This Border-Straddling U.S. Home Has a Door That Leads Right to Canada." *Global News*, June 29, 2017, https://globalnews.ca/news/3567283/this-border-straddling-u-s-home-has-a-door-that-leads-right-to-canada/.

Lipowicz, Alice. "Boeing's SBInet Contract Gets the Axe." *Washington Technology*, January 14, 2011, https://washingtontechnology.com/articles/2011/01/14/dhs-cancels-rest-of-sbinet-and-plans-mix-of-new-technologies-at-border.aspx.

Long Soldier, Layli. "Layli Long Soldier on Wounded Knee and the Murder of George Floyd." *Literary Hub*, June 3, 2020, https://lithub.com/layli-long-soldier-on-wounded-knee-and-the-murder-of-george-floyd/.

Los Angeles Times. "U.S.-Canada Border Cuts 20-Foot Swath." April 17, 1972.

Lounder, Jan. "This Town's a Tale of Two Countries." *Sunday Sun*, August 31, 1980.

Markon, Jerry. "Trump Says Building a U.S.-Mexico Wall Is 'Easy.' but Is It Really?" *Washington Post*, July 17, 2015, https://www.washingtonpost.com/politics/trump-on-the-us-mexico-border-building-a-wall-is-easy/2015/07/16/9a619668-2b0c-11e5-bd33-395c05608059_story.html.

Masanz, Sharon D. *History of the Immigration and Naturalization Service*. Congressional Research Service, 1980.

McKinley Jr., James. "With Beheadings and Attacks, Drug Gangs Terrorize Mexico." *New York Times*, October 26, 2006.

Morrissey, Kate. "Border Patrol Changes Rules at Friendship Park, Upsetting Frequent Visitors." *San Diego Union-Tribune*, February 14, 2018, https://www.sandiegouniontribune.com/news/immigration/sd-me-friendship-park-20180214-story.html.

Nesheim, David. "Machine Guns, Cows, and Quarantines: Foot and Mouth Disease in the United States, Mexico and Argentina." Paper presented at the James A. Rawley Graduate Conference in the Humanities, University of Nebraska, Lincoln, 2006.

New York Times. "Act to End Disease of Mexican Cattle." February 1, 1947, 19.

New York Times. "Ask Fence Along the Border." May 29, 1947.

New York Times. "Bush's Speech on Immigration." May 15, 2006, https://www.nytimes.com/2006/05/15/washington/15text-bush.html.

New York Times. "Hoof Disease Stirs U.S.-Mexico Action: Cattle Ailment Below Border Expected to Be Subject of Truman Talks on Trip." February 20, 1947.

Nickerson, Colin. "Haskell Library Straddles the Border." *The Chronicle*, April 20, 1978.

Nickerson, Colin. "International Border Slices Library in Half, Producing Unique Diplomatic Interactions." *Sunday Rutland Herald and Sunday Times Argus*, April 30, 1978.

Norman, Jim. "Solid Majority Still Opposes New Construction on Border Wall." *Gallup*, February 4, 2019, https://news.gallup.com/poll/246455/solid-majority-opposes-new-construction-border-wall.aspx.

Painter, William L., and Audrey Singer. *DHS Border Barrier Funding.* Congressional Research Service, January 29, 2020.

Passel, Jeffrey S. *Size and Characteristics of the Unauthorized Migrant Population in the U.S.* Pew Research Center, March 7, 2006, https://www.pewresearch.org/hispanic/2006/03/07/size-and-characteristics-of-the-unauthorized-migrant-population-in-the-us/.

Pear, Robert. "U.S. Strengthening Patrols Along the Mexican Border." *New York Times*, January 13, 1996.

Pierce, Sarah. *Change in the First Two Years of the Trump Administration.* Migration Policy Institute, May 2019.

Rayner, Richard. "What Immigration Crisis?: An Alien's Tour through the Back Rooms of What Is Becoming America's Most Exaggerated Threat." *New York Times*, January 7, 1996.

Scottish Rite News Bureau. "Unrestricted Immigration Not an Aid to Farmers." January 9, 1928.

Schmitt, Eric. "Milestones and Missteps on Immigration." *New York Times*, October 26, 1996.

Schmitt, Eric. "New Demands by White House Are Made on Immigration Bill." *New York Times*, September 27, 1996.

Shulevitz, Judith. "Bomb Trial to Feature Border-Line Testimony." *Burlington Free Press*, June 23, 1988.

Singer, Audrey. *Border Security between Ports of Entry: Homeland Security Issues in the 116th Congress.* Congressional Research Service, 2019.

Stanstead Journal. "Haskell Free Library." May 26, 1904.

Statistics Canada. "Census Profile, 2016 Census.", https://www12.statcan.gc.ca/census-recensement/index-eng.cfm.

Sullivan, Eileen, and Colbi Edmonds. "Biden, the Border, and Why a New Wall Is Going Up." *New York Times*, October 6 2023.

Sandia National Laboratories. Systematic Analysis of the Southwest Border. January 1993.

Theroux, Paul. "The Country Just over the Fence." *New York Times*, February 23, 2012, https://www.nytimes.com/2012/02/26/travel/nogales-mexico-a-few-steps-and-a-whole-world-away.html.

Timmons, Patrick. "El Paso Border Wall Rises at Place Once Marked by Unity." *United Press International*, October 2, 2018, https://www.upi.com/Top_News/US/2018/10/02/El-Paso-border-wall-rises-at-place-once-marked-by-unity/3151538421151/.

Torbati, Yeganeh. "Separated by Travel Ban, Iranian Families Reunite at Border Library." *Reuters*, November 28, 2018, https://www.reuters.com/article/us-usa-immigration-ban-insight/separated-by-travel-ban-iranian-families-reunite-at-border-library-idUSKCN1NX1P2.

Tran, Mark. "Mexico Fury as Bush Gives Go-Ahead to Border Fence." The Guardian, October 27, 2006, https://www.theguardian.com/world/2006/oct/27/usa.mexico.

USA Today. "The Wall." 2017, https://www.usatoday.com/border-wall/.

US Census Bureau. "American Fact Finder." https://factfinder.census.gov/faces/nav/jsf/pages/community_facts.xhtml.

US Customs and Border Protection. "Border Wall System." Updated July 24, 2023, https://www.cbp.gov/border-security/along-us-borders/border-wall-system.

US Customs and Border Protection. "CBP Announces New Path Forward for the Replacement of Deteriorated Border Barrier near Friendship Park." News release, January 17, 2023, https://www.cbp.gov/newsroom/local-media-release/cbp-announces-new-path-forward-replacement-deteriorated-border-barrier.

US Customs and Border Protection. "Large Groups of Aliens Encountered in Big Bend Sector." News release, March 7, 2019, https://www.cbp.gov/newsroom/local-media-release/large-groups-aliens-encountered-big-bend-sector.

US Customs and Border Protection. "Southwest Border Sectors: Total Illegal Alien Apprehensions by Fiscal Year." https://www.cbp.gov/newsroom/media-resources/stats.

US Customs and Border Protection. "United States Border Patrol: Border Patrol Agent Nationwide Staffing by Fiscal Year." https://www.cbp.gov/sites/default/files/assets/documents/2019-Mar/Staffing%20FY1992-FY2018.pdf.

US Department of Agriculture Animal and Plant Health Inspection Service. "Factsheet: Foot-and-Mouth Disease." https://www.aphis.usda.gov/aphis/ourfocus/animalhealth/animal-disease-information/fmd/index#:~:text=Foot%2Dand%2Dmouth%20disease%20(,health%20or%20food%20safety%20threat.

US Department of Defense. "More Troops Deploy to Support DHS/CBP Southwest Border Mission." News release, October 29, 2018.

US Department of Health and Human Services. "Separated Children Placed in Office of Refugee Resettlement Care." *HHS OIG Issue Brief*, January 2019, https://oig.hhs.gov/oei/reports/oei-BL-18-00511.pdf.

US Department of Justice. "Attorney General Announces Zero-Tolerance Policy for Criminal Illegal Entry." News release. April 6, 2018.

US Government Accountability Office. *Border Control: Revised Strategy Is Showing Some Positive Results*. March 1995.

US Government Accountability Office. *Border Security: Progress and Challenges with the Use of Technology, Tactical Infrastructure, and Personnel to Secure the Southwest Border*. March 2018.

US Government Accountability Office. *Secure Border Initiative: DHS Has Faced Challenges Deploying Technology and Fencing Along the Southwest Border*. May 2010.

US Government Accountability Office. *Secure Border Initiative: SBInet Expenditure Plan Needs to Better Support Oversight and Accountability*. February 2007.

US Government Accountability Office. *Southwest Border: Additional Actions Needed to Address Cultural and Natural Resource Impacts from Barrier Construction* September 2023.

US Government Accountability Office. *Southwest Border: Information on Federal Agencies' Process for Acquiring Private Land for Barriers*. November 2020.

US Government Accountability Office. *Southwest Border: Issues Related to Private Property Damage*. April 2015.

Vanderboegh, Mike. "The Botany of Illegal Immigration." *Free Republic*, 2005, http://www.freerepublic.com/focus/f-news/1471676/posts.

Wall Street Journal. "Cuba's Backyard Exiles." January 16, 2015, https://www.wsj.com/articles/cuban-refugees-fled-to-the-u-s-naval-base-in-guantanamo-bay-a-half-century-agoand-never-left-1421427942?mod=article_inline.

Washington Post. "Full Text: Donald Trump Announces a Presidential Bid." June 16, 2015, https://www.washingtonpost.com/news/post-politics/wp/2015/06/16/full-text-donald-trump-announces-a-presidential-bid/.

We Build the Wall. "About Us." https://webuildthewall.us/about-us/.

Index

Note: Page numbers in italics refer to figures, and endnotes are indicated by "n" followed by the endnote number.

abjectification vs. dehumanization, 213n195
Achiume, Tendayi E., 7, 20, 94, 156
Act of August 19, 1935: adoption of, 10, 38–44, 181n94; author's approach and, 3, 5, 32; comparative obscurity of, 85, 111, 153; proposed fencing under, 44–53, *45*, *50–52*; as unjust precedent, 153. *See also* historical and cultural context
Act of February 27, 1925, 37–38
aesthetic dimensions of law, 8, 12, 23–27, 105, 115–16, 119. *See also* materiality
Agnew, John, 30
Ahmed, Sara, 21, 28, 95, 106, 144, 173n54
alien criminality, 98–101
Ambos Nogales community, 35–36, 132–36, 141, 146, *162*
American Civil War (1861–1865), 35
Anderson, Benedict, 30, 41
Anzaldúa, Gloria: chapter epigraphs, 30, 75, 113; on exclusion and division, 114, 135, 142, 143–45, 149; on Mexican and Chicano identities, 6–7; on settler-colonial history, 30, 75
architecture, and spatial knowledge, 24–25, 143–44, 156, 175n95. *See also* materiality
Arizona: border community interactions, 35–36; fences near Yuma, 162, *163–64*; initiatives for additional fencing, 109–11; Nogales-Nogales border, 39, 44, 59, 132–36, 141, 146, *162*; Operation Safeguard, 79; proposed fencing, 1930s, 39, 43, 44; provisions under Secure Fence Act, 85
Army Corps of Engineers, 79
Ashworth, Gregory, 123
awe vs. wonder, 143

Baja California, 1, 36, 53, 125, 127–32, *130–32*, 142, 146
Balint, Kathryn, 129
Bannon, Stephen, 110
Barad, Karen, 22, 173n59
barbed wire, symbolism of, 123–24
barriers, author's usage, 8–9

Bayoumi, Moustafa, 56
Berlin Wall, 123–24, 135, 207n68
Bhabha, Homi, 56, 60, 72, 95
Biden, Joseph, 109, 139
Binational Garden, 129, 142, 209n105
Blomley, Nicholas K., 26
bollard walls, *132*, 134, 159, 161, 162, 166
Border Angels, 146
"border culture," 36
Border Field State Park, 127–32, *130–32*, 142, 146, *165*, 166, 209n105
Borderlands/La Frontera (Anzaldúa), 75
Border Meetup Group, 146
Border Protection, Antiterrorism, and Illegal Immigration Control Act (2005), 87–93
"The Botany of Illegal Immigration" (Vanderboegh), 100
Boundaries of Discourse in the International Court of Justice (Burgis-Kasthala), 18
Boyle, T. C., 193n24
Bracero Program, 68, 69
Braverman, Irus, 27–28
Brewer, Janice K., 110
Brossat, Alain, 123
Brown, Wendy, 96, 121–22
Brownsville, Texas, 35, 49–50, *51–52*, 85, 159–60, *160*, 187n186, 191n240
Bruce, David, 123
Bruyneel, Kevin, 113, 151, 214n1
built environments, and spatial knowledge, 24–25, 156, 175n95. *See also* materiality
Burgis-Kasthala, Michelle, 18
Bush, George W., 90–91, 102, 197n86

Calderón, Felipe, 124
Calexico, California, 36, 48, 52, 53, 85
California: border community interactions, 36; erected fencing, 1930s, 52, 53; Friendship Park, 125, 127–32, *130–32*, 142, 146, *165*, 209n105; increased securitization, 1980s, 78–79; proposed fencing, 43, 44, 48, 49–50, *50*; provisions under Secure Fence Act, 85; Sand Dragon fence, 164, *164*. *See also* San Diego, California
California National Guard, 79
Canada–United States Safe Third Country Agreement, 157
Canadian–American International Boundary Commission, 126
Casey, Edward, 135–36
Catholicism, 33–34, 177n26
Chacón, Jennifer, 93
Channel Tunnel, 66, 117
Chapman, Leonard F., 78
China, 2, 19, 122, 135
citizenship: immigration reform and, 89, 93; national belonging vs., 41–42
Ciudad Juárez, Chihuahua, 39, 40–46, *45*
Clark, Tom C., 48
Clinton, Bill, 195n50
Cold War, 4, 96, 124
collective memory, 113–14, 153
colonialism: centrality of otherness in, 60, 150–51; collective memory and, 113–14, 153; colorblind positivism, 94; "exoticized" violence, 101; race, habit, and, 144; settler colonialism vs., 5–6, 30–31. *See also* settler colonialism
colorblind positivism, 94
Columbus, New Mexico, 85
Comprehensive Immigration Reform Act (2006) bill, 88–89
Connally, Tom, 65
constitutive rhetoric, 19, 57–58, 70, 72
"constructed social spaces," 27
constructivism, 120
contagion, fear of, 2, 39, 47, 49, 62–68, 189n209.
Conyers, John, 84
Cooper, Davina, 28, 141, 147
Cordova Island, 44
Cornell, Sidney, 128
Cousar, R. M., 39, 133

Cover, Robert, 18, 20, 54, 172n44
COVID-19 pandemic, 66, 131
crime: conflation with immigration, 60, 82–83, 86, 88, 98–101; as justification for wall-building, 2, 11, 39, 48; narratives around women, 40–41, 42, 51–52, 59; race and criminal predisposition, 41. *See also* smuggling

Dallas Morning News, 102
danger, border as space of, 96–98
Darian-Smith, Eve, 20, 27, 66–67, 116, 117, 152, 204n18
Davies, Margaret: on home metaphor, 121; on identity formation, 54–55; on law as process of exclusion, 158; on legal materiality, 116; on material-immaterial binary, 26–27; pathways concept, 141; on subjectivity and law, 16, 19; on walls as law, 15
Dawes Act (1887), 38, 179n61
Dear, Michael, 35
dehumanization vs. abjectification, 213n195
de jure and de facto pathways, 28, 141, 144, 147, 157–58
Delaney, David, 117, 204n24
De La Viña, Gustavo, 80
Democratic Review periodical, 33
Department of Agriculture, 46, 54, 63
Department of Homeland Security (DHS): calls for additional fencing and, 109–10; directions under IIRIRA, 82, 84, 85, 86; introduction of, 102
Department of Justice, 84, 111
Department of Labor, 43, 44
Department of the Interior, 84
Derby Line-Stanstead border, 136–40, *140*, 141, 212n158
design, and spatial knowledge, 24–25, 156, 175n95. *See also* materiality
Dhamoon, Rita, 6, 31, 151
"discursive coherence," 56
disease, fear of, 2, 39, 47, 49, 62–68, 189n209
Dobbs, Lou, 102
Douglas, Arizona, 85, 162
Douglas, Mary, 120
Dreier, David, 103
Ducey, Doug, 110

economics: increasing immigration due to, 78, 82; market liberalization, 79; perceptions of migrant dependency, 40, 42, 78, 83; Sonora-Arizona border restrictions and, 134
El Paso, Texas: extant scholarship, 5; McAllen to El Paso fencing, 160–61, *161*; Operation Blockade, 79; proposed fencing, 39, 40–46, *45*, 59; provisions under Secure Fence Act, 85; "Tortilla Curtain," 78, 193nn23–24
emotion: border as space of danger, 96–98; constructing fear and vulnerability, 94–96; constructing spatialized terror, 101–4; in legal discourse, 21–22, 54, 95, 173n54; responses to terrorism, 106. *See also* Secure Fence Act (2006)
Endangered Species Act (ESA), 84
England, 66–67, 117
environmental law, encroachments on, 15, 84, 196n66
Environmental Policy Act (NEPA), 84
exclusion: identity formation based on, 54–55; law as process of, 158; legal discourse as exclusionary, 19–20; magnified by border walls, 135; symbolism of walls, 121–23. *See also* otherness; race
Executive Order 13767 (2017), 154
Executive Order 13780 (2017), 139
"exoticized" violence, 101
experience, meaning through, 24, 113–14, 116–17, 119, 141, 144, 147. *See also* materiality

Fabri, Hélène Ruiz, 15
fear and vulnerability, construction of, 94–96
fences, author's usage, 8–9
Fernandez, Janet, 131
Fernández-Kelly, Patricia, 79
Fishman, Joshua, 17
Foley, Neil, 178n40
Folk, R. G., 40
foot-and-mouth disease, 47, 49, 62–65, 67, 69, 189n209
Ford, Richard, 118
Foxx, Virginia, 87–88
France, 66–67, 117
Friendship Park (San Diego–Tijuana), 125, 127–32, *130–32*, 142, 146, *165*, 209n105
Frist, Bill, 92
"frontier myth," 31

gender. *See* women
Gerstle, Gary, 90, 197n86
Geslin, Albane, 9, 123–24
Glackman, William, 95
Glenn, Evelyn Nakano, 6, 31
globalization, 2, 4, 170n3
Global North/Global South, 7, 104, 157
Gohmert, Louie, 97
Good Neighbor Policy, 191n240
Goodrich, Peter, 23, 115
Gordon, Linda, 36
Great Depression (1929–1939), 37, 42, 44
Great Wall of China, 2, 122, 135
Guardino, Peter, 34
Gulasekaram, Pratheepan, 121, 170n3

habit, whiteness and, 144–45
Hall, Stuart, 23, 76–78, 89–90, 94
Harrison, George, 139
Hartman, Saidiya, 76
Haskell, Carlos, 138
Haskell, Martha, 138
Haskell Free Library, 137, 138, 139, 211n149
Hayden, Carl, 47
health, as rhetorical weapon, 65–66
Herzog, Benno, 22
"hierarchies of otherness," 6
historical and cultural context: Act of August 19, 1935, adoption of, 38–44, 181n94; border delimitation, 32–38, 149, 177n26, 178n40; constructing Mexican difference, 54–62, 150–51; fear of contagion, 62–68, 189n209; opposition to border fences, 68–72, 191n240; precedents of injustice, 13, 20, 108–11, 112, 152–54; proposed fences, 44–53, *45*, *50–52*; settler-colonial myths, 53–54; territoriality and national identity, 30–31, 72–73
Hoeven, Charles B., 67
home, symbolism of, 120–21
humiliation-generating practices, 143–44
Hunter, Duncan Lee, 83
Hurst, Walter, 69–70

identity. *See* national identity
ideology. *See* knowledge production
Illegal Immigration Reform and Immigration Responsibility Act (IIRIRA): adoption of, 81; provisions under Section 102, 84–86; scope of, 82–83, 84, 111, 195n50
immigration: competing visions for, 85–93; conflation with crime and disease, 2, 64–65, 98–101; early restrictions on, 37–38; globalization and, 4, 170n3; Global North/South mobility divide, 7, 104, 157; media depictions of, 77–78; terrorism and, 101–4, 106–7; wall-building and immigration law, 81–85
Immigration Act of 1917, 37
Immigration and Naturalization Service (INS): completed projects, 52–53; IIRIRA waivers and, 84; inflammatory discourse, 78; proposed fencing,

Texas, 43, 44, 46, 49, 51; San Diego border enforcement, 79–80
Imperial Sand Dunes, 164, *164*
indigeneity: colonialism vs. settler colonialism, 5–6, 30–31; delimitation of Mexico-US border and, 33–34; indigenous presence in Mexico, 6–7, 214n1. *See also* race; settler colonialism
inferential racism, 77
Intelligence Reform and Terrorism Prevention Act (2004), 139
International Boundary and Water Commission (IBWC), 48, 49, 54, 63
International Boundary Commission (IBC), 43–44, 46, 47, 181n94
international boundary fence project: disease as justification for, 62–68; opposition to, 68–72; proposals for, 46–53, *50–52*
International Peace Garden, 124, 125–27, 142
International Water Company, 137
invasion, as metaphor and theme, 62–68, 78, 88, 91, 98, 107
Israel, 28

Jackson, Andrew, 151
Johnson, Kevin R., 193n24
Jones, Reece, 102

Kang, Deborah, 5, 52, 58–59, 192n10
Keenen, Sarah, 116, 117
Kelly, Willard F., 53
Kennedy, Ted, 87, 89
King, Peter, 92, 103
knowledge production: fear as rhetorical tool, 95; legal rhetoric, 17–22, 56–57, 70, 72, 89–90, 104–5; material dimensions of law, 22–29, 115–19, 173n59; media discourse in, 77–78. *See also* legislative debate; materiality
Kolfage, Brian, 110
Konrad, Victor, 139

labor: citizenship and, 183n118; exploitative, 86, 89; guest worker programs, 68, 69, 87–88, 89, 92; illegal, 68–69
Laclau, Ernesto, 22
landscape: material normativity of, 116–19; national identity and, 27–28, 117, 204n18. *See also* space; walled landscapes
language: discourse and materiality, 22–23, 115, 173n59; fear as rhetorical tool, 95; in identity-formation, 54–55; in influencing emotion, 24, 173n54; law as, 17–22, 56–57, 70, 72, 89–90, 151, 172n44; politics of performativity, 9; race-neutral discourse, 94, 151
law: criminal- and immigration law, convergence of, 98; derived from physical experience, 10; in eliciting emotion, 21–22, 170n3, 173n54; as exclusionary, 19–20; legal geography, 25–26; legal materiality, 8, 22–28, 115–19, 146–47, 154–57; legal positivism, 14–17, 115; precedents of injustice, 13, 20, 108–11, 112, 152–54; as process of exclusion, 158; as rhetorical, 17–22, 56–57, 70, 72, 89–90, 151, 172n44; settler-colonial myths and, 53–54
"lawscape" vs. "landscape," 117, 204n22
legislative debate: alien criminality, 98–101; border as space of danger, 96–98; competing visions, 85–93; constructing fear and vulnerability, 94–96; constructing spatialized terror, 101–4; embedded narratives, 105–8; evolving discourses, 75–77; increasing border controls, 77–81; normative power, 104–5; Secure Fence Act as legal precedent, 108–11, 112; wall-building and immigration law, 82–85
Lennon, John, 139
Leuenberger, Christine, 120, 124
Lodge, Henry C., Jr., 64
Long Soldier, Layli, 119

MacCormak, Daniel W., 40
Manderson, Desmond, 20–21, 24, 65, 96, 116, 119, 146
"manifest destiny," 33
Manitoba, 124, 125–27
Martínez, Oscar, 5
Massey, Douglas, 79
Matamoros, Tamaulipas, 35, 49, 187n186
materiality: Derby Line-Stanstead border and, 136–40, *140*, 141, 212n158; Friendship Park and, 125, 127–32, *130–32*; International Peace Garden, 125–27; material dimensions of law, 22–28, 154–57; material-immaterial binary, 26–27; material narratives, 113–14; performing walled landscapes, 140–46; Sonora-Arizona border and, 132–36; symbolism of walls, 119–24, 206n50; wall as normative object, 115–19, 146–47
materiality–inflicted approaches, 25
Matoreyna, Jose M., 133
McAllen, Texas, 160
McAllen Chamber of Commerce, 70, 71
McCain, John, 87
McCaul, Michael, 100, 103
McDowell, John, 48
McGuire, Randall, 133
media, ideological production, 77–78
Meinig, Donald, 116
Meissner, Doris, 87
"metonymic slide," 106
Mexicali, Baja California, 36
Mexican–American War (1846–1848), 2, 11, 32, 150
Mexican Revolution (1910–1920), 36
Mexico: constructing Mexican difference, 54–62, 73, 150–51; delimitation of Mexico-US border, 32–38, 149, 177n26, 178n40; discourse around disease, 2, 39, 47, 49, 62–68, 189n209; indigenous presence, 6–7, 214n1. *See also* historical and cultural context; legislative debate; materiality; walls as legal objects
Miller, David, 41
Mitchell, W.J.T., 116
mobility. *See* immigration
Montague, Joe G., 61, 63
Moore, Henry J., 126
Mouffe, Chantal, 22

national identity: "American community/identity," 176n13; centrality to wall building, 3–4; citizenship vs. national belonging, 41–42; constructing Mexican difference, 54–62, 73, 150–51; delimitation of Mexico-US border, 32–38, 149–50, 178n40; extant scholarship, 14; as imagined, 30; law, landscape, and, 27–28, 117, 204n18; perceived dilution of, 96–97; territorial appropriation and, 30–31, 72–73. *See also* historical and cultural context; legislative debate; materiality; walls as legal objects
National Prohibition Act (1919), 58
national security, 78–79, 87, 101–4
National Wool Growers Convention, 63
Navarro, Ed, 129
Neal, Mary, 213n195
neutrality of law, 15–16, 18, 150
Nevins, Joseph, 193n23
New Deal programs, 44
New Mexico, 43, 85, 110, 161
The New York Times, 60, 63, 78, 97
Ngai, Mae, 59
Nicol, Heather, 139
Nixon, Patricia, 128
Nogales-Nogales border: border fencing, 39, 44, 59, 132–36, 141, 146, *162*; cross-border interactions, 35–36
nomos (normative universe), 20, 172n44
"nomoscapes," 117, 204n24
North American Free Trade Agreement (NAFTA), 79

North Dakota, 124, 125–27
Nussbaum, Martha, 21, 95, 143

Operation Blockade (1993), 79
Operation Gatekeeper (1994), 79, 128
Operation Safeguard (1994), 79
Operation Wetback (1954), 77, 192n10
Orientalism, 19, 55–56
Orientalism (Said), 19
otherness: abjectification, 213n195; constructing Mexican difference, 54–62, 73, 150–51; "exoticized" violence, 101; fear as rhetorical tool, 95; humiliation-generating practices, 143; identity formation based on, 54–55; persistence in tropes, 94; symbolism of walls and, 121, 206n50. *See also* exclusion; race; Secure Fence Act (2006)

Palestine, 28
Passport Act (1918), 37
pathways, de jure and de facto, 28, 141, 144, 147, 157–58
pedestrian fencing, 159, 162
Pelosi, Nancy, 154
performativity, politics of, 9
Perkins, Frances, 44
Philippopoulos-Mihalopoulos, Andreas, 26, 27, 117, 204n22
"plastic presence" of the law, 23
politics as source of law, 18
Polk, James K., 33
positivist approaches, 14–17, 115, 150
precedents of injustice, 13, 20, 108–11, 112, 152–54
property rights, 15, 121
protection, walls as, 120–22
Protestantism, 33–34

Quebec, 136–40, *140*, 141
Quétel, Claude, 2, 120

rabies, 66–67
race: Act of August 19, 1935 and, 38–44; alien criminality, 98–101; constructing fear and vulnerability, 94–96; constructing Mexican difference, 54–62, 73, 150–51; delimitation of Mexico-US border, 33–35, 36, 72; fear of contagion and, 2, 39, 62–68; humiliation-generating practices, 143–44; inferential racism, 77; international borders as racial borders, 7, 104, 156; media and, 77–78; preceded by colonialism, 73; precedents of injustice and, 20, 152–53; race-neutral discourse, 94, 151; responses to terrorism and, 106–7; space, habit, and, 144–45. *See also* historical and cultural context; legislative debate; settler colonialism
racial amnesia vs. racial aphasia, 94, 153
rape trees, 100
REAL ID Act (2005), 84, 196n64
"religiously inflicted multiculturalism," 90, 197n86
repatriation campaigns, 38
Rio Grande, 43, 159–60, 181n94
Rio Grande Border Fence Project, 46–53, *50–52*, 182n110
Rio Grande Valley, 68–70
Ritaine, Evelyn, 71, 143, 157
Roman limes, 122, 206n58
Roosevelt, Theodore, 68
Roosevelt Reservation, 68
Royce, Edward R., 103
Rubin, Andrew, 56
Ruskola, Teemu, 18, 19

Sabal Palm Sanctuary, *160*
Sacco, Vincent, 95
Safe Third Country Agreement, 157
Said, Edward, 19, 55–56
Sand Dragon wall, California, 164, *164*

Sandia National Laboratories, 80–81, 82, 84
San Diego, California: fence southeast of, 164–66, *165*; Friendship Park, 125, 127–32, *130–32*, 142, 146, *165*, 209n105; IIRIRA and, 82; Operation Gatekeeper, 79; three-tier border fence, 79–81, 83–85; "Tortilla Curtain," 78, 193nn23–24
San Luis, Arizona, 78
Santorum, Rick, 98–99
San Ysidro, San Diego, 78
Saussure, Ferdinand de, 54, 114
Saxton, Jim, 84
Secure Fence Act (2006): adoption of, 1, 85–86, 92–93; alien criminality, 98–101; border as space of danger, 96–98; constructing fear and vulnerability, 94–96; constructing spatialized terror, 101–4; in eliciting emotion, 21–22; embedded narratives, 105–8; Friendship Park access, 129; as legal precedent, 108–11, 152–54; performative challenges to, 146; reifying racial distinctions, 11. *See also* legislative debate; materiality
securitization, 78–79, 87, 101–4
Send-a-Brick campaign, 91
Sensenbrenner, James, 87–88
"Sensenbrenner Bill," 87–93
September 11th attacks, 101–4, 112, 139
Sessions, Jeff, 91
settler colonialism: constructing Mexican difference, 54–62, 151; Dawes Act, 38; discourse around disease, 62–68; exclusionary narratives, 19; material narratives, 28, 113–14, 141, 144, 147; as ongoing, 75, 111; opposition to border fencing and, 68–72; as process of erasure, 5–7; settler-colonial myths, 53–54; supported by legal discourses, 27; territorial gain and, 5, 30–32
sexual violence, 100–101
Shamir, Ronen, 170n3
Shields, Rob, 175n95
"silent invasion" trope, 78
slavery, 34, 76
Slotkin, Richard, 34
Smith, Lamar, 82–84
smuggling: at Friendship Park, 128; as justification for fencing, 38, 40, 43, 46–49, 64–65, 83; during prohibition period, 58–59; as referent of Mexican criminality, 61; San Diego border fence and, 80–81; South American drug trade, 78
Snow, David, 49
Sonora, Mexico, 35–36, 39, 132–36, 141, 146, *162*
South American drug trade, 78
South Bay Historical Society, 127–28
space: border as space of danger, 96–98; built environments, knowledge through, 24–25, 156, 175n95; home, symbolism of, 120–21; law, materiality and, 25–26, 116–19; national identity and, 27–28, 117, 204n18; openness as site of danger, 95–96; race, habit, and, 144–45; spatialized terror, 11, 101–4
spatial justice, 26
Stanstead, Quebec, 136–40, *140*, 141, 212n158
St. John, Rachel, 36
subjectivity of law, 15–17, 18, 54
Sunland Park wall, New Mexico, 110
surveillance, 2, 130, 134
symbolism of walls, 14, 24, 28, 119–24, 155–56, 170n3, 206n50
Szary, Anne-Laure Amilhat, 145–46

Tecate, California, 85
territory: delimitation of Mexico-US border, 32–34, 149, 177n26, 178n38; sovereignty protection, 121–22, 206n50; territorial gain and settler

colonialism, 5, 30–31; territorial jurisdiction, 118–19
terrorism: conflation with immigration, 86, 106–7; constructing spatialized terror, 101–4; emotional responses to, 106; symbolism of walls and, 206n50
Texas: border community interactions, 35; Brownsville wall, 159–60, *160*; opposition to border fencing, 68–72, 191n240; proposed fencing, 39, 40–46, *45*; provisions under Secure Fence Act, 85; Western Land Boundary Fence Project, 46–52, *50–52*. *See also* El Paso, Texas
Texas and Southwestern Cattle Raisers Association, 63
Theiss-Morse, Elizabeth, 41–42
Theroux, Paul, 135
Thomason, Robert Ewing, 40
Thompson, Debra, 94, 153
threat narratives, 77–78
tick fever, 63–64
Ticktin, Miriam, 101
Tijuana, Baja California, 53, 125, 127–32, *130–32*, 142, 146, *165*, 209n105
Time magazine, 78
"Tortilla Curtain," 78, 193nn23–24
touch, 141, 144
Treaty of Guadalupe Hidalgo, 10, 32, 34–35, 72, 135, 149, 214n1
Trump administration: Executive Order 13767, 154; Executive Order 13780, 139; modifications to Sonora-Arizona wall, 135; performative use of language, 9; wall-building as theme of, 1, 109, 151
Tuan, Yi-Fu, 24–25, 119

Un–American Activities Committee (HUAC), 49
United States: "American" used herein, 176n13; territorial expansion, 30–31, 32–38, 149; war on drugs, 78, 106, 128; war on terror, 102–4, 106. *See also* historical and cultural context; legislative debate; materiality; walls as legal objects
US attorney general, 82, 85
US Border Patrol: creation of, 37–38, 52, 149; Friendship Park management, 128–29, 131, 209n105; increase in border operations, 79; international boundary fence project and, 51; Operation Wetback and, 192n10; opposition to San Diego border fence, 84; proposed fencing, El Paso, 43
US–Canada border: Derby Line-Stanstead, 136–40, *140*, 141, 212n158; International Peace Garden, 125–27, 142; political violence and, 104; US-Mexico border vs., 12, 70–71, 107–8, 141–43, 147, 156–57
US–Mexico border: author's approach, 3, 9–13; legal history and, 148–54; Nogales-Nogales border, 39, 44, 59, 132–36, 141, 146, *162*; San Diego-Tijuana border, 125, 127–32, *130–32*, 146, *165*, 209n105; Trump administration and, 1, 109; US-Canada border vs., 12, 70–71, 107–8, 141–43, 147, 156–57; visual tour of, 159–66, *160–65*, 216n1; walled landscape concept and, 27. *See also* historical and cultural context; legislative debate; materiality; walls as legal objects
US News & World Report, 78
US State Department, 46, 51, 64

Vanderboegh, Mike, 100
vehicle fences, 159
Veracini, Lorenzo, 5–6
Vermont, 136–40, *140*, 141, 212n158
vice, 58–59
vulnerability, 95–96

wall building: American support for, 202n179, 203n182; author's approach, 8–13, 167n5, 168n22; as continuous process, 1–5, 168n9; extant scholarship, 14–15; as process of colonial settlement, 5–7; symbolism of walls, 14, 24, 28, 119–24, 155–56, 170n3, 206n50; as technique of division, 10. *See also* historical and cultural context; legislative debate; materiality; walls as legal objects
walled landscapes: author's usage, 8–9; characterized, 27; materiality of, 8, 12, 22–28, 115–19, 146–47, 154–57; performance within, 140–46. *See also* materiality; space
Walled States, Waning Sovereignty (Brown), 121–22
walls as legal objects: beyond legal positivism, 15–17, 115; extant scholarship, 14–15; law as language, 17–22; material dimensions of law, 22–29, 173n59. *See also* materiality
war on drugs, 78, 106, 128
war on terror, 102–4, 106
Watkins, Mary, 135–36
Watman, Dan, 209n105
Webster–Ashburton Treaty (1842), 136
"We Build the Wall" initiative, 110
welfare: perceptions of migrant dependency, 40, 42, 78, 83; reduced access for migrants, 82, 195n50
West, Milton, 43, 47
Western Hemisphere Travel Initiative (WHTI), 139
Western Land Boundary Fence Project, 46–53, *50–52*
"wetbacks," 60, 77, 192n10
White, James Boyd, 17, 18, 56–57, 70, 72, 89–90
whiteness: persistent tropes of white supremacy, 94; privileging of, 7, 12; space, habit, and, 144–45; white settlement, 6. *See also* race; settler colonialism
Wilson, Pete, 90
Wolfe, Patrick, 6, 31, 73
women: sexual violence against, 100–101; as threat, 40–41, 42, 51–52, 59
wonder vs. awe, 143
Works Progress Administration (WPA), 44
World Trade Center bombing (1993), 82
World War I (1914–1918), 37, 39
World War II (1939–1945), 123, 159

xenophobia, 36, 109

Young, Iris Marion, 120
Yuma, Arizona, 162, *163–64*

THE CULTURAL LIVES OF LAW
Austin Sarat, Editor

The Cultural Lives of Law series brings insights and approaches from cultural studies to law and tries to secure for law a place in cultural analysis. Books in the series focus on the production, interpretation, consumption, and circulation of legal meanings. They take up the challenges posed as boundaries collapse between as well as within cultures, and as the circulation of legal meanings becomes more fluid. They also attend to the ways law's power in cultural production is renewed and resisted.

Joseph Mello, *Pot for Profit: Cannabis Legalization, Racial Capitalism, and the Expansion of the Carceral State*
2024

Chloé Deambrogio, *Judging Insanity, Punishing Difference: A History of Mental Illness in the Criminal Court*
2024

Daniel LaChance and Paul Kaplan, *Crimesploitation: Crime, Punishment, and Pleasure on Reality Television*
2022

Nesam McMillan, *Imagining the International: Crime, Justice, and the Promise of Community*
2020

Jeffrey R. Dudas, *Raised Right: Fatherhood in Modern American Conservatism*
2017

Renée Ann Cramer, *Pregnant with the Stars: Watching and Wanting the Celebrity Baby Bump*
2015

Sora Y. Han, *Letters of the Law: Race and the Fantasy of Colorblindness*
2015

Marianne Constable, *Our Word Is Our Bond: How Legal Speech Acts*
2014

Joshua C. Wilson, *The Street Politics of Abortion: Speech, Violence, and America's Culture Wars*
2013

Irus Braverman, *Zooland: The Institution of Captivity*
2012

Nora Gilbert, *Better Left Unsaid: Victorian Novels, Hays Code Films, and the Benefits of Censorship*
2012

Edited by Winnifred Fallers Sullivan, *Robert A. Yelle, and Mateo Taussig-Rubbo, After Secular Law*
2011

Keith J. Bybee, *All Judges Are Political—Except When They Are Not: Acceptable Hypocrisies and the Rule of Law*
2010

Susan Sage Heinzelman, *Riding the Black Ram: Law, Literature, and Gender*
2010

David M. Engel and Jaruwan S. Engel, *Tort, Custom, and Karma: Globalization and Legal Consciousness in Thailand*
2010

Ruth A. Miller, *Law in Crisis: The Ecstatic Subject of Natural Disaster*
2009

Ravit Reichman, *The Affective Life of Law: Legal Modernism and the Literary Imagination*
2009

Edited by David M. Engel and Michael McCann, *Fault Lines: Tort Law as Cultural Practice*
2008

William P. MacNeil, *Lex Populi: The Jurisprudence of Popular Culture*
2007

Edited by Austin Sarat and Christian Boulanger, *The Cultural Lives of Capital Punishment: Comparative Perspectives*
2005